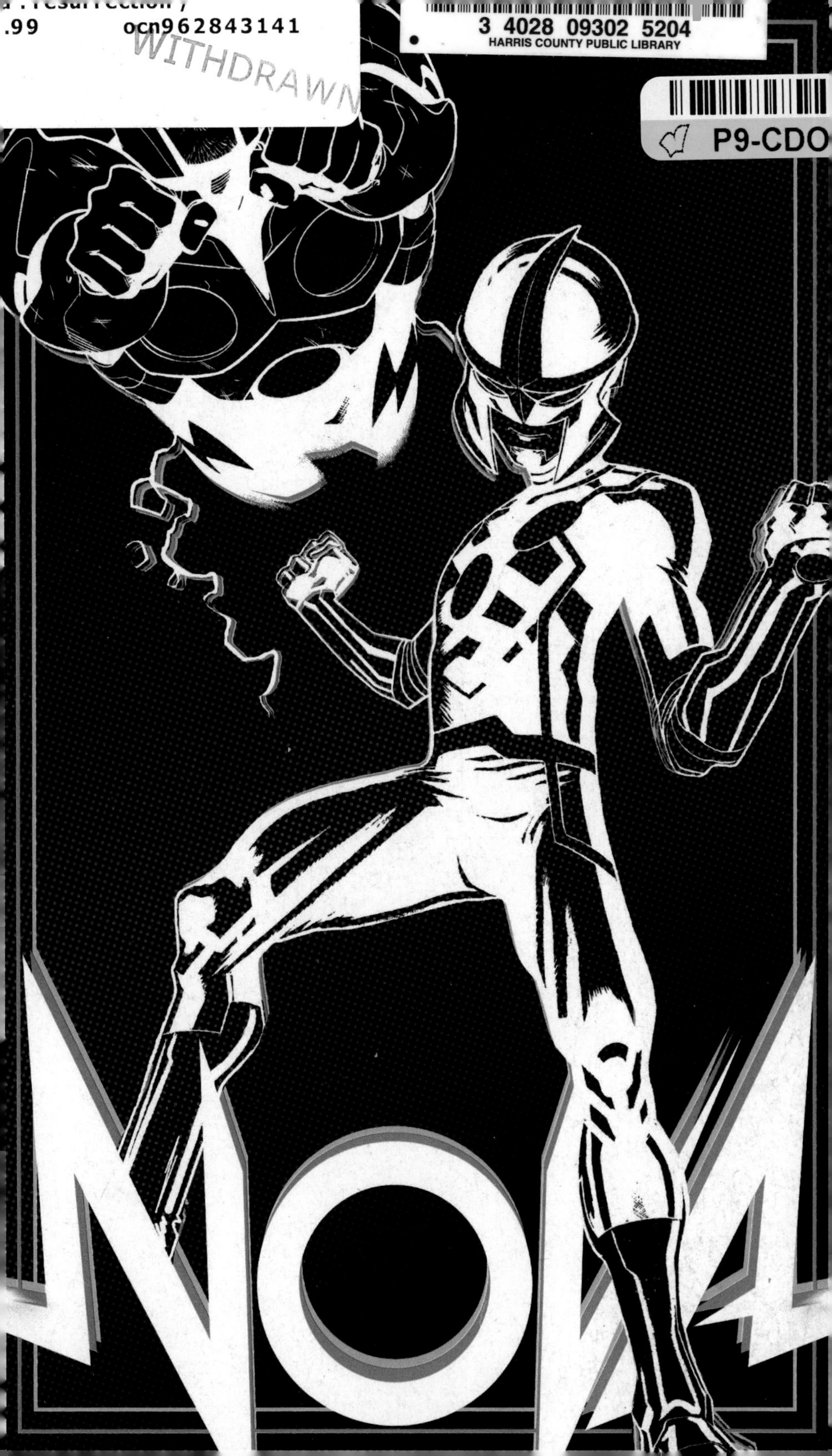

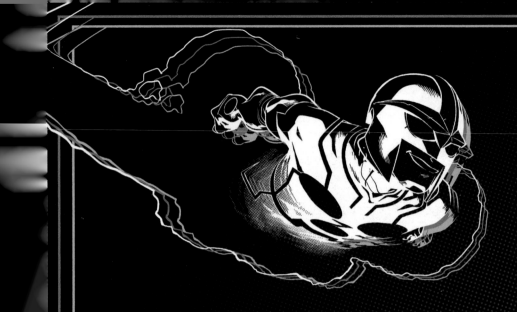

AS A HIGH SCHOOLER, RICHARD RIDER WAS DRAFTED INTO THE INTERGALACTIC PEACEKEEPING
TASK FORCE CALLED THE NOVA CORPS. AFTER A DEVASTATING ATTACK BY ANNIHILUS WIPED OUT ALL
THE OTHER MEMBERS OF THE CORPS, RICHARD HAD NO CHOICE BUT TO PATROL THE GALAXY ALONE
FOR YEARS. HE VALIANTLY DEFENDED IT FROM EVIL UNTIL HE MET HIS UNTIMELY END AT THE HANDS
OF THANOS IN A PARALLEL DIMENSION CALLED THE CANCERVERSE. BUT HE MYSTERIOUSLY APPEARED
ON HIS MOTHER'S DOORSTEP ALIVE AND WELL, THOUGH HE HAS NO IDEA HOW OR WHY.

15-YEAR-OLD SAM ALEXANDER'S FATHER WAS A NOVA AS WELL, SERVING AS A MEMBER OF
THE ELITE BLACK NOVA UNIT. WITH MORE POWERFUL HELMETS THAN THE REST OF THE CORPS,
THE BLACK NOVAS WERE ONLY SENT ON THE MOST DANGEROUS ASSIGNMENTS. BUT WHEN HIS
FATHER WENT MISSING, IT WAS UP TO SAM TO LOOK AFTER HIS MOTHER, HIS SISTER,
AND HIS PLANET BY TAKING UP THE MANTLE AND BECOMING THE LAST AND ONLY NOVA.

FOR A TIME…

COLLECTION EDITOR **JENNIFER GRÜNWALD**
ASSISTANT EDITOR **CAITLIN O'CONNELL**
ASSOCIATE MANAGING EDITOR **KATERI WOODY**
EDITOR, SPECIAL PROJECTS **MARK D. BEAZLEY**
VP PRODUCTION & SPECIAL PROJECTS **JEFF YOUNGQUIST**
SVP PRINT, SALES & MARKETING **DAVID GABRIEL**
BOOK DESIGNER **ADAM DEL RE**

EDITOR IN CHIEF **AXEL ALONSO**
CHIEF CREATIVE OFFICER **JOE QUESADA**
PRESIDENT **DAN BUCKLEY**
EXECUTIVE PRODUCER **ALAN FINE**

NOVA: RESURRECTION. Contains material originally published in magazine form as NOVA #1-7. First printing 2017. ISBN# 978-1-302-90529-3. Published by MARVEL WORLDWIDE, INC., a subsidiary of MARVEL ENTERTAINMENT, LLC. OFFICE OF PUBLICATION: 135 West 50th Street, New York, NY 10020. Copyright © 2017 MARVEL. No similarity between any of the names, characters, persons, and/or institutions in this magazine with those of any living or dead person or institution is intended, and any such similarity which may exist is purely coincidental. **Printed in the U.S.A.** DAN BUCKLEY, President, Marvel Entertainment; JOE QUESADA, Chief Creative Officer; TOM BREVOORT, SVP of Publishing; DAVID BOGART, SVP of Business Affairs & Operations, Publishing & Partnership; C.B. CEBULSKI, VP of Brand Management & Development, Asia; DAVID GABRIEL, SVP of Sales & Marketing, Publishing; JEFF YOUNGQUIST, VP of Production & Special Projects; DAN CARR, Executive Director of Publishing Technology; ALEX MORALES, Director of Publishing Operations; SUSAN CRESPI, Production Manager; STAN LEE, Chairman Emeritus. For information regarding advertising in Marvel Comics or on Marvel.com, please contact Vit DeBellis, Integrated Sales Manager, at vdebellis@marvel.com. For Marvel subscription inquiries, please call 888-511-5480. **Manufactured between 6/2/2017 and 7/3/2017 by QUAD/GRAPHICS WASECA, WASECA, MN, USA.**

10 9 8 7 6 5 4 3 2 1

NOVA

RESURRECTION

JEFF LOVENESS & RAMÓN PÉREZ
WRITERS

RAMÓN PÉREZ (NOS. 1-5, NO. 7) &
SCOTT HEPBURN (NOS. 6-7)
ARTISTS

IAN HERRING
COLOR ARTIST

RAMÓN PÉREZ (NOS. 1-3, NO. 5),
VID MARQUEZ & LAURA MARTIN (NO. 4) &
DAN MORA & IAN HERRING (NOS. 6-7)
COVER ART

ALLISON STOCK
ASSISTANT EDITOR

DEVIN LEWIS
EDITOR

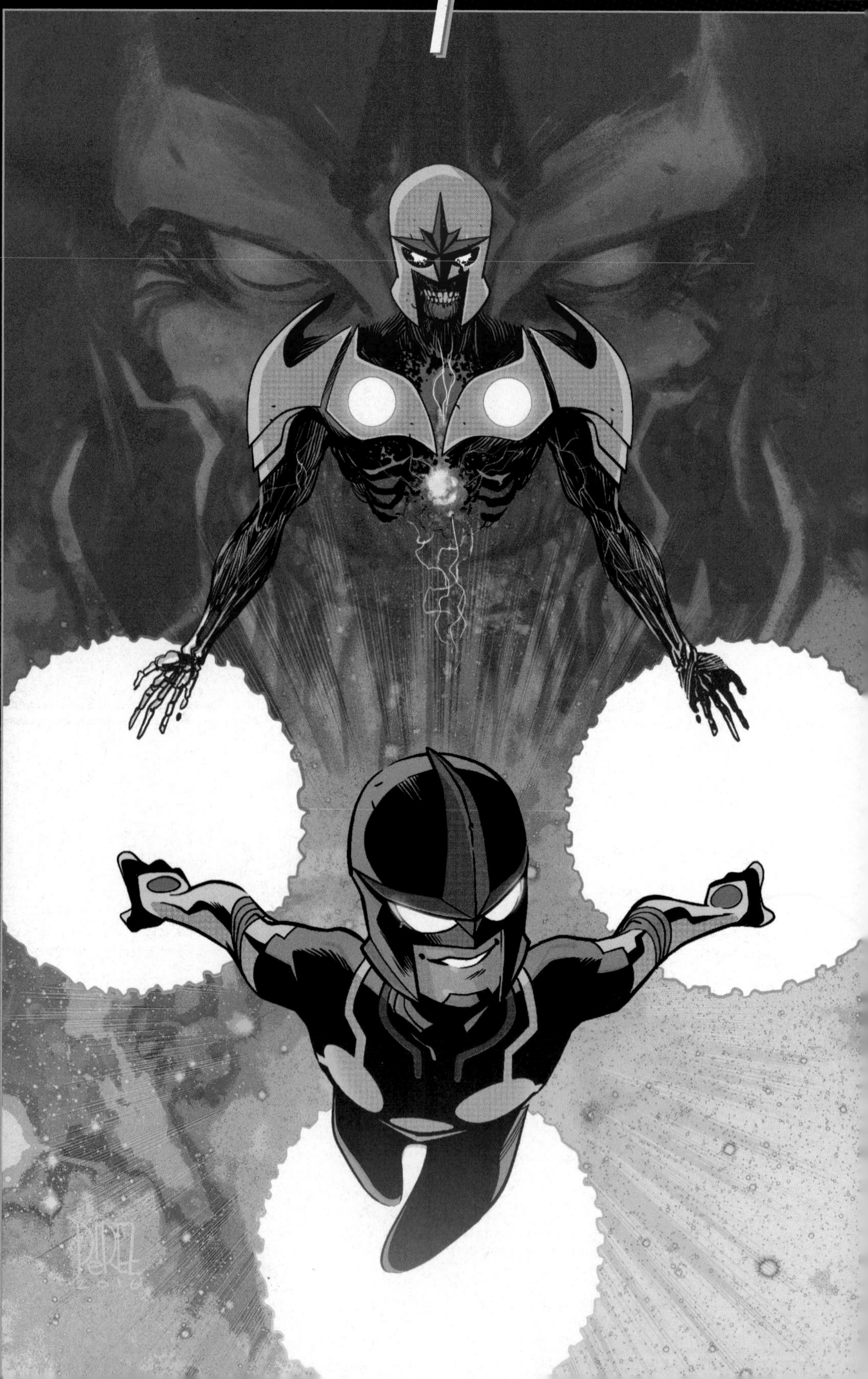

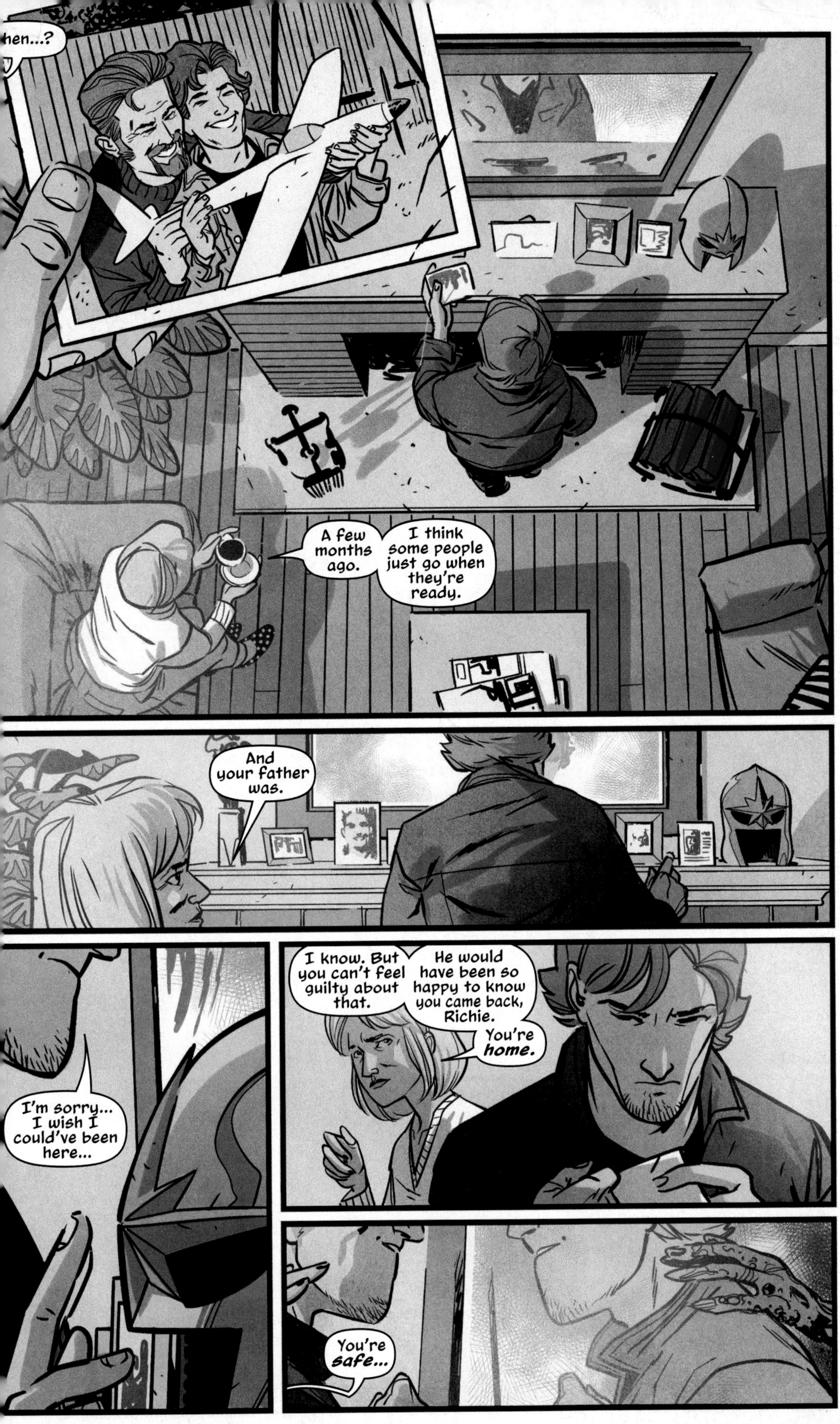
hen...?
A few months ago.
I think some people just go when they're ready.
And your father was.
I'm sorry... I wish I could've been here...
I know. But you can't feel guilty about that.
He would have been so happy to know you came back, Richie.
You're *home.*
You're *safe...*

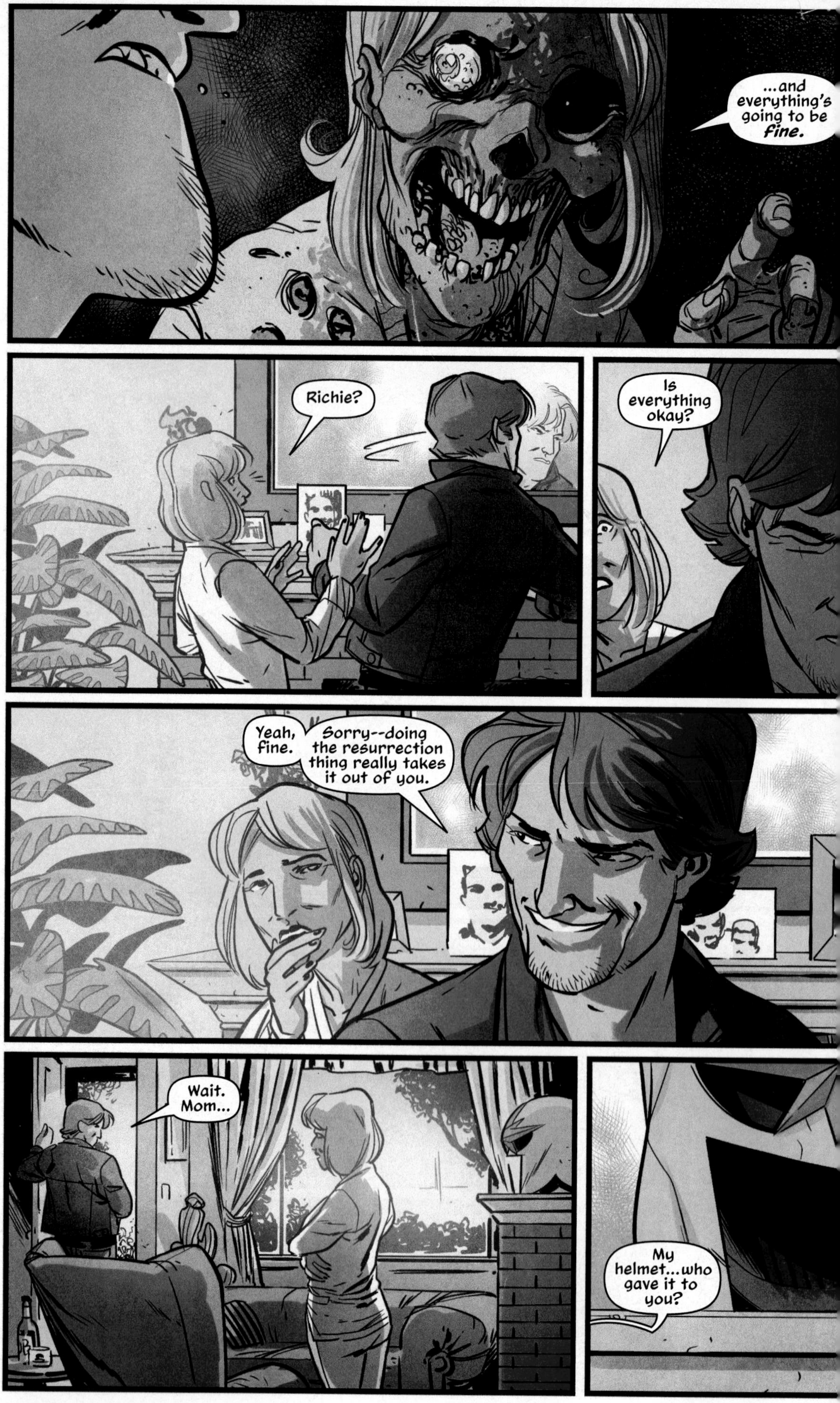
...and everything's going to be *fine.*
Richie?
Is everything okay?
Yeah, fine.
Sorry--doing the resurrection thing really takes it out of you.
Wait. Mom...
My helmet...who gave it to you?

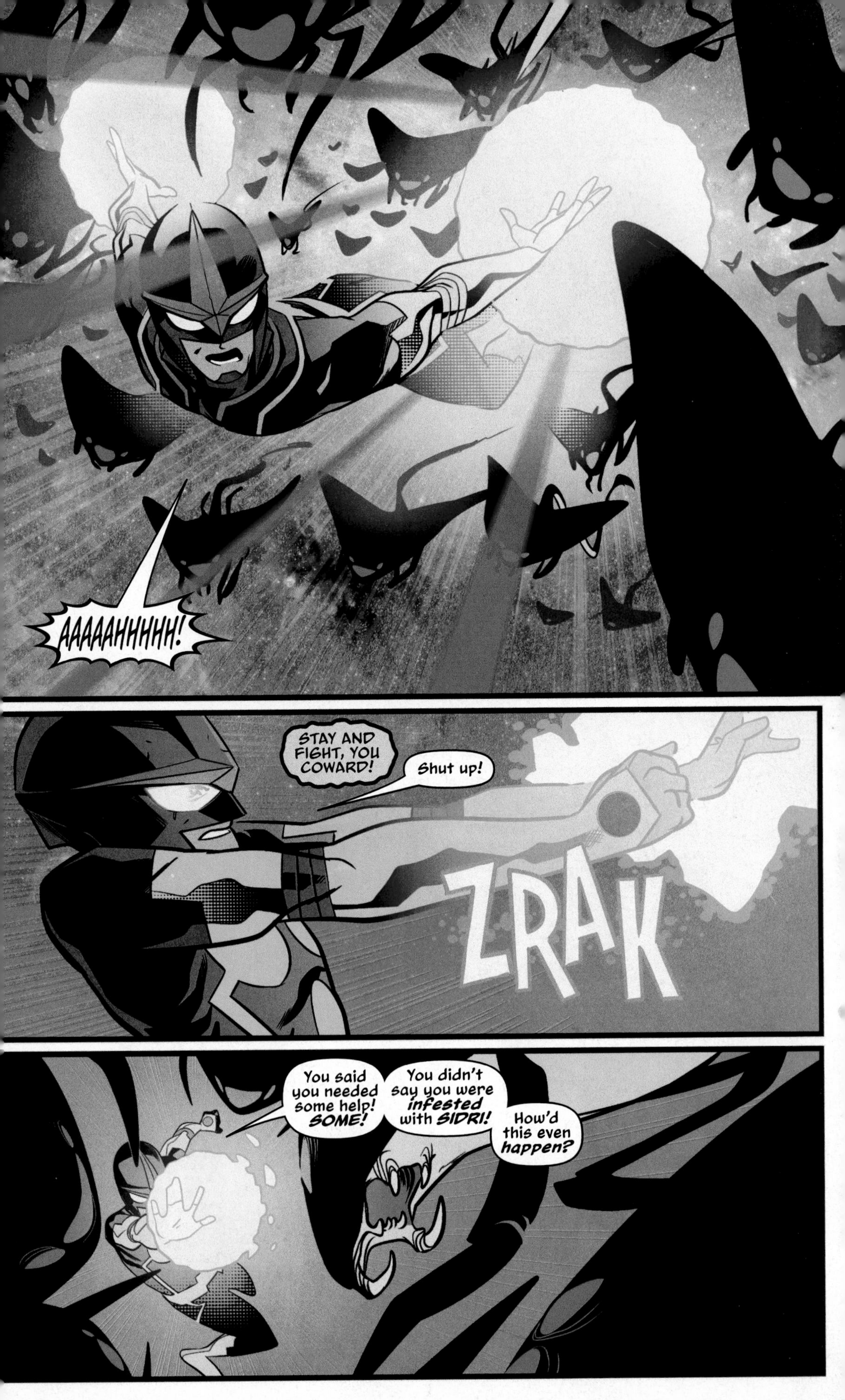
AAAAAHHHHH!
STAY AND FIGHT, YOU COWARD!
Shut up!
ZRAK
You said you needed some help! SOME!
You didn't say you were infested with SIDRI!
How'd this even happen?

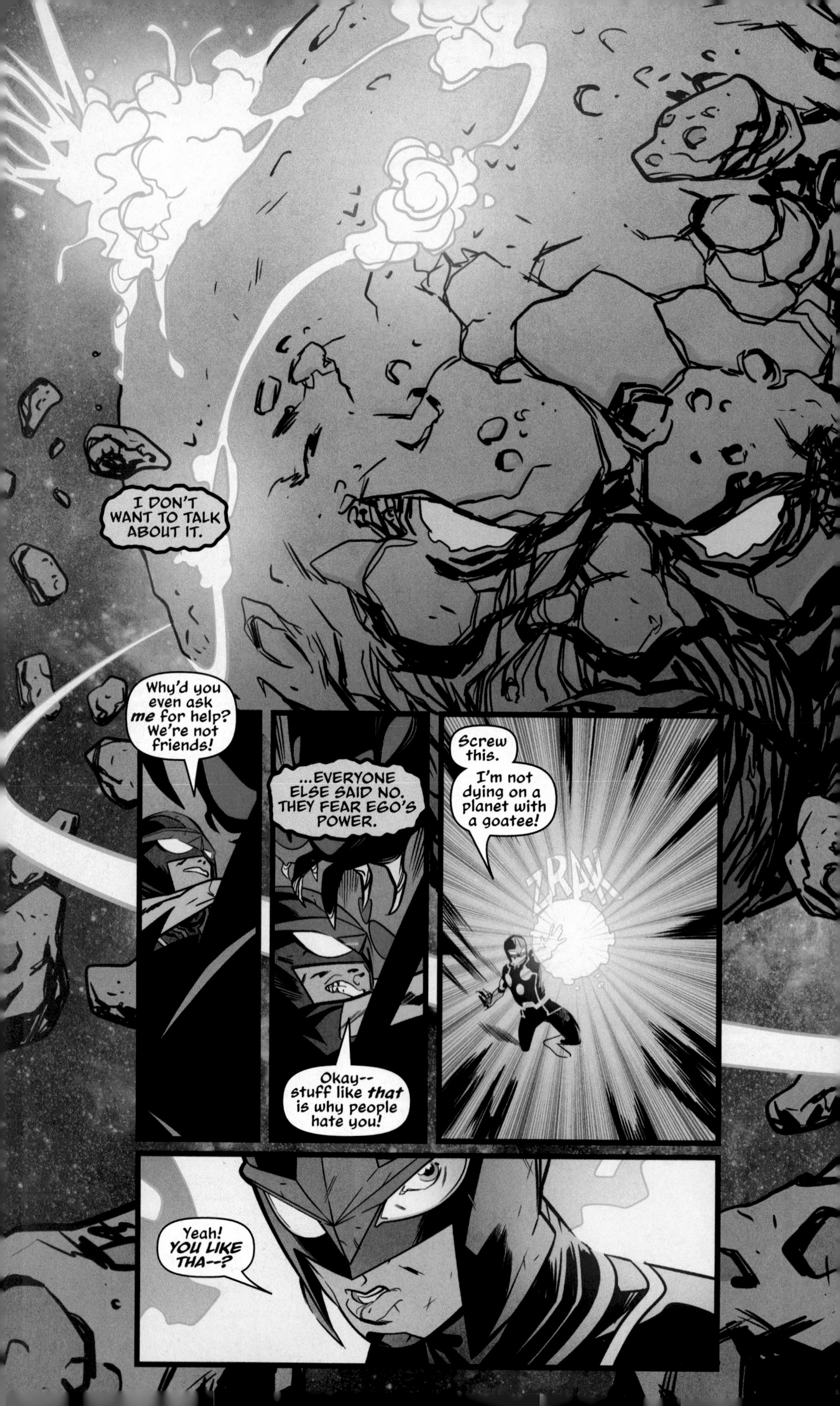

I DON'T WANT TO TALK ABOUT IT.
Why'd you even ask *me* for help? We're not friends!
...EVERYONE ELSE SAID NO. THEY FEAR EGO'S POWER.
Okay-- stuff like *that* is why people hate you!
Screw this.
I'm not dying on a planet with a goatee!
ZRAK!
Yeah! YOU LIKE THA--?

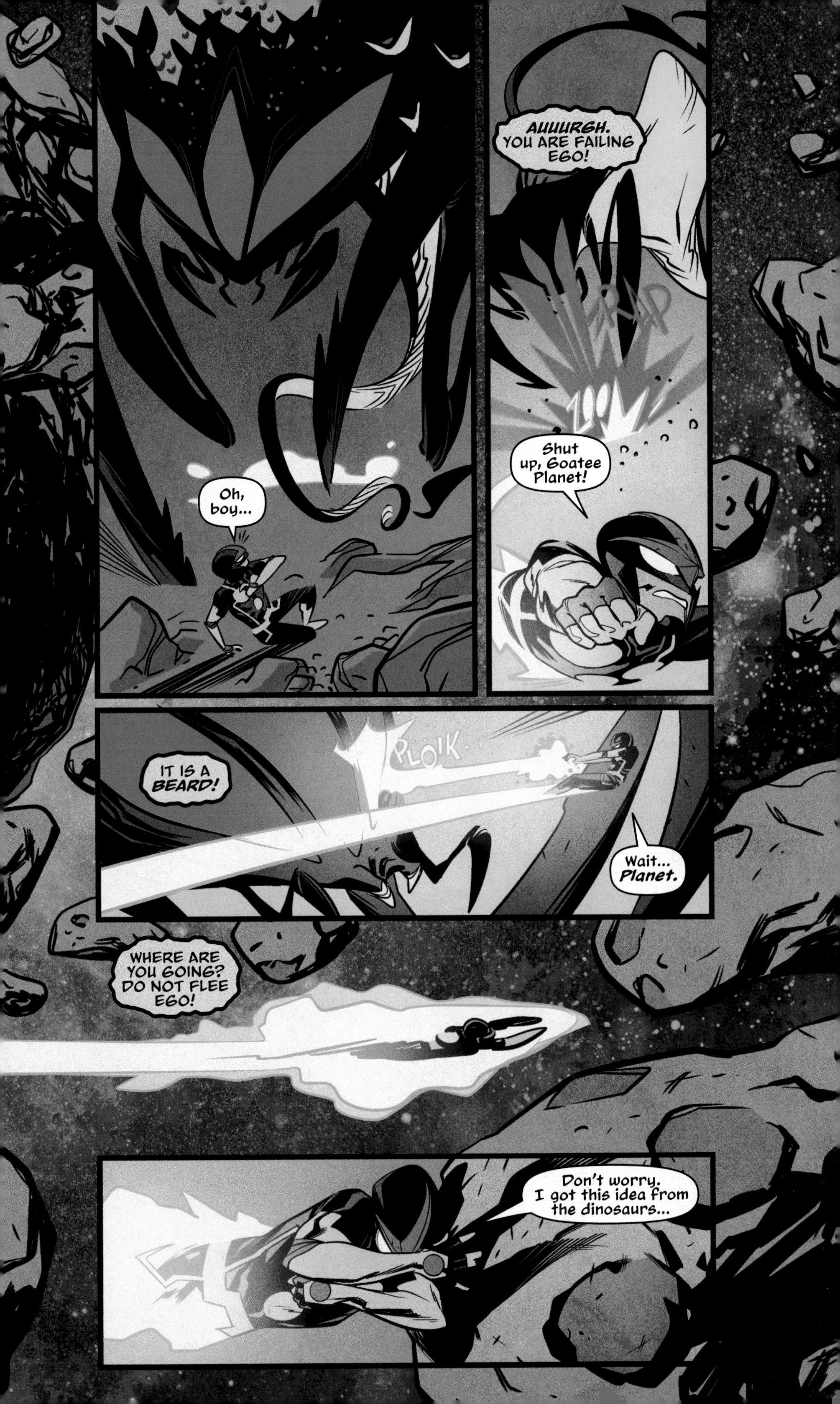
Oh, boy...
AUUURGH. YOU ARE FAILING EGO!
Shut up, Goatee Planet!
IT IS A BEARD!
PLOIK
Wait... Planet.
WHERE ARE YOU GOING? DO NOT FLEE EGO!
Don't worry. I got this idea from the dinosaurs...

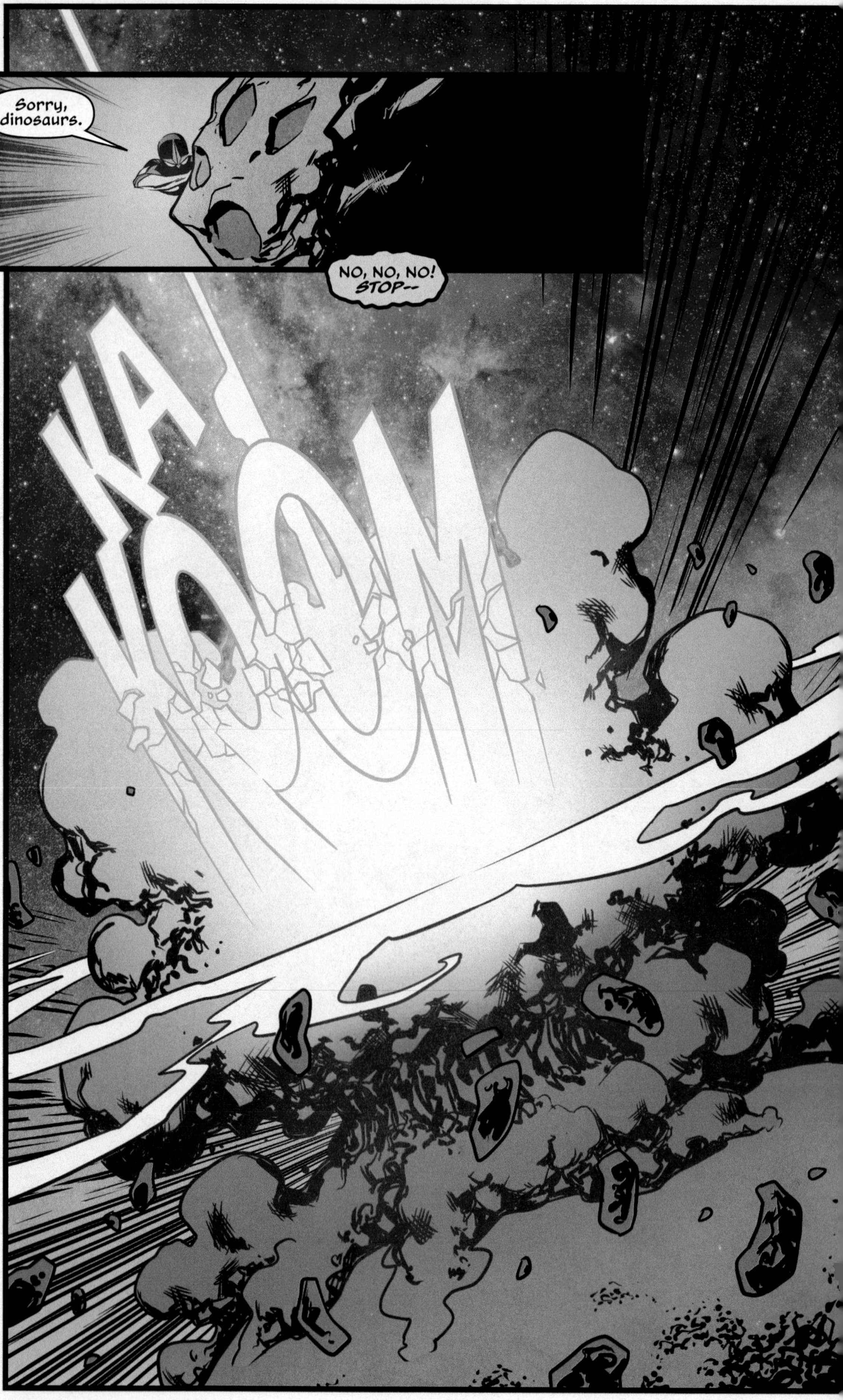
Sorry, dinosaurs.
NO, NO, NO! STOP--
KA-VOOM

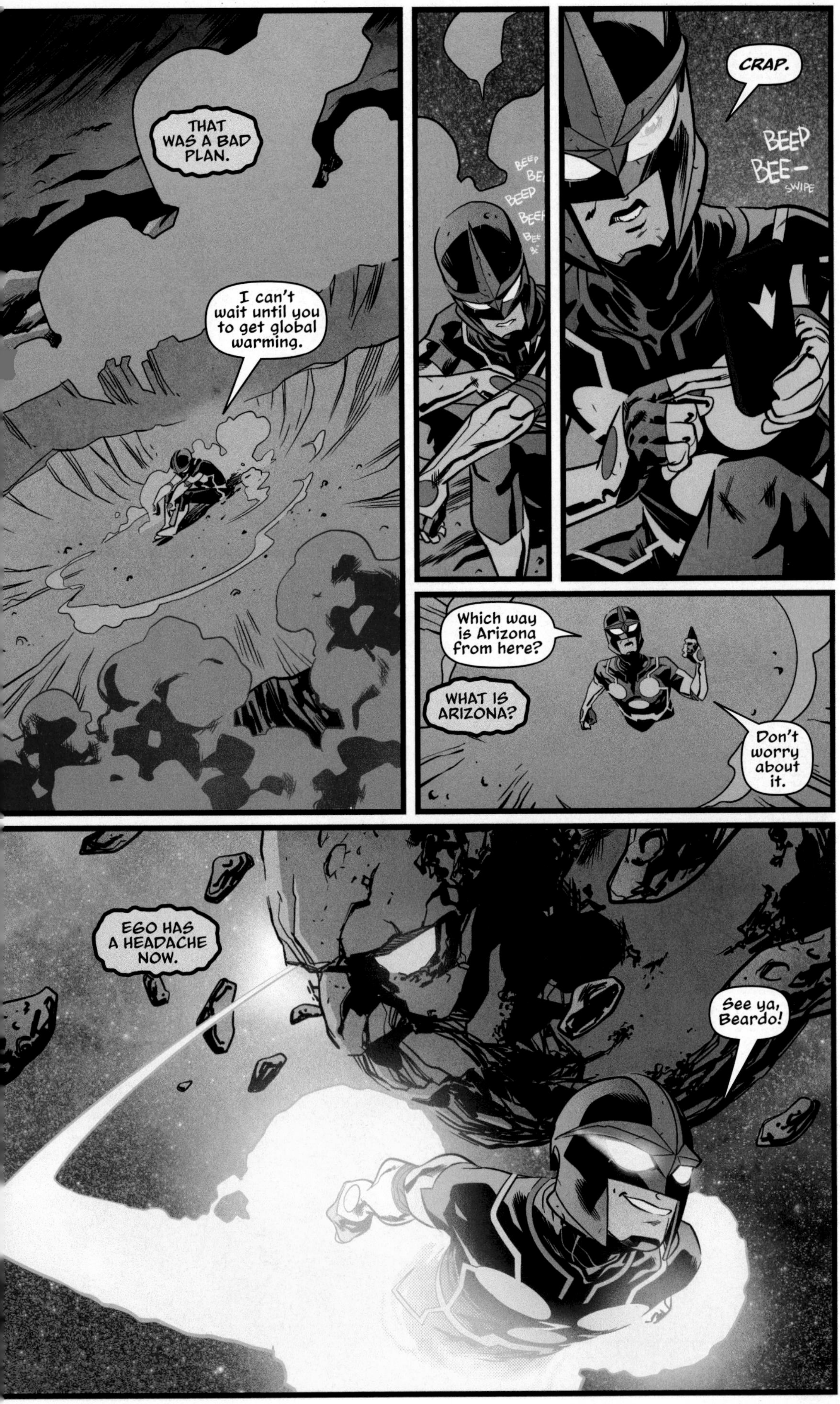
THAT WAS A BAD PLAN.
I can't wait until you to get global warming.
BEEP
BEEP
BEEP
CRAP.
BEEP BEE-
SWIPE
Which way is Arizona from here?
WHAT IS ARIZONA?
Don't worry about it.
EGO HAS A HEADACHE NOW.
See ya, Beardo!

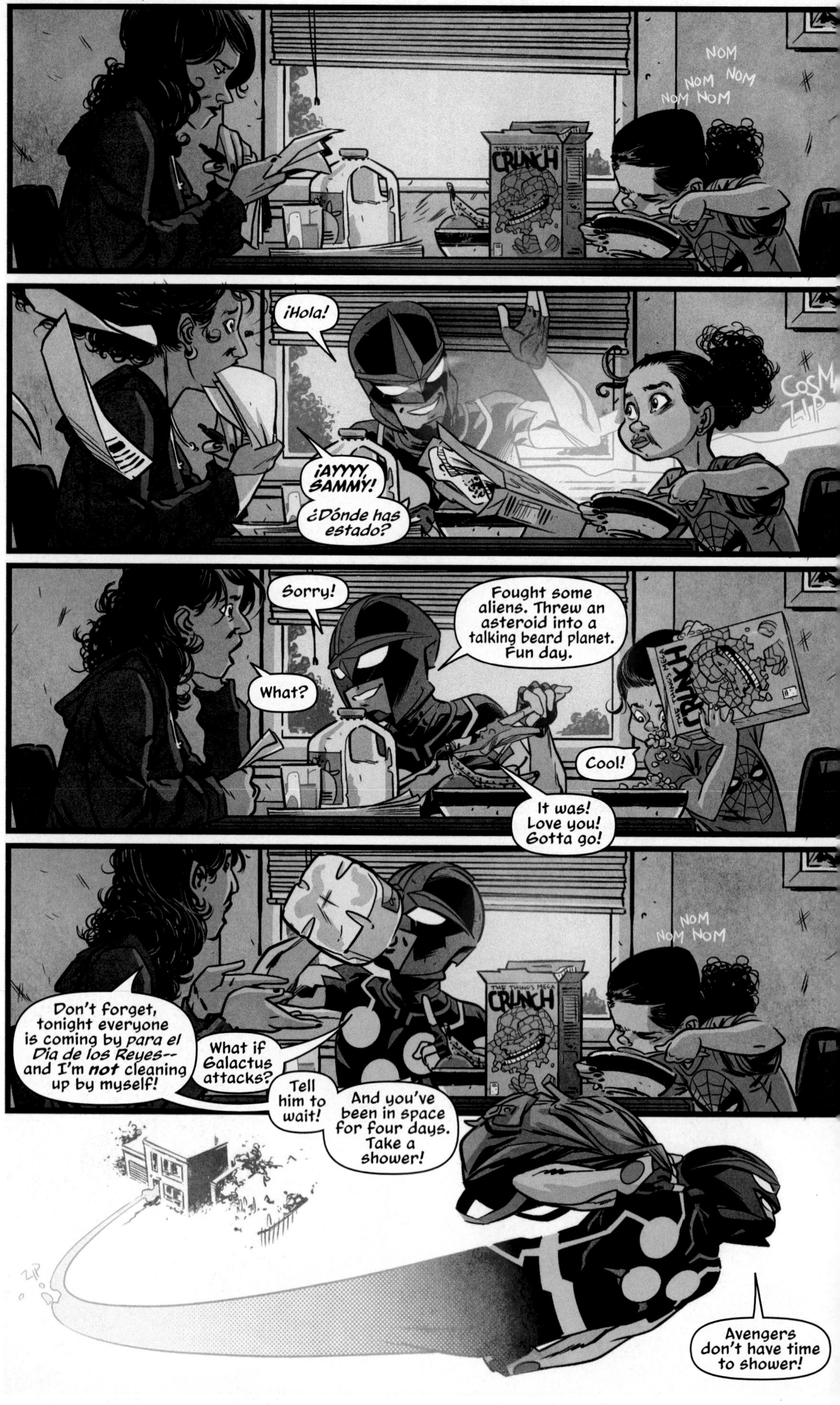
NOM
NOM NOM
NOM NOM
THE THING'S MEGA CRUNCH
¡Hola!
¡AYYYY, SAMMY!
¿Dónde has estado?
COSM ZIP
Sorry!
Fought some aliens. Threw an asteroid into a talking beard planet. Fun day.
What?
Cool!
It was! Love you! Gotta go!
NOM
NOM NOM
THE THING'S MEGA CRUNCH
Don't forget, tonight everyone is coming by *para el Dia de los Reyes*-- and I'm **not** cleaning up by myself!
What if Galactus attacks?
Tell him to wait!
And you've been in space for four days. Take a shower!
ZIP
Avengers don't have time to shower!

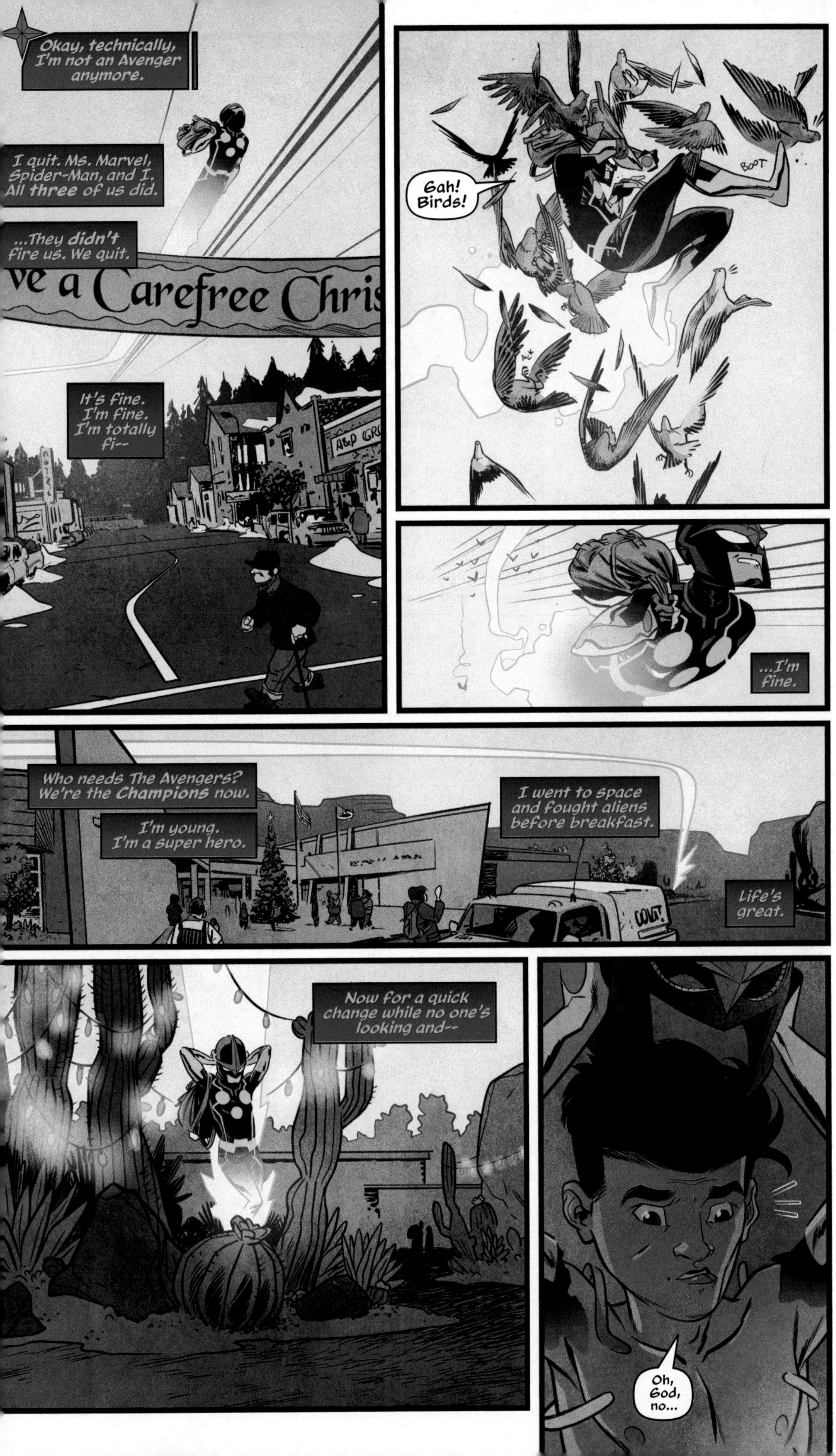
Okay, technically, I'm not an Avenger anymore.
I quit. Ms. Marvel, Spider-Man, and I. All three of us did.
...They didn't fire us. We quit.
ve a Carefree Chris
It's fine. I'm fine. I'm totally fi--
A&P GR
Gah! Birds!
BOOT
...I'm fine.
Who needs The Avengers? We're the Champions now.
I'm young. I'm a super hero.
I went to space and fought aliens before breakfast.
Life's great.
Now for a quick change while no one's looking and--
Oh, God, no...

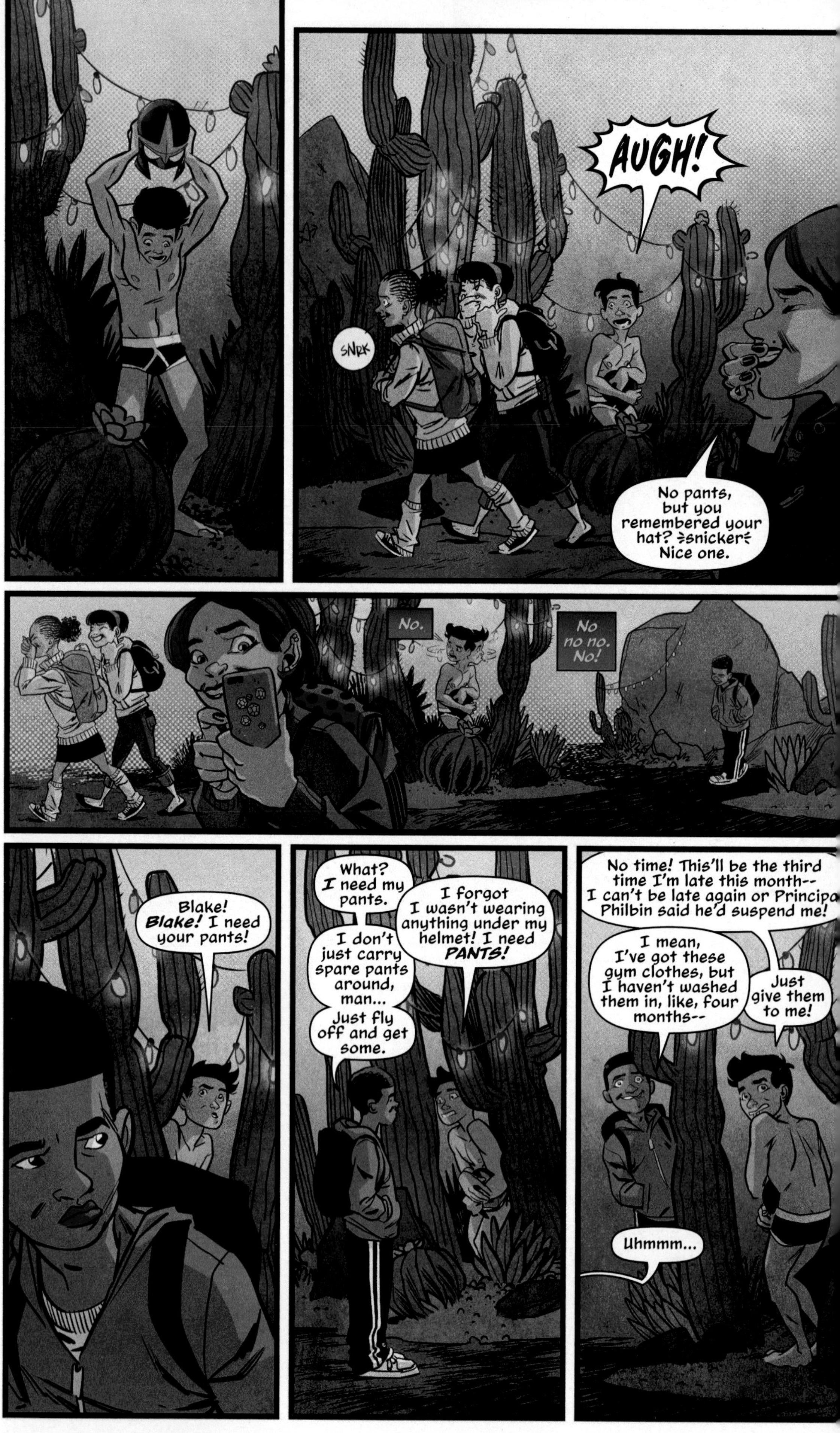
AUGH!
SNRK
No pants, but you remembered your hat? ≑snicker≑ Nice one.
No.
No no no. No!
Blake! Blake! I need your pants!
What? I need my pants.
I don't just carry spare pants around, man... Just fly off and get some.
I forgot I wasn't wearing anything under my helmet! I need PANTS!
No time! This'll be the third time I'm late this month-- I can't be late again or Principa Philbin said he'd suspend me!
I mean, I've got these gym clothes, but I haven't washed them in, like, four months--
Just give them to me!
Uhmmm...

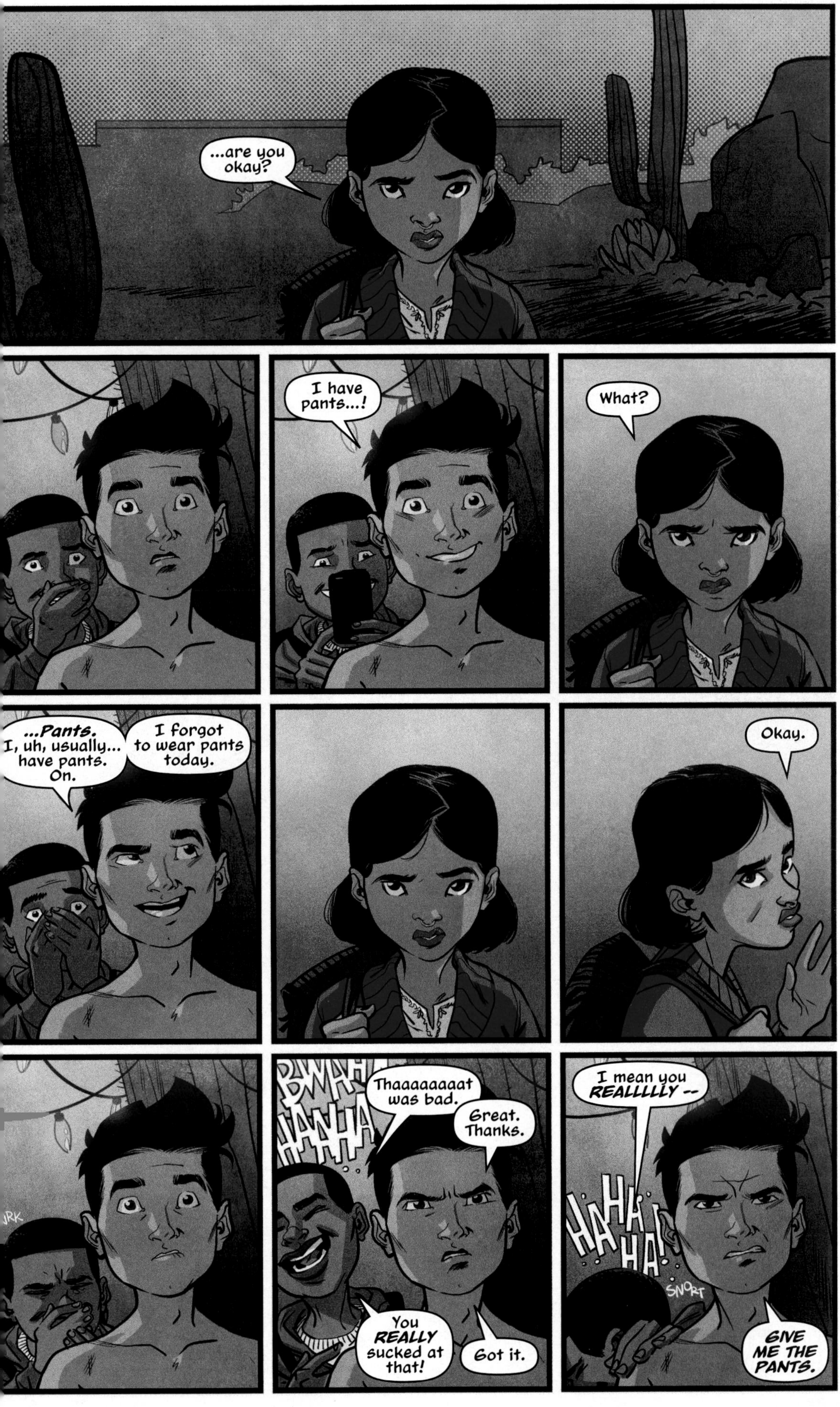
...are you okay?
I have pants...!
What?
...Pants. I, uh, usually... have pants. On.
I forgot to wear pants today.
Okay.
Thaaaaaaaat was bad.
Great. Thanks.
You REALLY sucked at that!
Got it.
I mean you REALLLLLY --
HAHA HA!
SNORT
GIVE ME THE PANTS.

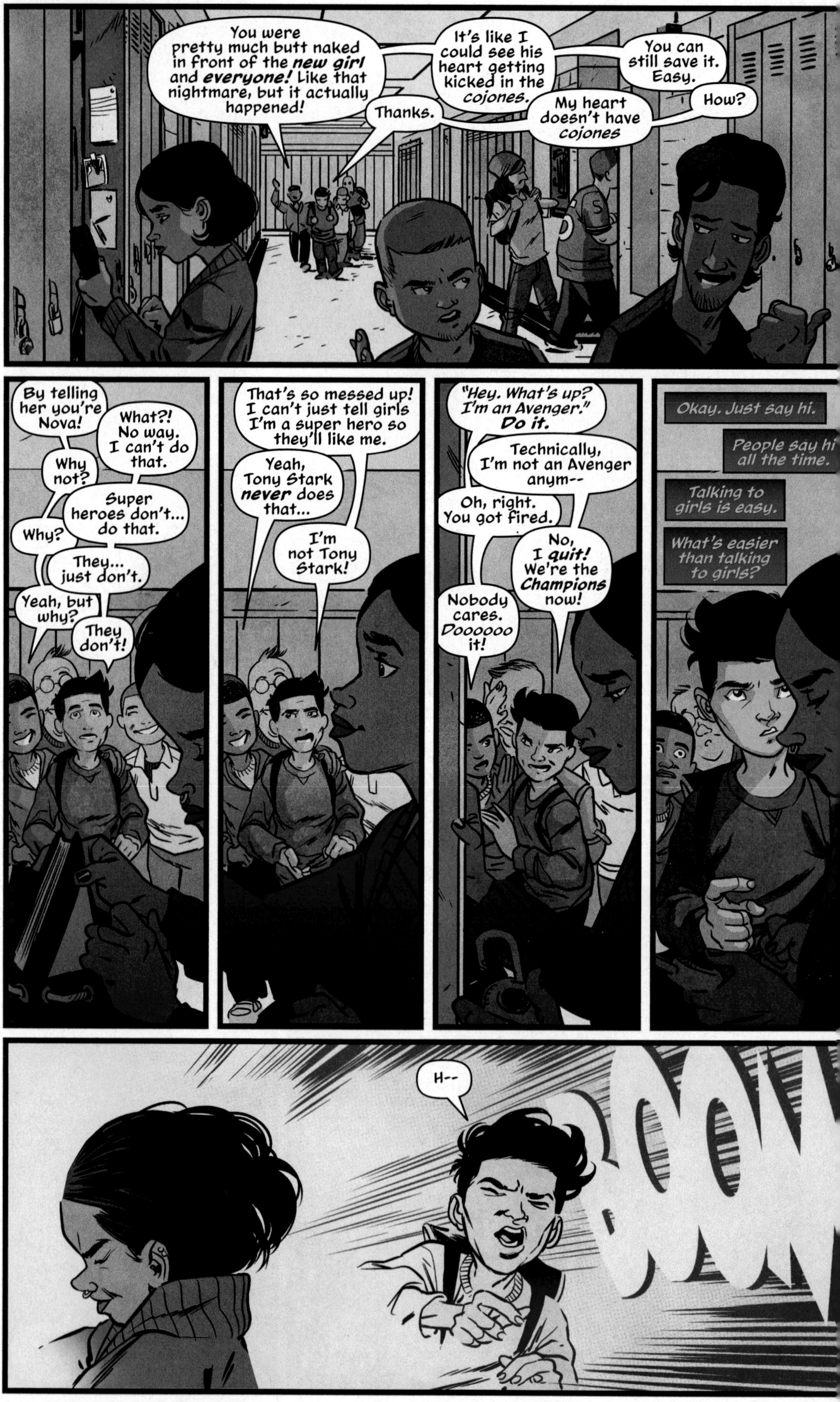
You were pretty much butt naked in front of the *new girl* and *everyone!* Like that nightmare, but it actually happened!
Thanks.
It's like I could see his heart getting kicked in the *cojones*.
My heart doesn't have *cojones*
You can still save it. Easy.
How?
By telling her you're Nova!
What?! No way. I can't do that.
Why not?
Super heroes don't... do that.
Why?
They... just don't.
Yeah, but why?
They don't!
That's so messed up! I can't just tell girls I'm a super hero so they'll like me.
Yeah, Tony Stark *never* does that...
I'm not Tony Stark!
"Hey. What's up? I'm an Avenger." Do it.
Technically, I'm not an Avenger anym--
Oh, right. You got fired.
No, I *quit!* We're the *Champions* now!
Nobody cares. *Doooooo it!*
Okay. Just say hi.
People say hi all the time.
Talking to girls is easy.
What's easier than talking to girls?
H--

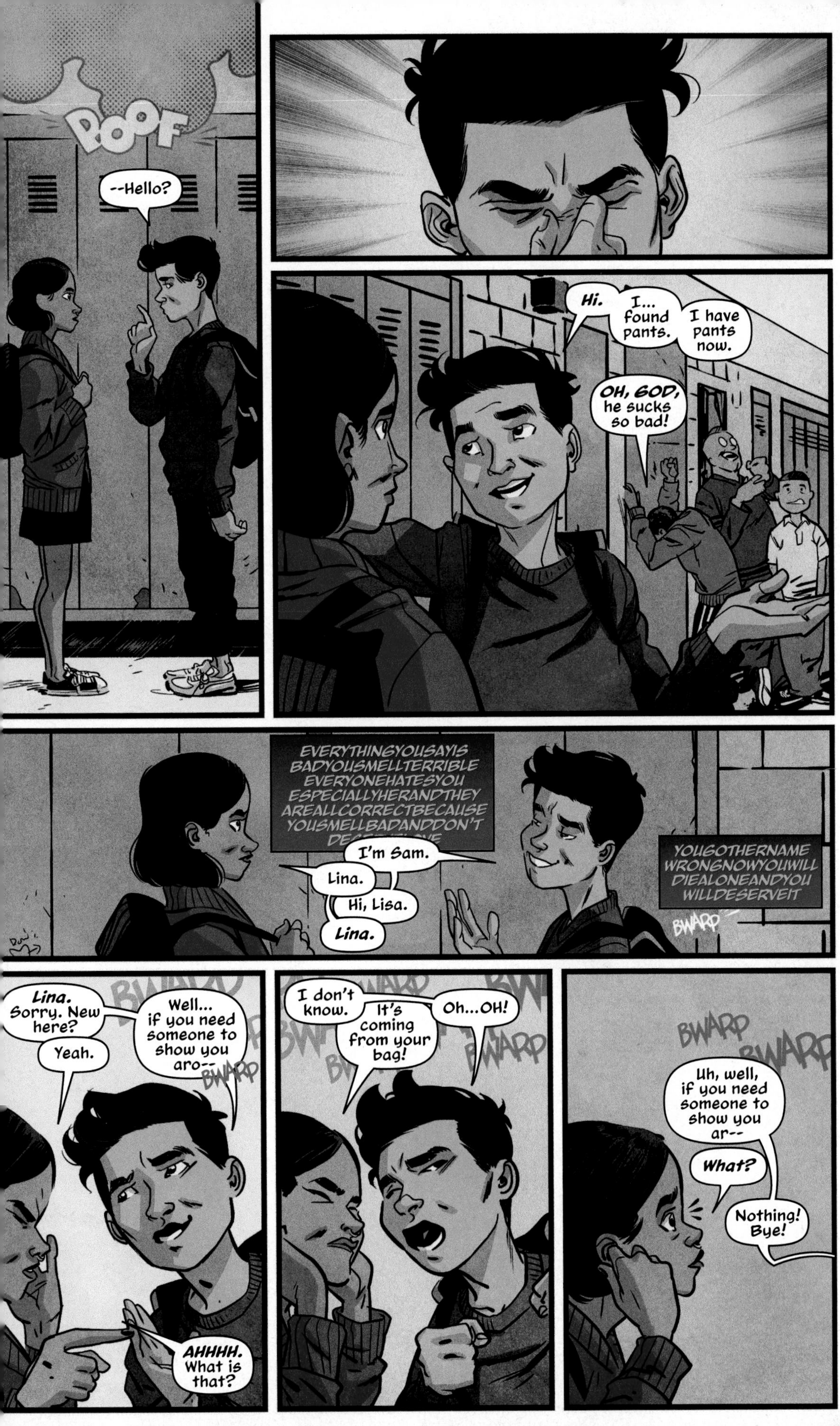
POOF
--Hello?
Hi.
I... found pants.
I have pants now.
OH, GOD, he sucks so bad!
EVERYTHINGYOUSAYIS BADYOUSMELLTERRIBLE EVERYONEHATESYOU ESPECIALLYHERANDTHEY AREALLCORRECTBECAUSE YOUSMELLBADANDDON'T
I'm Sam.
Lina.
Hi, Lisa.
Lina.
YOUGOTHERNAME WRONGNOWYOUWILL DIEALONEANDYOU WILLDESERVEIT
BWARP
Lina. Sorry. New here?
Yeah.
Well... if you need someone to show you aro--
BWARP
AHHHH. What is that?
I don't know.
It's coming from your bag!
Oh...OH!
BWARP
BWARP
BWARP
Uh, well, if you need someone to show you ar--
What?
Nothing! Bye!

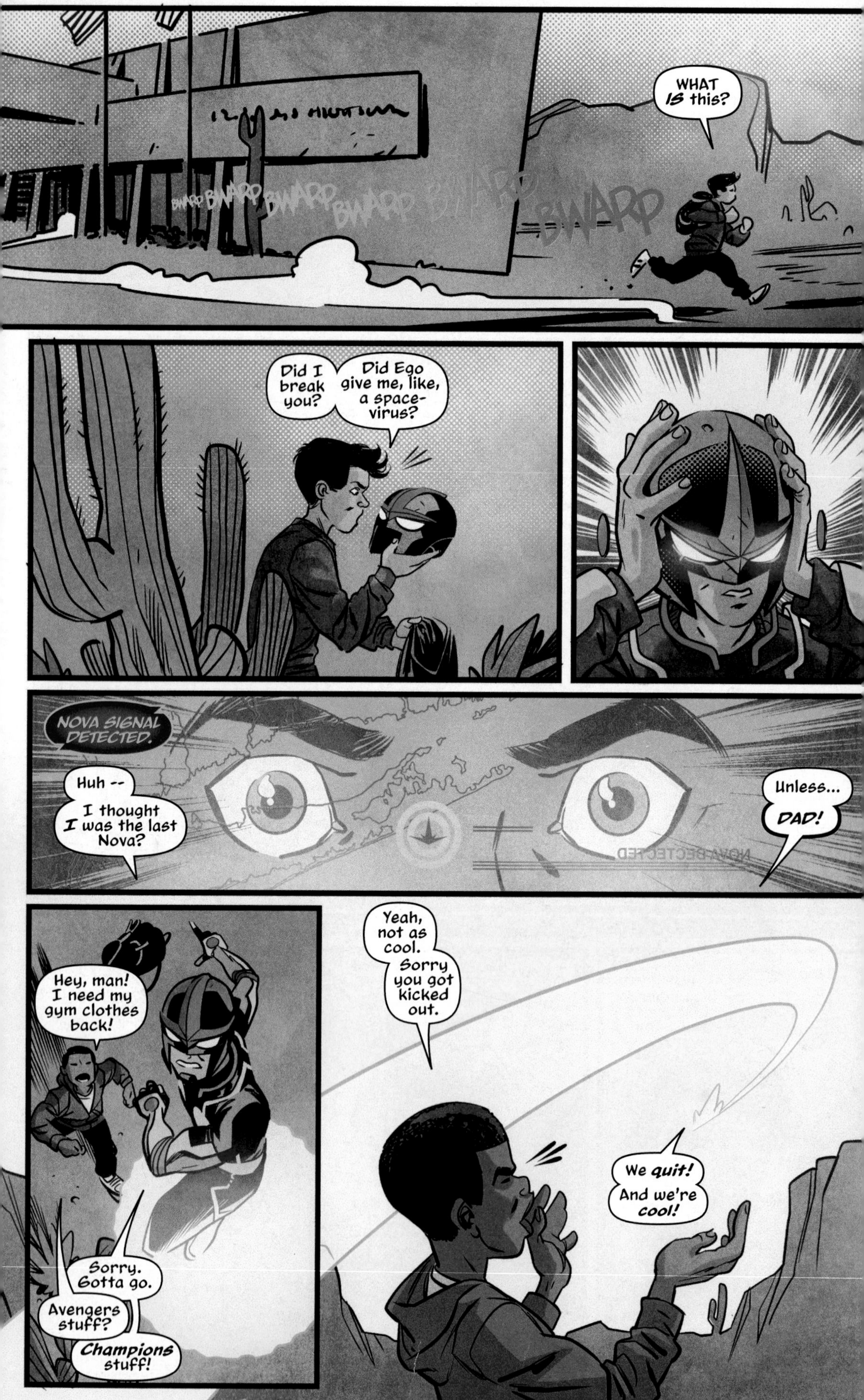
WHAT IS this?
BWARP BWARP BWARP BWARP BWARP BWARP
Did I break you?
Did Ego give me, like, a space-virus?
NOVA SIGNAL DETECTED.
Huh -- I thought I was the last Nova?
Unless... DAD!
Hey, man! I need my gym clothes back!
Sorry. Gotta go.
Avengers stuff?
Champions stuff!
Yeah, not as cool.
Sorry you got kicked out.
We quit! And we're cool!

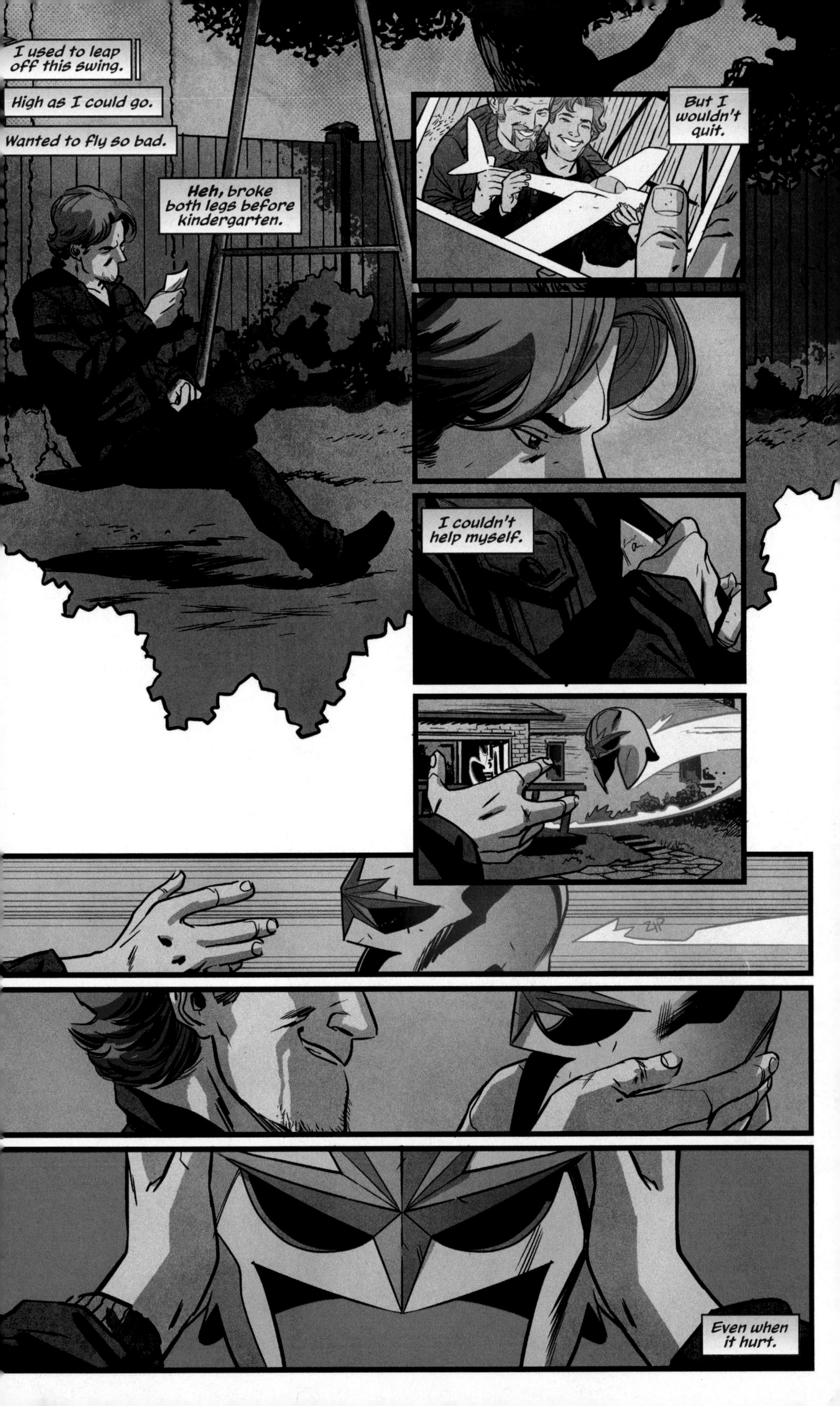
I used to leap off this swing.
High as I could go.
Wanted to fly so bad.
Heh, broke both legs before kindergarten.
But I wouldn't quit.
I couldn't help myself.
Even when it hurt.

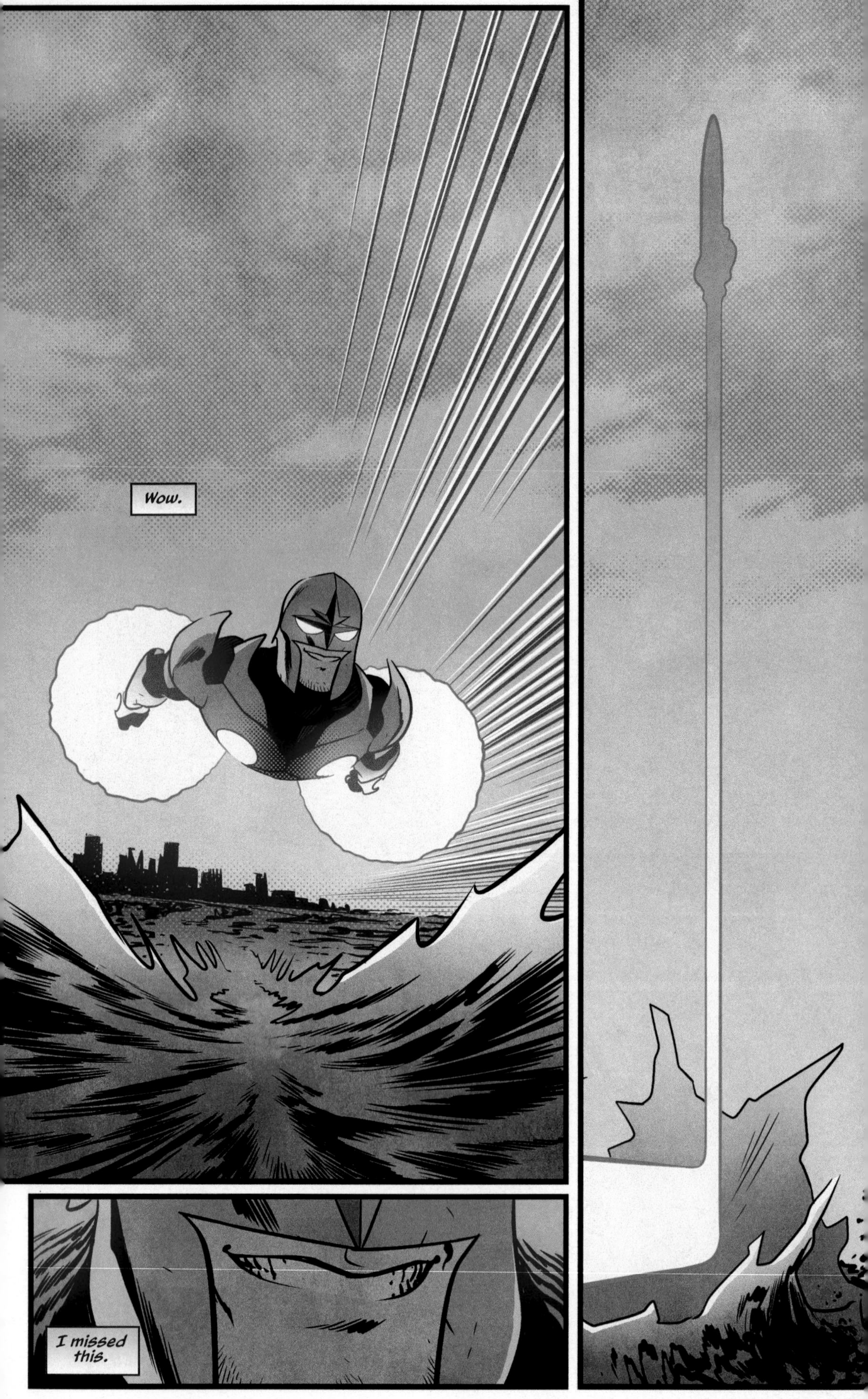
Wow.
I missed this.

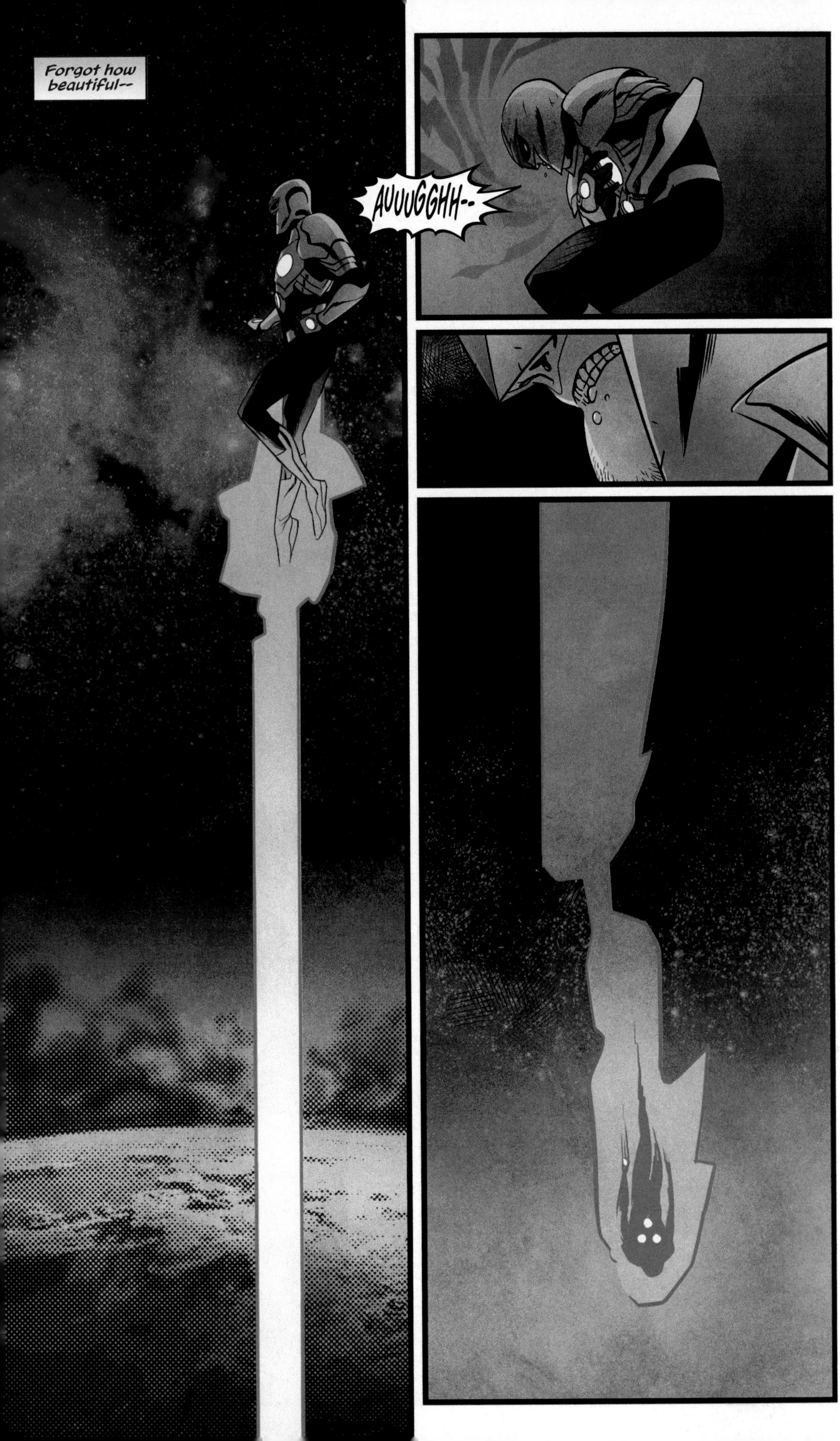
Forgot how beautiful--
AUUUGHH--

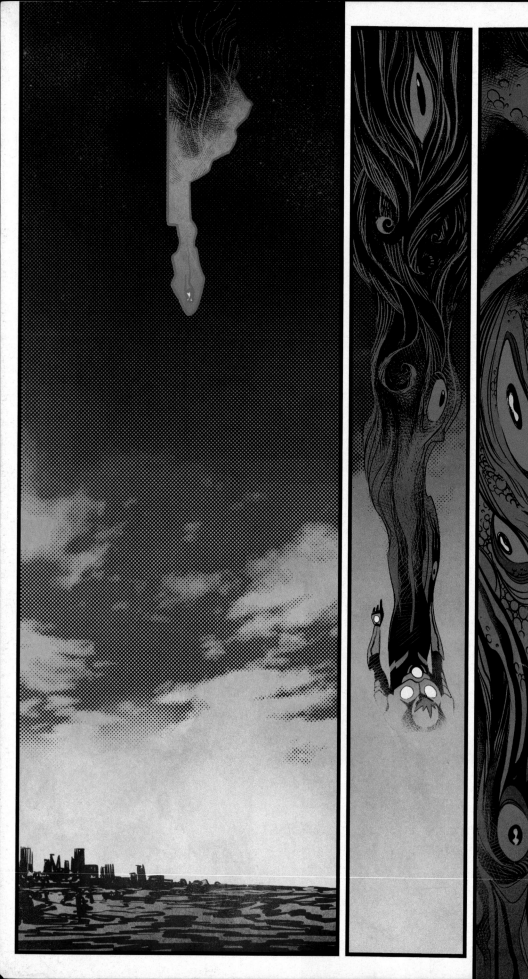

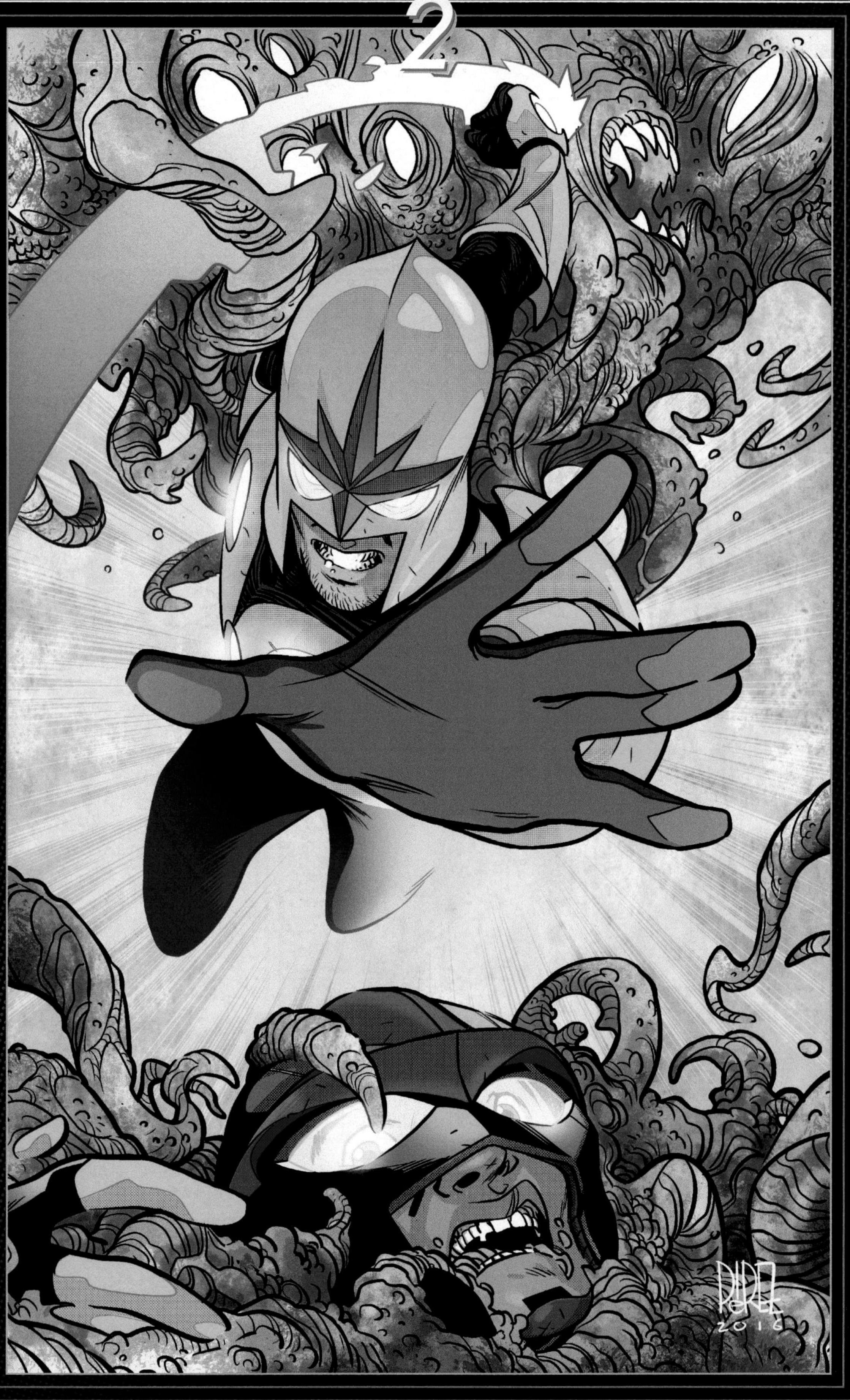
2

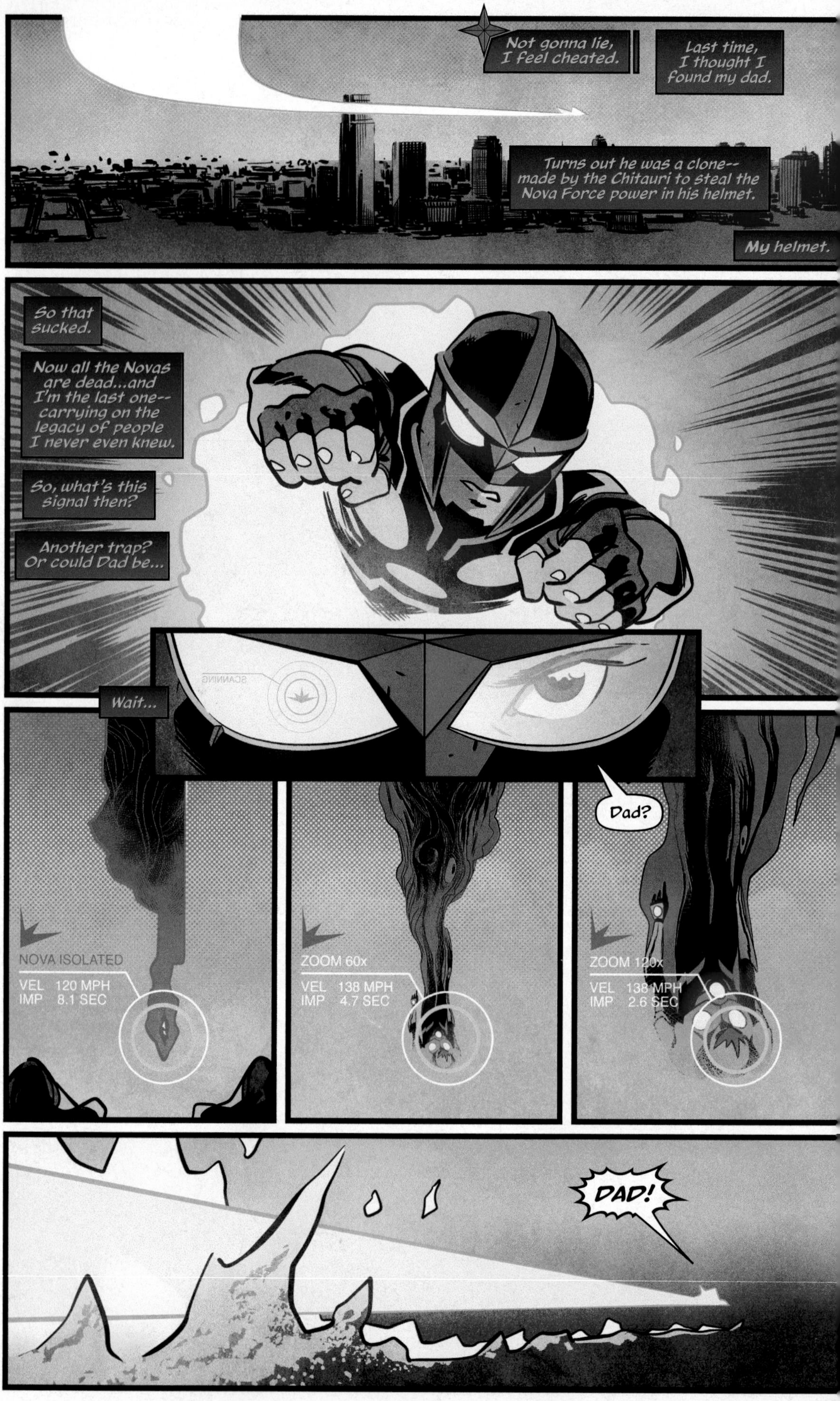
Not gonna lie, I feel cheated.
Last time, I thought I found my dad.
Turns out he was a clone-- made by the Chitauri to steal the Nova Force power in his helmet.
My helmet.
So that sucked.
Now all the Novas are dead...and I'm the last one-- carrying on the legacy of people I never even knew.
So, what's this signal then?
Another trap? Or could Dad be...
SCANNING
Wait...
NOVA ISOLATED
VEL 120 MPH
IMP 8.1 SEC
ZOOM 60x
VEL 138 MPH
IMP 4.7 SEC
Dad?
ZOOM 120x
VEL 138 MPH
IMP 2.6 SEC
DAD!

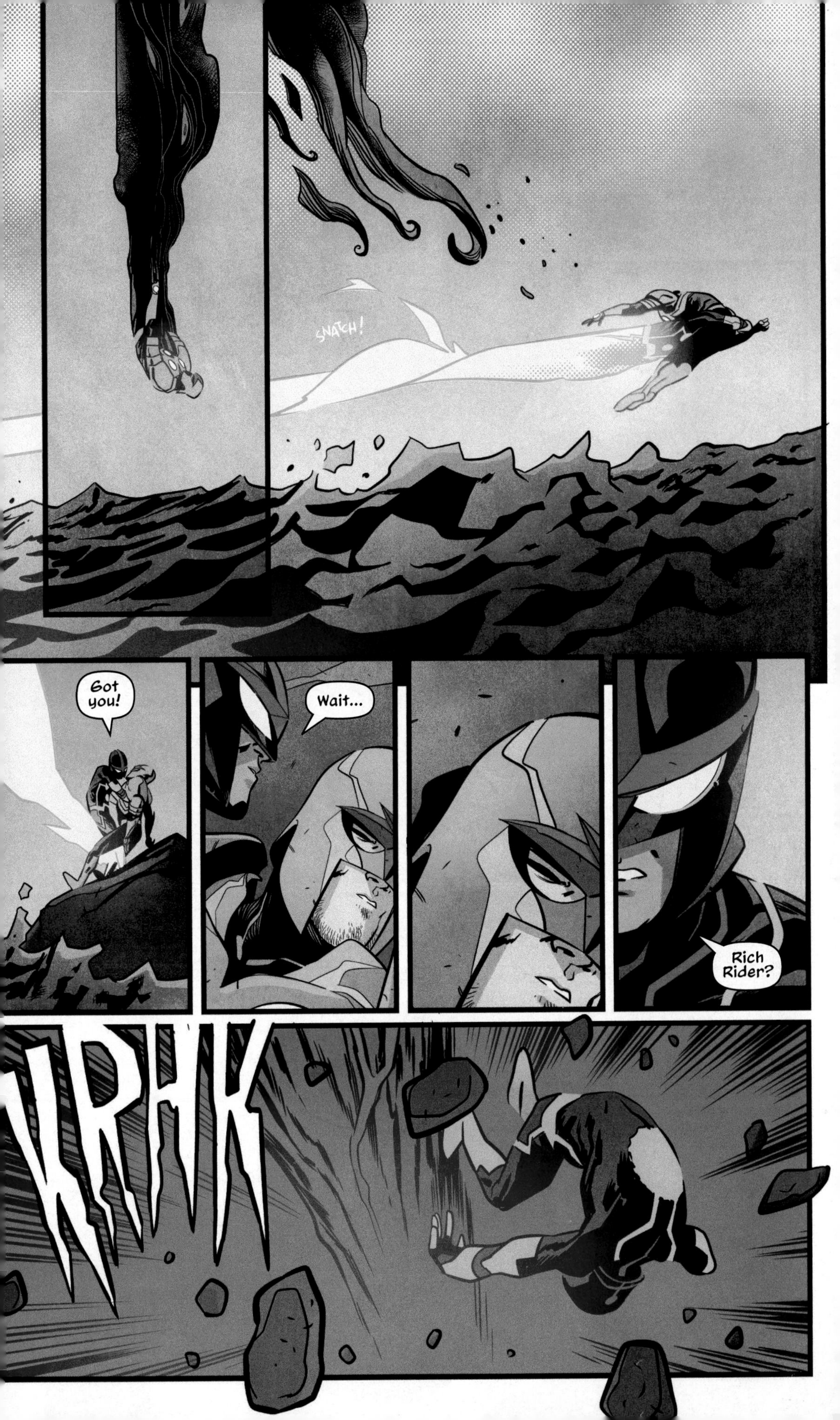
SNATCH!
Got you!
Wait...
Rich Rider?
KRAK

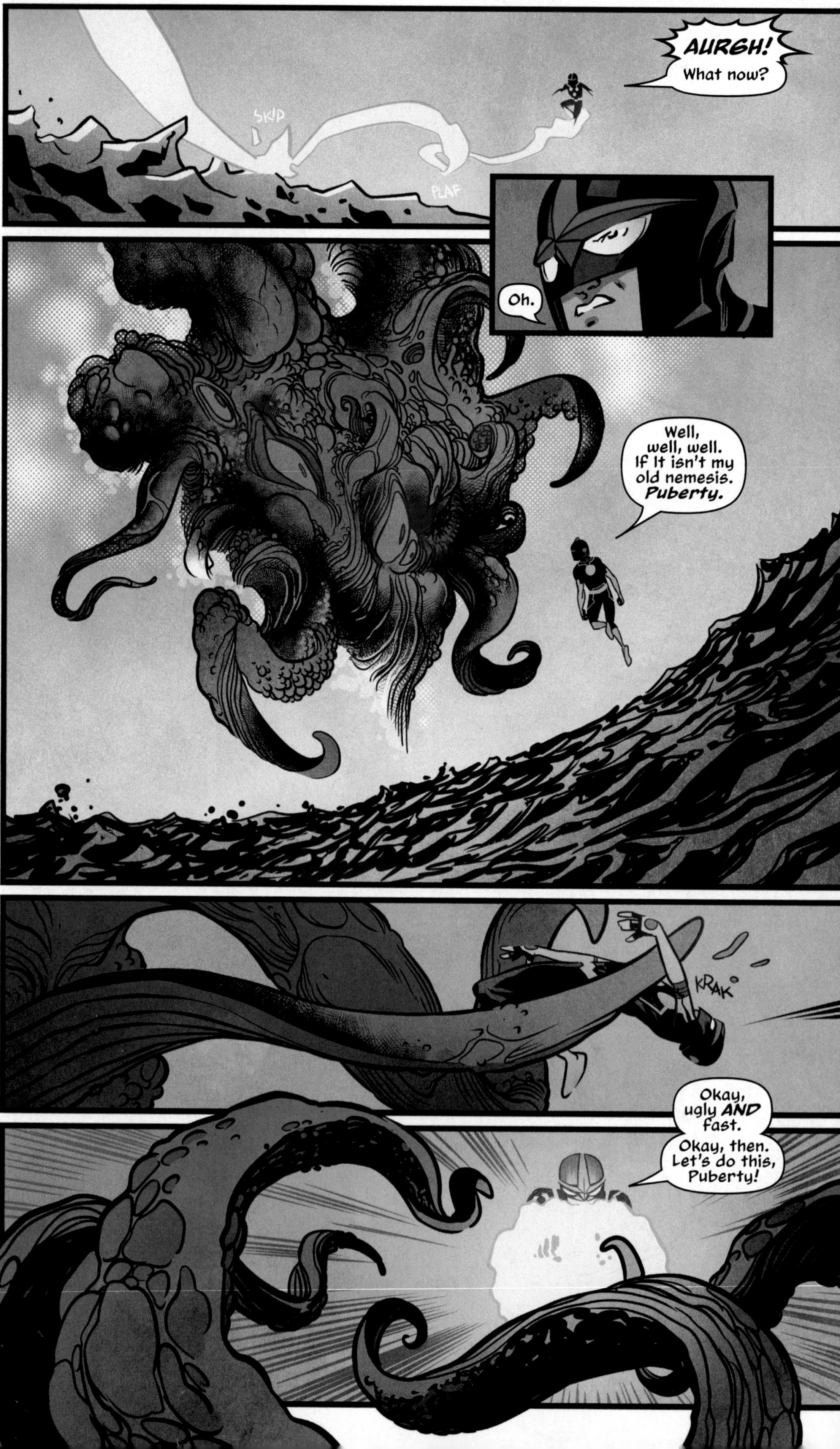
AURGH! What now?
SKIP
PLAF
Oh.
Well, well, well. If It isn't my old nemesis. *Puberty.*
KRAK
Okay, ugly AND fast. Okay, then. Let's do this, Puberty!

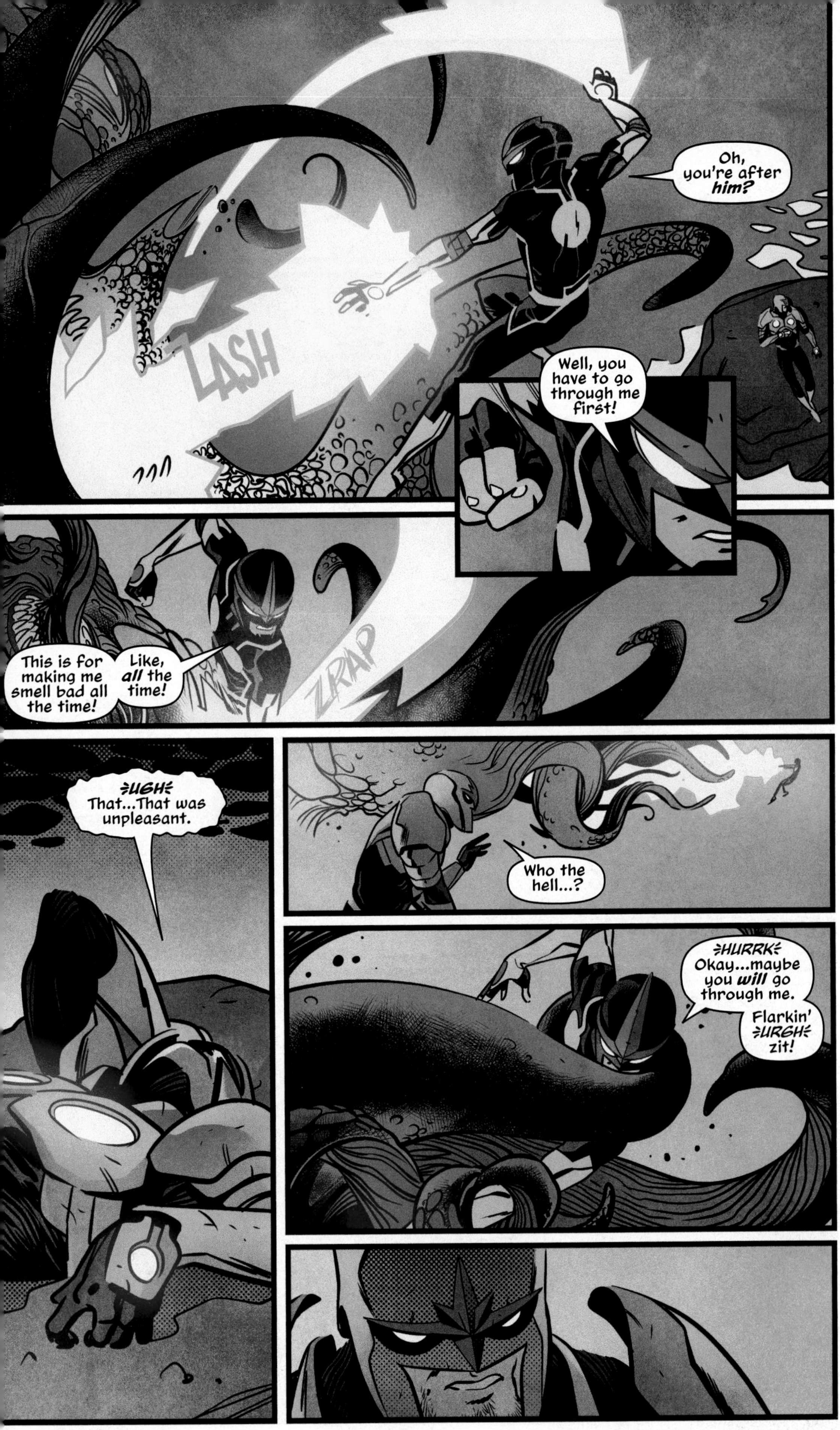
Oh, you're after him?
LASH
Well, you have to go through me first!
This is for making me smell bad all the time!
Like, all the time!
ZRAP
UGH
That...That was unpleasant.
Who the hell...?
HURRK
Okay...maybe you will go through me.
Flarkin' URGH zit!

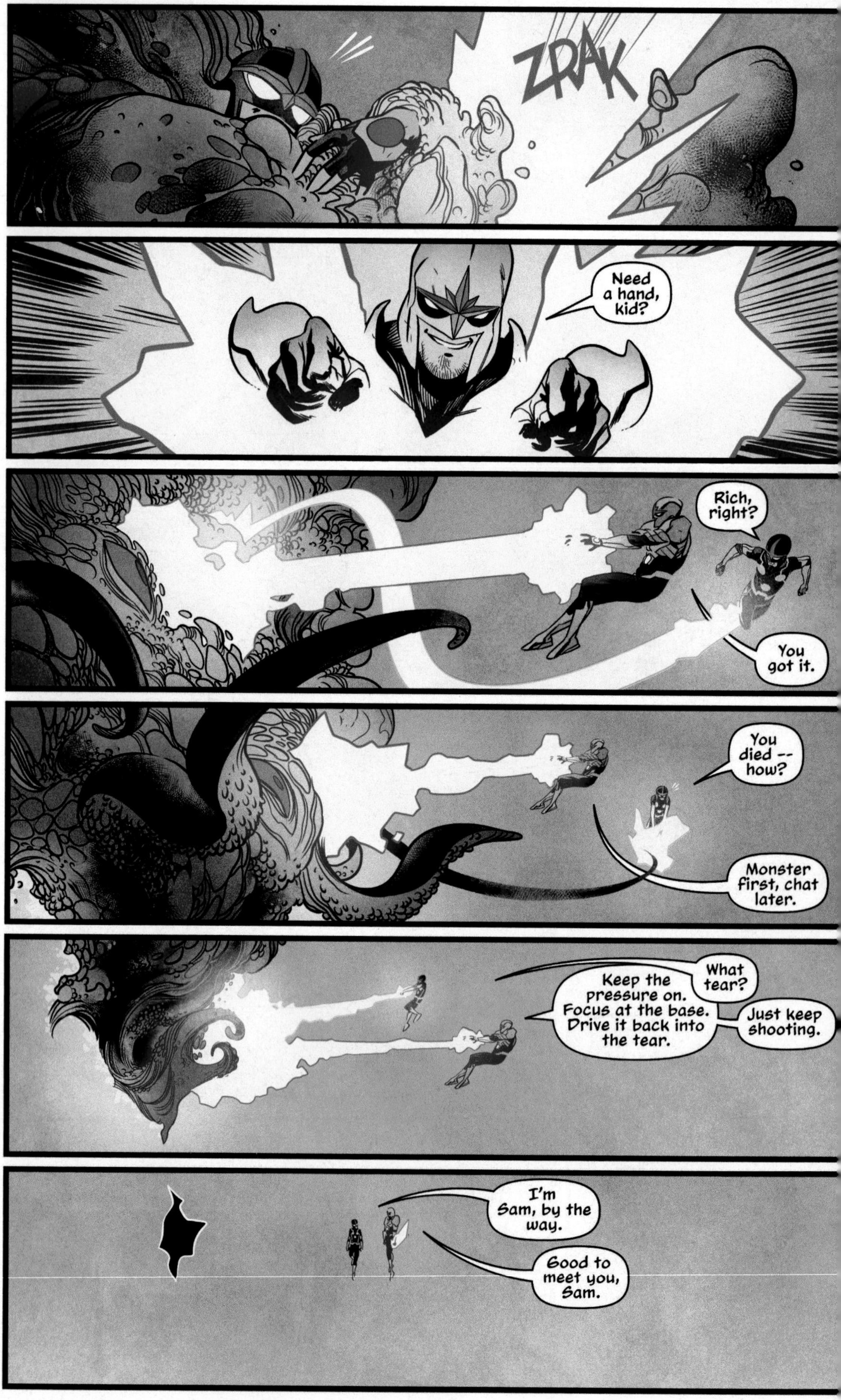
ZRAK
Need a hand, kid?
Rich, right?
You got it.
You died -- how?
Monster first, chat later.
What tear?
Keep the pressure on. Focus at the base. Drive it back into the tear.
Just keep shooting.
I'm Sam, by the way.
Good to meet you, Sam.

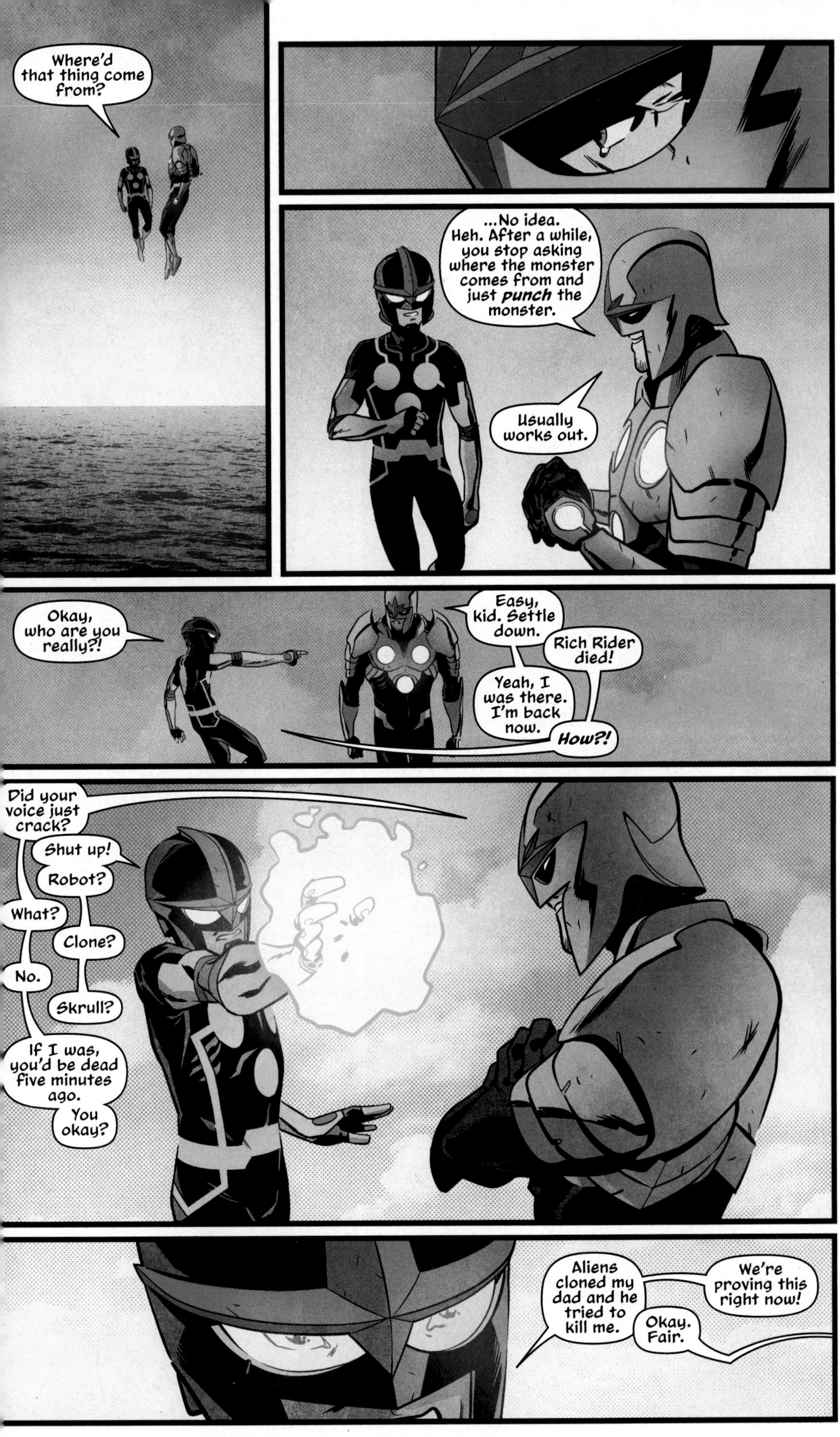
Where'd that thing come from?
...No idea. Heh. After a while, you stop asking where the monster comes from and just *punch* the monster.
Usually works out.
Okay, who are you really?!
Easy, kid. Settle down.
Rich Rider died!
Yeah, I was there. I'm back now.
How?!
Did your voice just crack?
Shut up!
Robot?
What?
Clone?
No.
Skrull?
If I was, you'd be dead five minutes ago.
You okay?
Aliens cloned my dad and he tried to kill me.
We're proving this right now!
Okay. Fair.

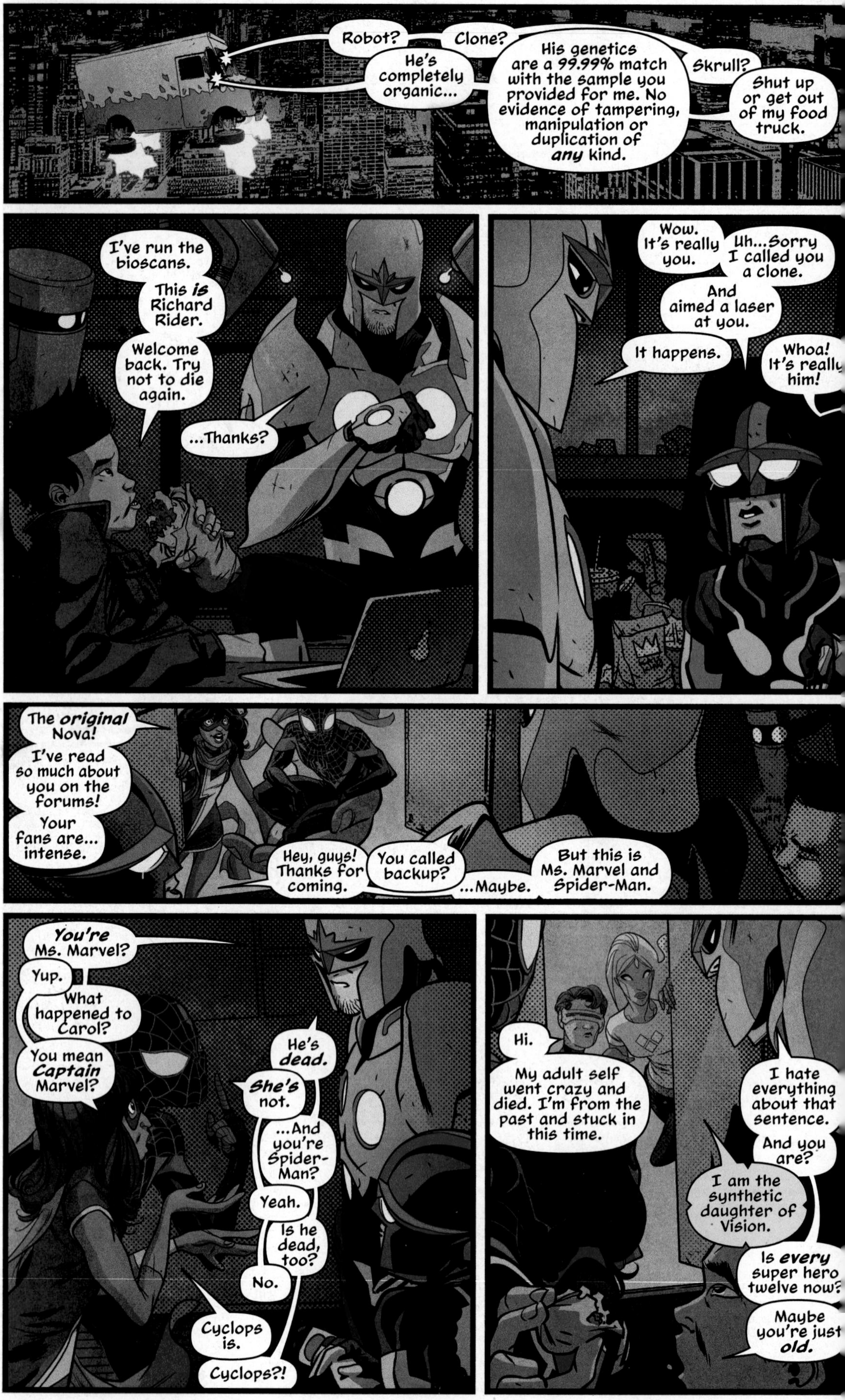

Robot?
Clone?
He's completely organic...
His genetics are a 99.99% match with the sample you provided for me. No evidence of tampering, manipulation or duplication of *any* kind.
Skrull?
Shut up or get out of my food truck.
I've run the bioscans.
This *is* Richard Rider.
Welcome back. Try not to die again.
...Thanks?
Wow. It's really you.
Uh...Sorry I called you a clone.
And aimed a laser at you.
It happens.
Whoa! It's really him!
The *original* Nova!
I've read so much about you on the forums!
Your fans are... intense.
Hey, guys! Thanks for coming.
You called backup?
...Maybe.
But this is Ms. Marvel and Spider-Man.
You're Ms. Marvel?
Yup.
What happened to Carol?
You mean *Captain* Marvel?
He's *dead.*
She's not.
...And you're Spider-Man?
Yeah.
Is he dead, too?
No.
Cyclops is.
Cyclops?!
Hi.
My adult self went crazy and died. I'm from the past and stuck in this time.
I hate everything about that sentence.
And you are?
I am the synthetic daughter of Vision.
Is *every* super hero twelve now?
Maybe you're just *old.*

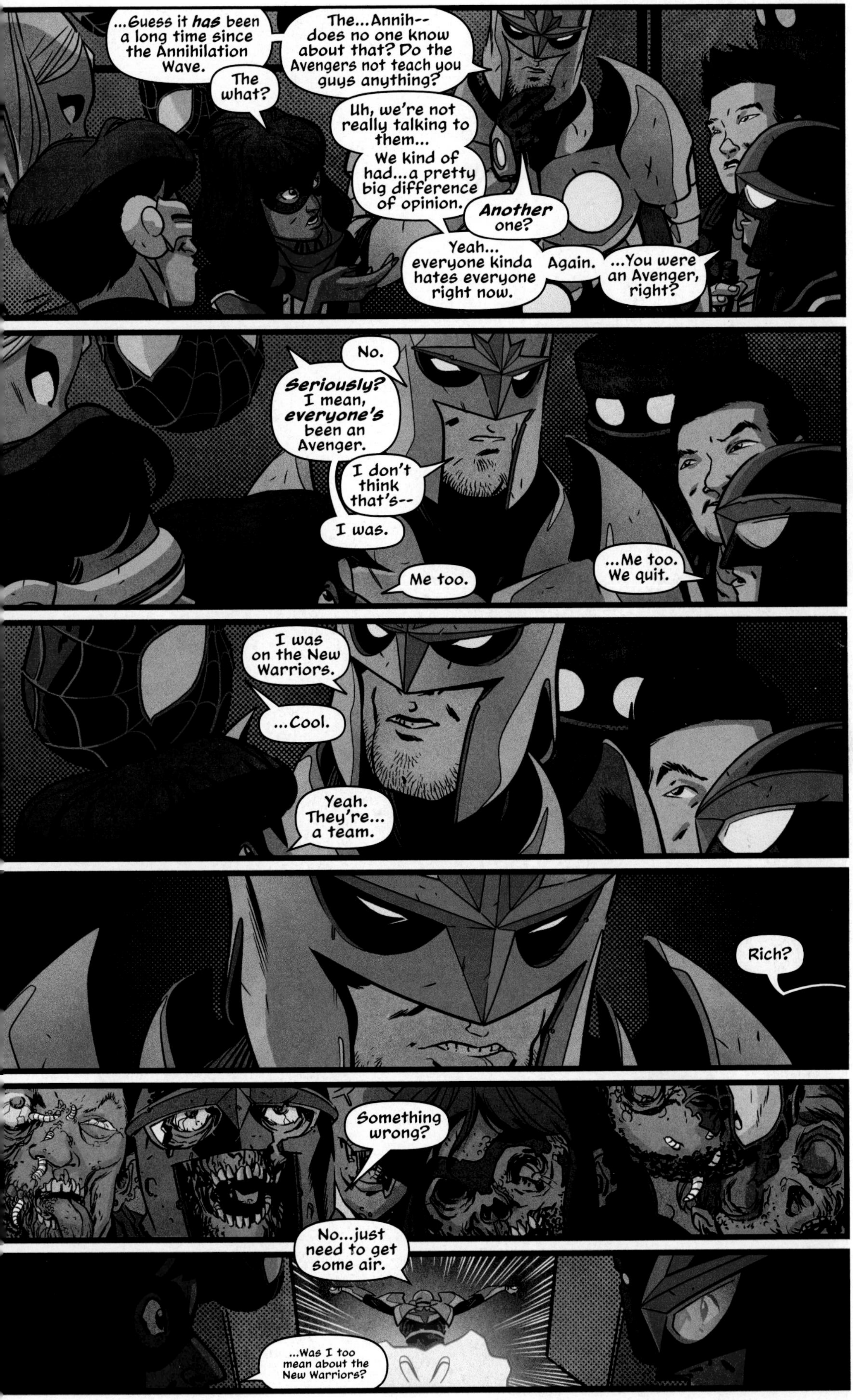
...Guess it *has* been a long time since the Annihilation Wave.
The...Annih-- does no one know about that? Do the Avengers not teach you guys anything?
The what?
Uh, we're not really talking to them...
We kind of had...a pretty big difference of opinion.
Another one?
Yeah... everyone kinda hates everyone right now.
Again.
...You were an Avenger, right?
No.
Seriously? I mean, *everyone's* been an Avenger.
I don't think that's--
I was.
Me too.
...Me too. We quit.
I was on the New Warriors.
...Cool.
Yeah. They're... a team.
Rich?
Something wrong?
No...just need to get some air.
...Was I too mean about the New Warriors?

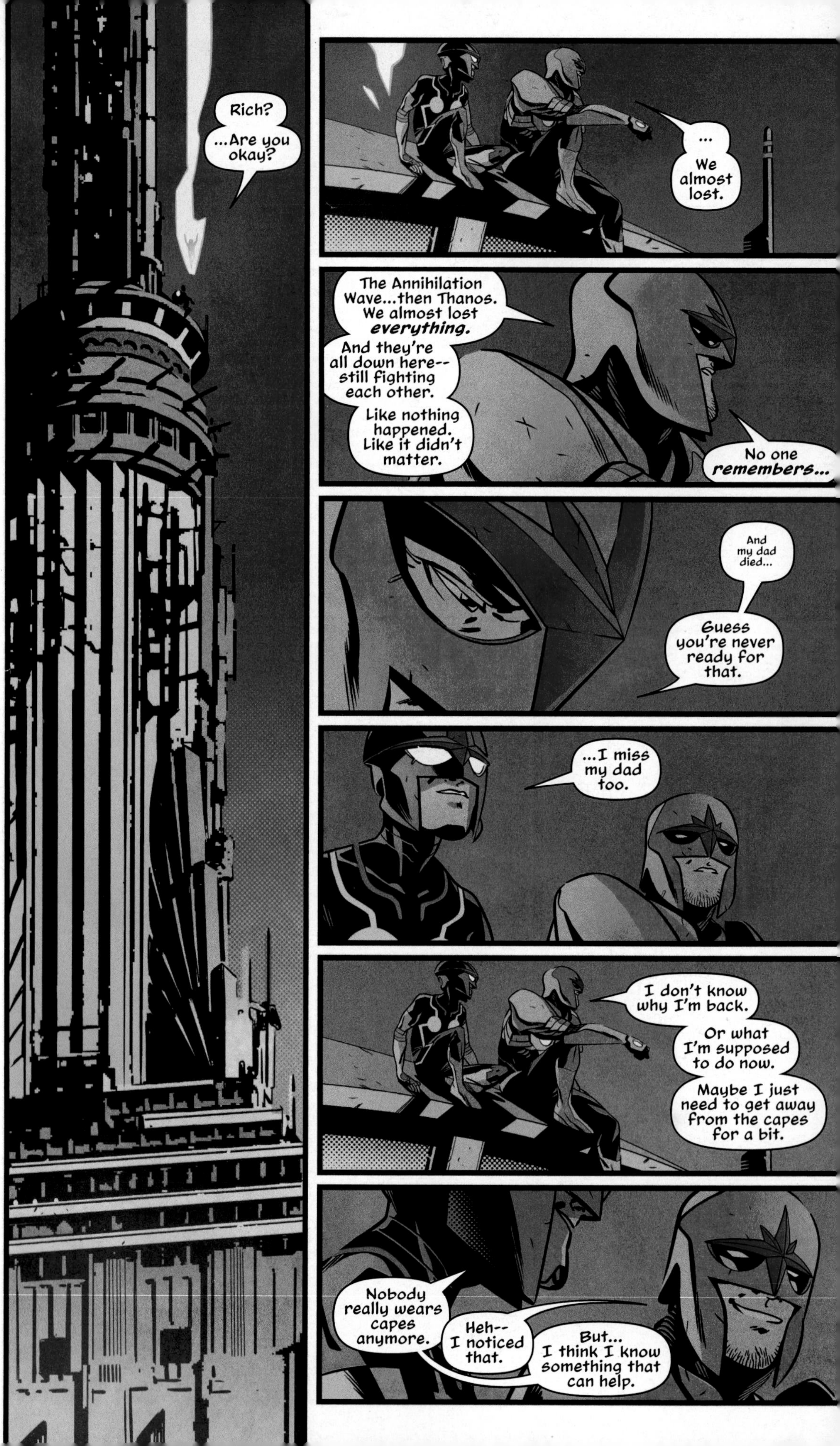

Rich?
...Are you okay?
...
We almost lost.
The Annihilation Wave...then Thanos. We almost lost *everything.*
And they're all down here--still fighting each other.
Like nothing happened. Like it didn't matter.
No one *remembers...*
And my dad died...
Guess you're never ready for that.
...I miss my dad too.
I don't know why I'm back.
Or what I'm supposed to do now.
Maybe I just need to get away from the capes for a bit.
Nobody really wears capes anymore.
Heh--I noticed that.
But... I think I know something that can help.

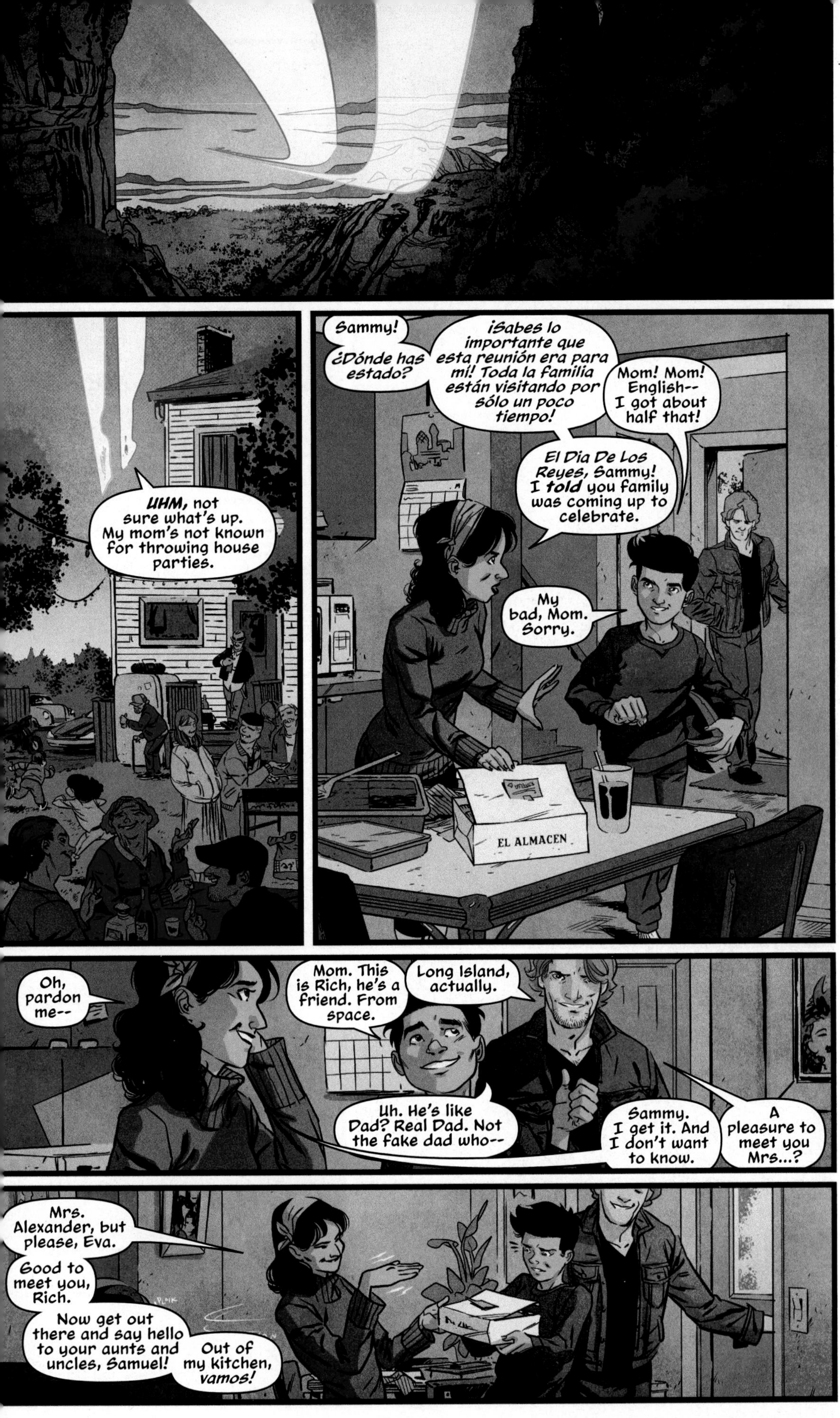

UHM, not sure what's up. My mom's not known for throwing house parties.
Sammy! ¿Dónde has estado?
¡Sabes lo importante que esta reunión era para mí! Toda la familia están visitando por sólo un poco tiempo!
Mom! Mom! English-- I got about half that!
El Dia De Los Reyes, Sammy! I told you family was coming up to celebrate.
My bad, Mom. Sorry.
EL ALMACEN
Oh, pardon me--
Mom. This is Rich, he's a friend. From space.
Long Island, actually.
Uh. He's like Dad? Real Dad. Not the fake dad who--
Sammy. I get it. And I don't want to know.
A pleasure to meet you Mrs...?
Mrs. Alexander, but please, Eva.
Good to meet you, Rich.
Now get out there and say hello to your aunts and uncles, Samuel!
Out of my kitchen, vamos!

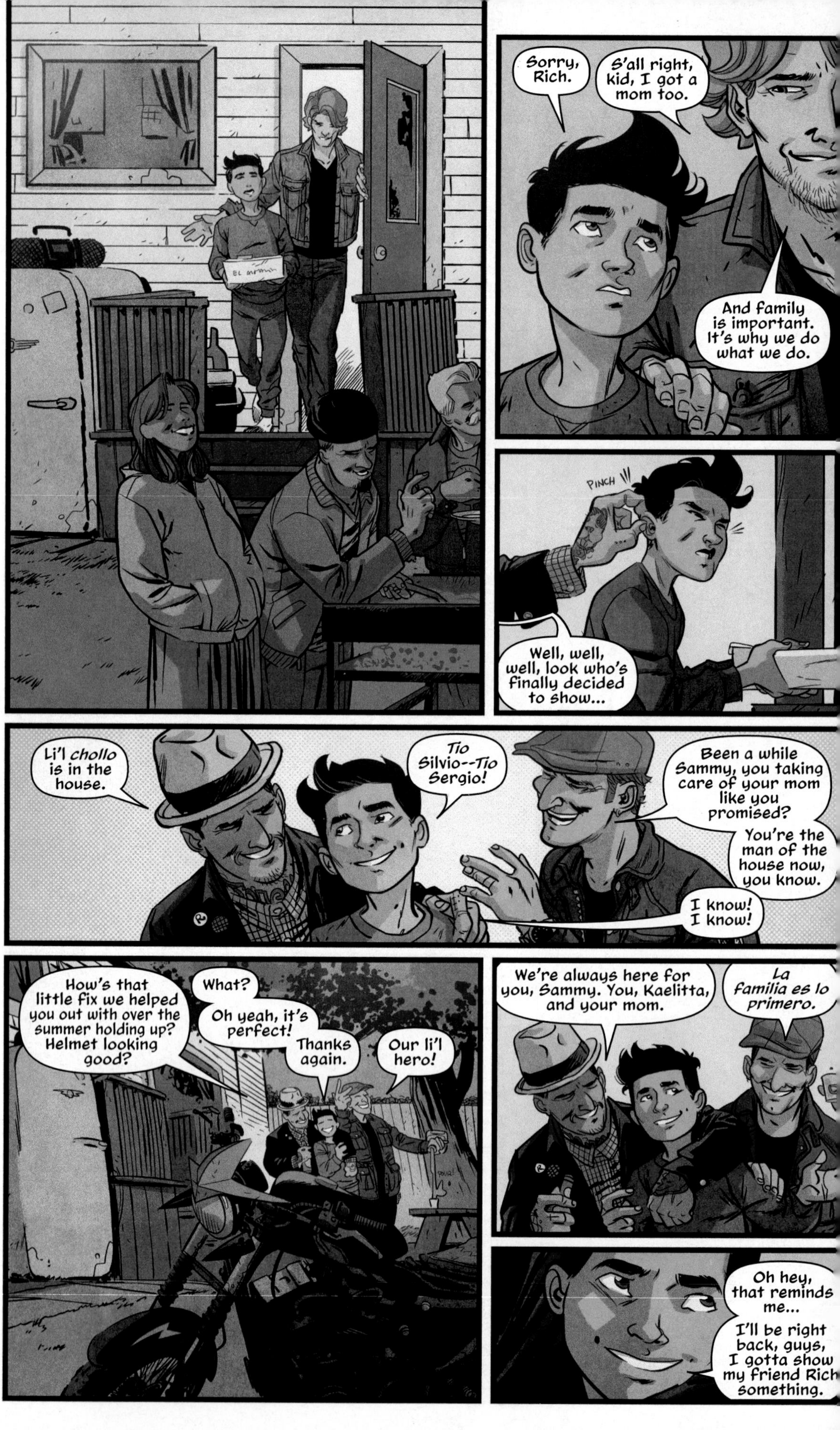
EL ARMA
Sorry, Rich.
S'all right, kid, I got a mom too.
And family is important. It's why we do what we do.
PINCH
Well, well, well, look who's finally decided to show...
Li'l *chollo* is in the house.
Tio Silvio--Tio Sergio!
Been a while Sammy, you taking care of your mom like you promised?
You're the man of the house now, you know.
I know! I know!
How's that little fix we helped you out with over the summer holding up? Helmet looking good?
What?
Oh yeah, it's perfect!
Thanks again.
Our li'l hero!
POUR
We're always here for you, Sammy. You, Kaelitta, and your mom.
La familia es lo primero.
Oh hey, that reminds me...
I'll be right back, guys, I gotta show my friend Rich something.

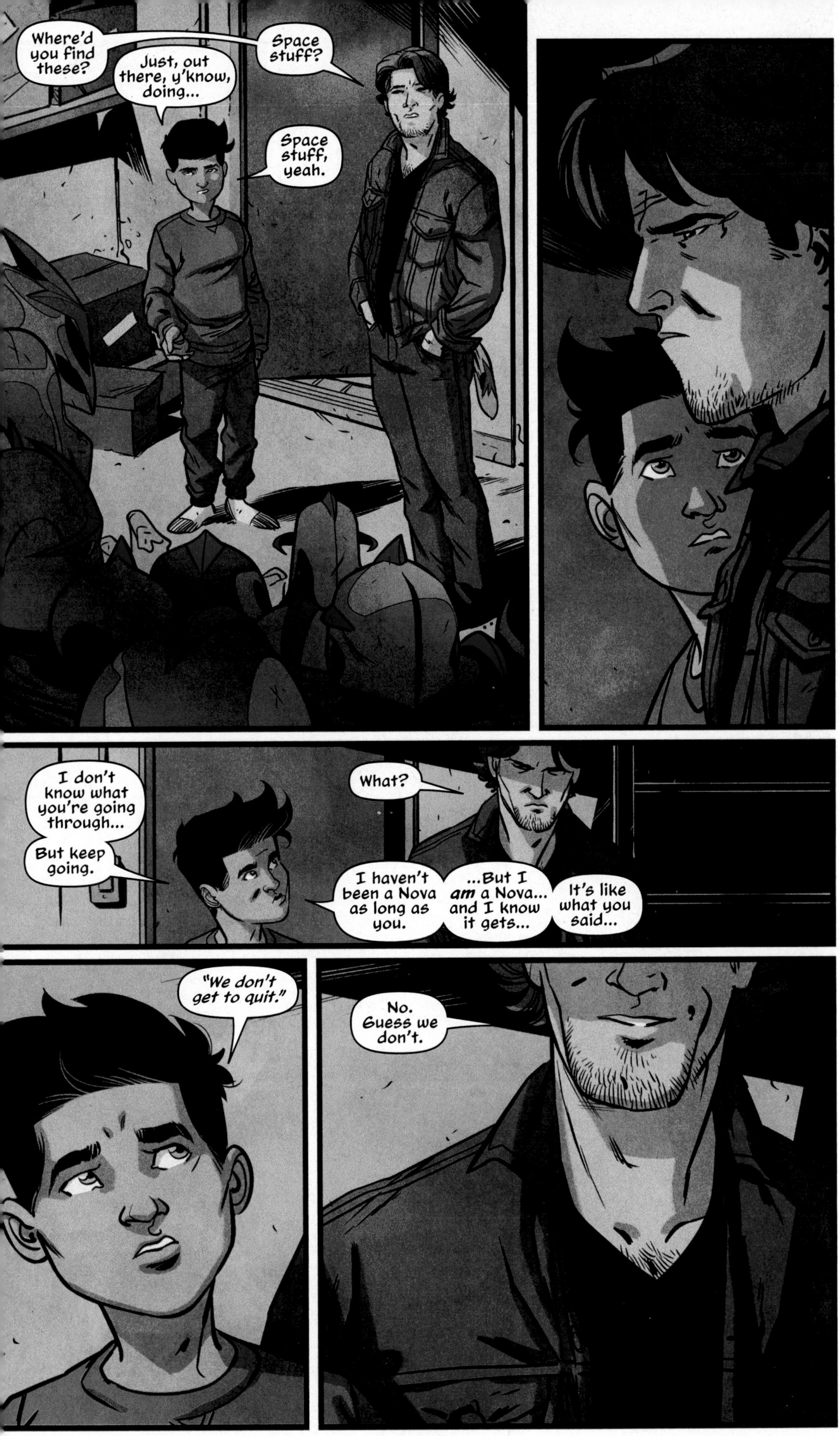
Where'd you find these?
Space stuff?
Just, out there, y'know, doing...
Space stuff, yeah.
I don't know what you're going through...
But keep going.
What?
I haven't been a Nova as long as you.
...But I *am* a Nova... and I know it gets...
It's like what you said...
"We don't get to quit."
No. Guess we don't.

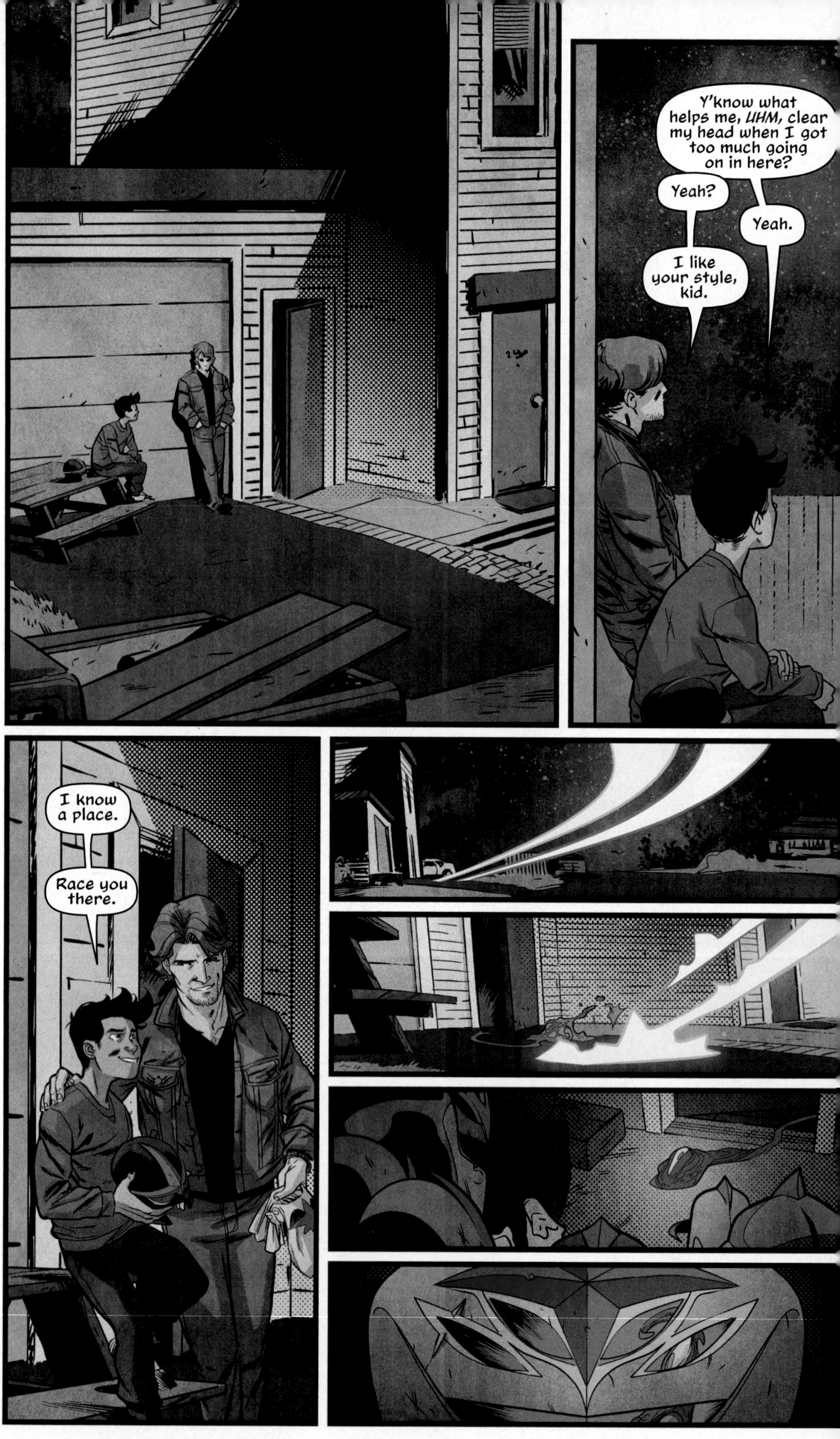
Y'know what helps me, *UHM*, clear my head when I got too much going on in here?
Yeah?
Yeah.
I like your style, kid.
I know a place.
Race you there.

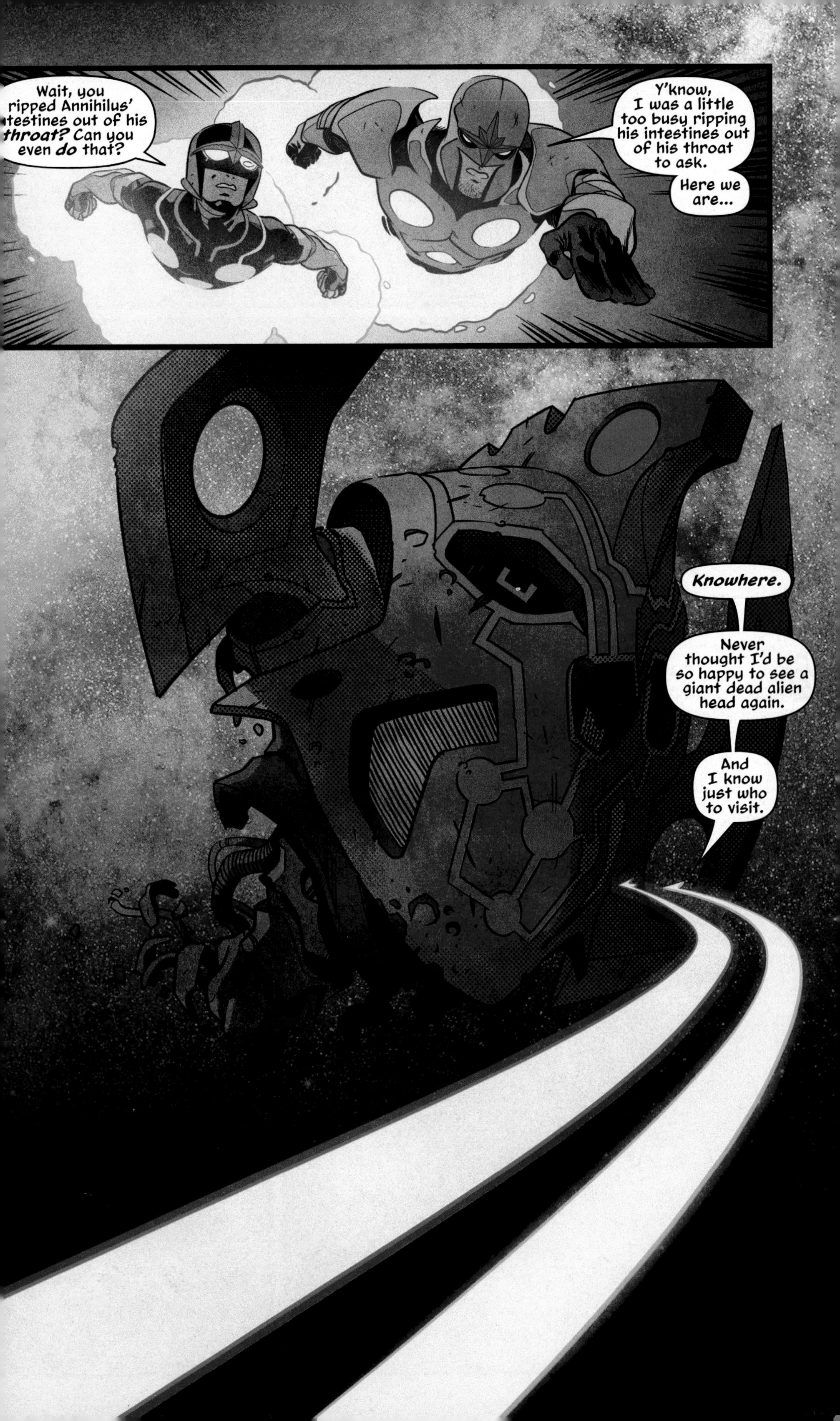
Wait, you ripped Annihilus' intestines out of his *throat?* Can you even *do* that?
Y'know, I was a little too busy ripping his intestines out of his throat to ask.
Here we are...
Knowhere.
Never thought I'd be so happy to see a giant dead alien head again.
And I know just who to visit.

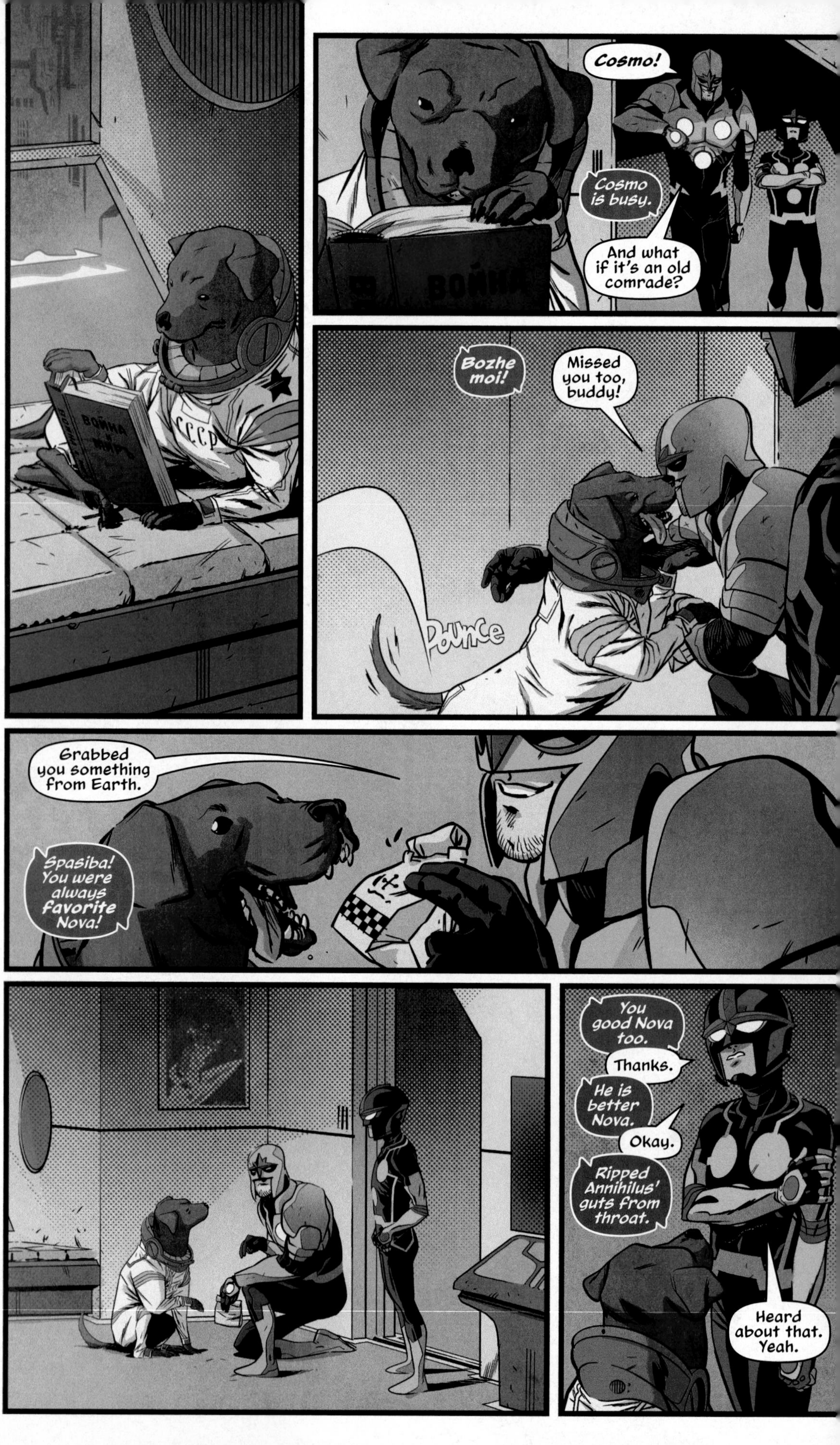
Cosmo!
Cosmo is busy.
And what if it's an old comrade?
Bozhe moi!
Missed you too, buddy!
Pounce
Grabbed you something from Earth.
Spasiba! You were always *favorite* Nova!
You good Nova too.
Thanks.
He is better Nova.
Okay.
Ripped Annihilus' guts from throat.
Heard about that. Yeah.

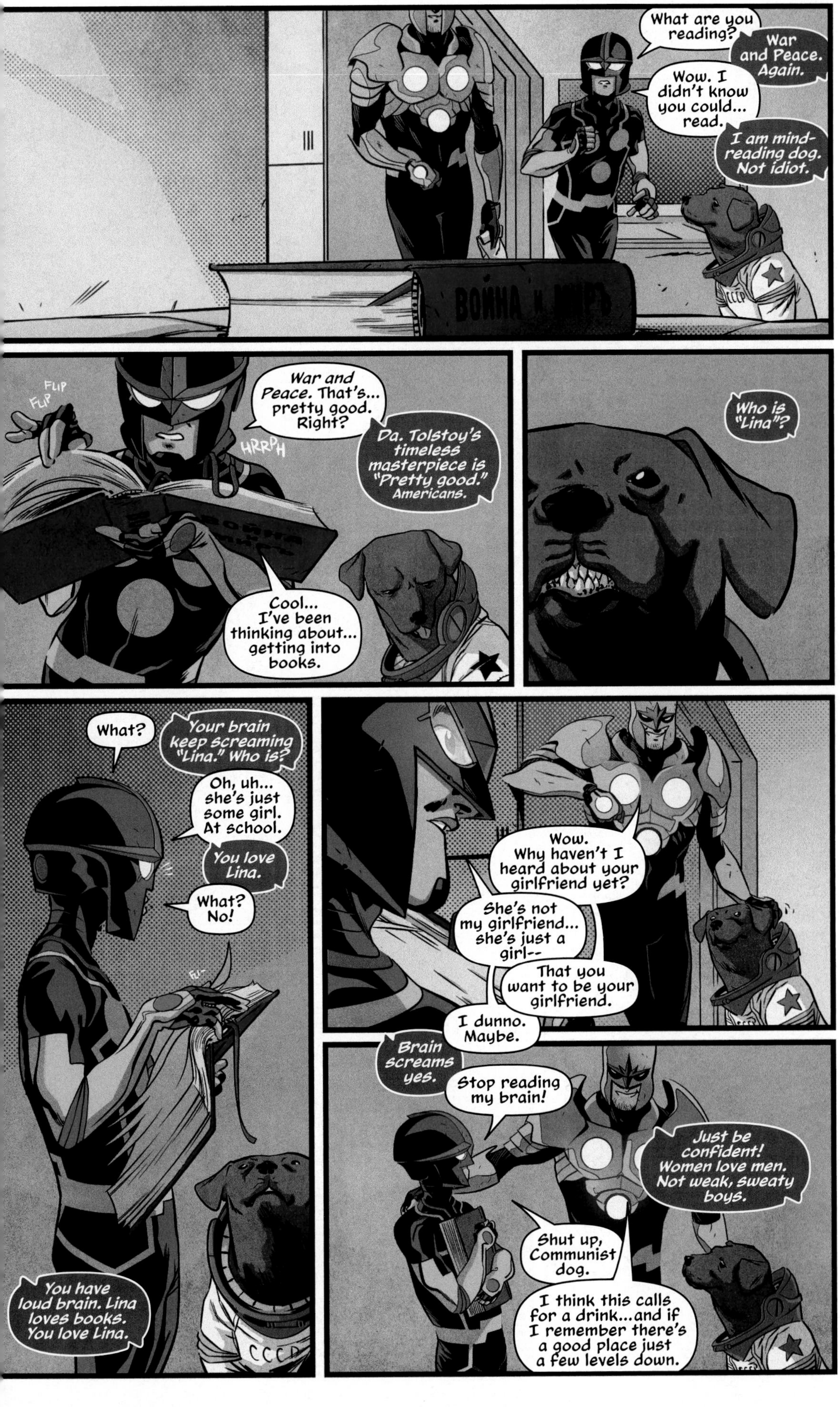

What are you reading?
War and Peace. Again.
Wow. I didn't know you could... read.
I am mind-reading dog. Not idiot.
ВОЙНА И МИРЪ
FLIP
FLIP
War and Peace. That's... pretty good. Right?
HRRPH
Da. Tolstoy's timeless masterpiece is "Pretty good." Americans.
Cool... I've been thinking about... getting into books.
Who is "Lina"?
What?
Your brain keep screaming "Lina." Who is?
Oh, uh... she's just some girl. At school.
You love Lina.
What? No!
You have loud brain. Lina loves books. You love Lina.
Wow. Why haven't I heard about your girlfriend yet?
She's not my girlfriend... she's just a girl--
That you want to be your girlfriend.
I dunno. Maybe.
Brain screams yes.
Stop reading my brain!
Just be confident! Women love men. Not weak, sweaty boys.
Shut up, Communist dog.
I think this calls for a drink...and if I remember there's a good place just a few levels down.

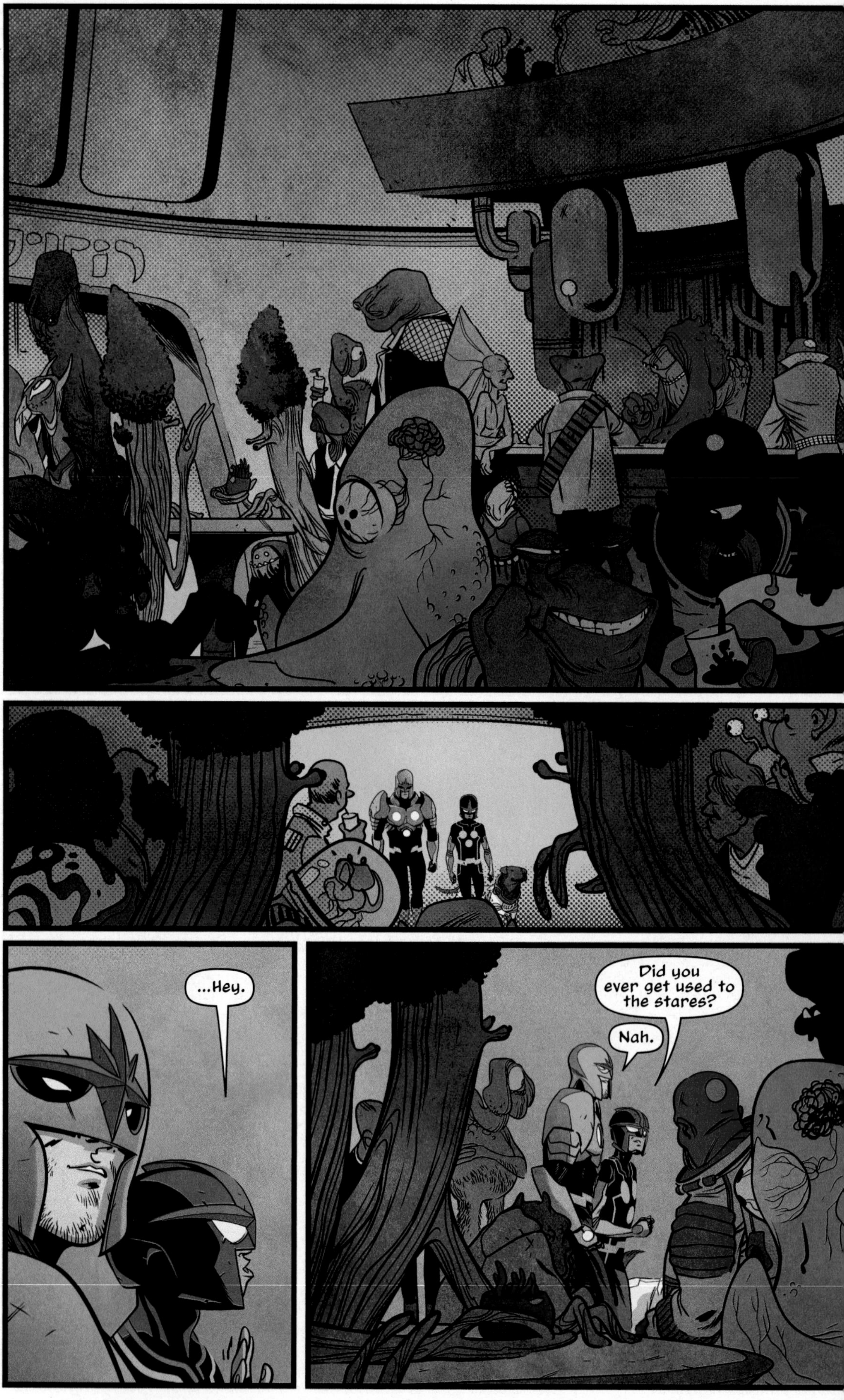
...Hey.
Did you ever get used to the stares?
Nah.

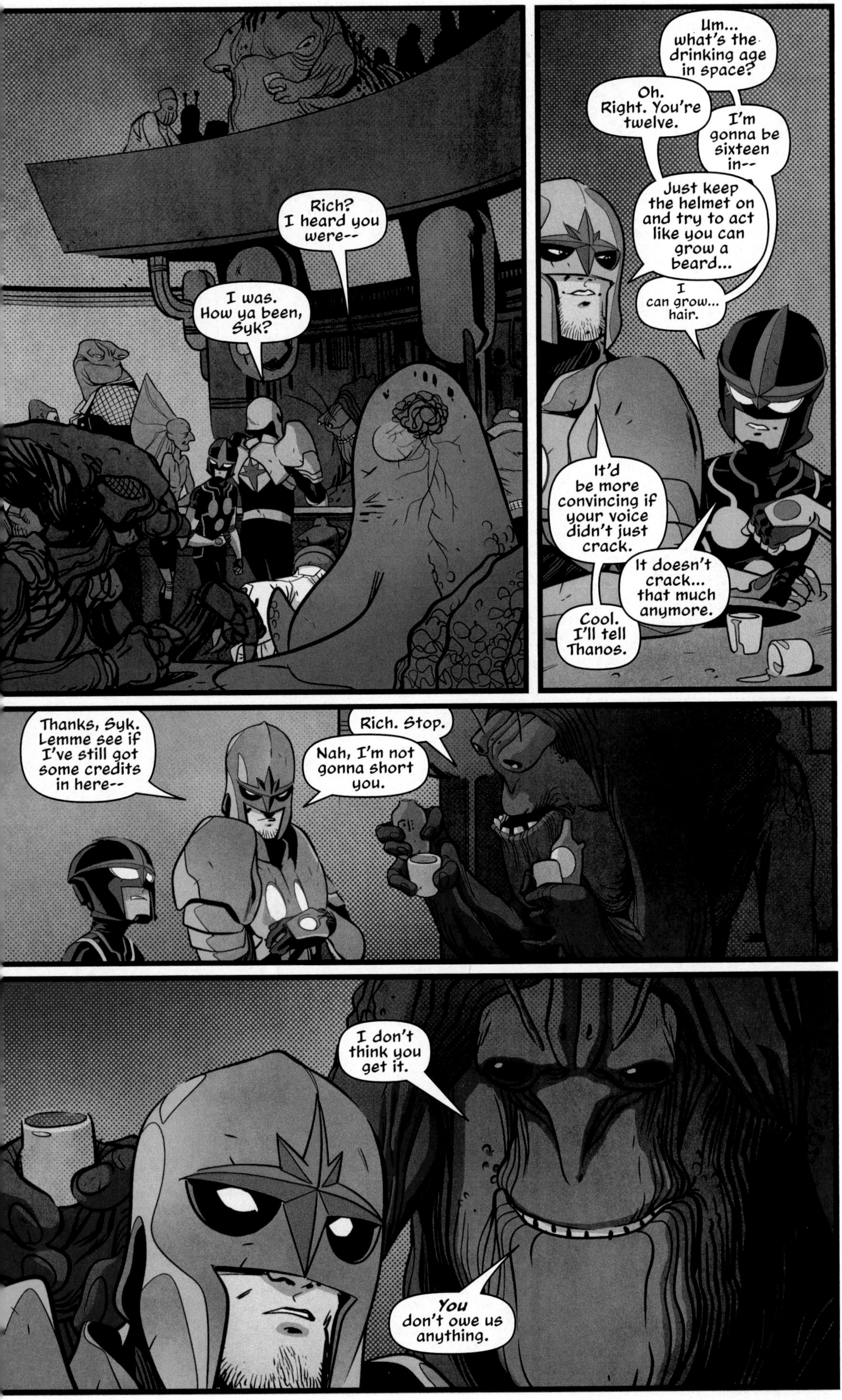
Rich?
I heard you
were--
I was.
How ya been,
Syk?
Um...
what's the
drinking age
in space?
Oh.
Right. You're
twelve.
I'm
gonna be
sixteen
in--
Just keep
the helmet on
and try to act
like you can
grow a
beard...
I
can grow...
hair.
It'd
be more
convincing if
your voice
didn't just
crack.
It doesn't
crack...
that much
anymore.
Cool.
I'll tell
Thanos.
Thanks, Syk.
Lemme see if
I've still got
some credits
in here--
Rich. Stop.
Nah, I'm not
gonna short
you.
I don't
think you
get it.
You
don't owe us
anything.

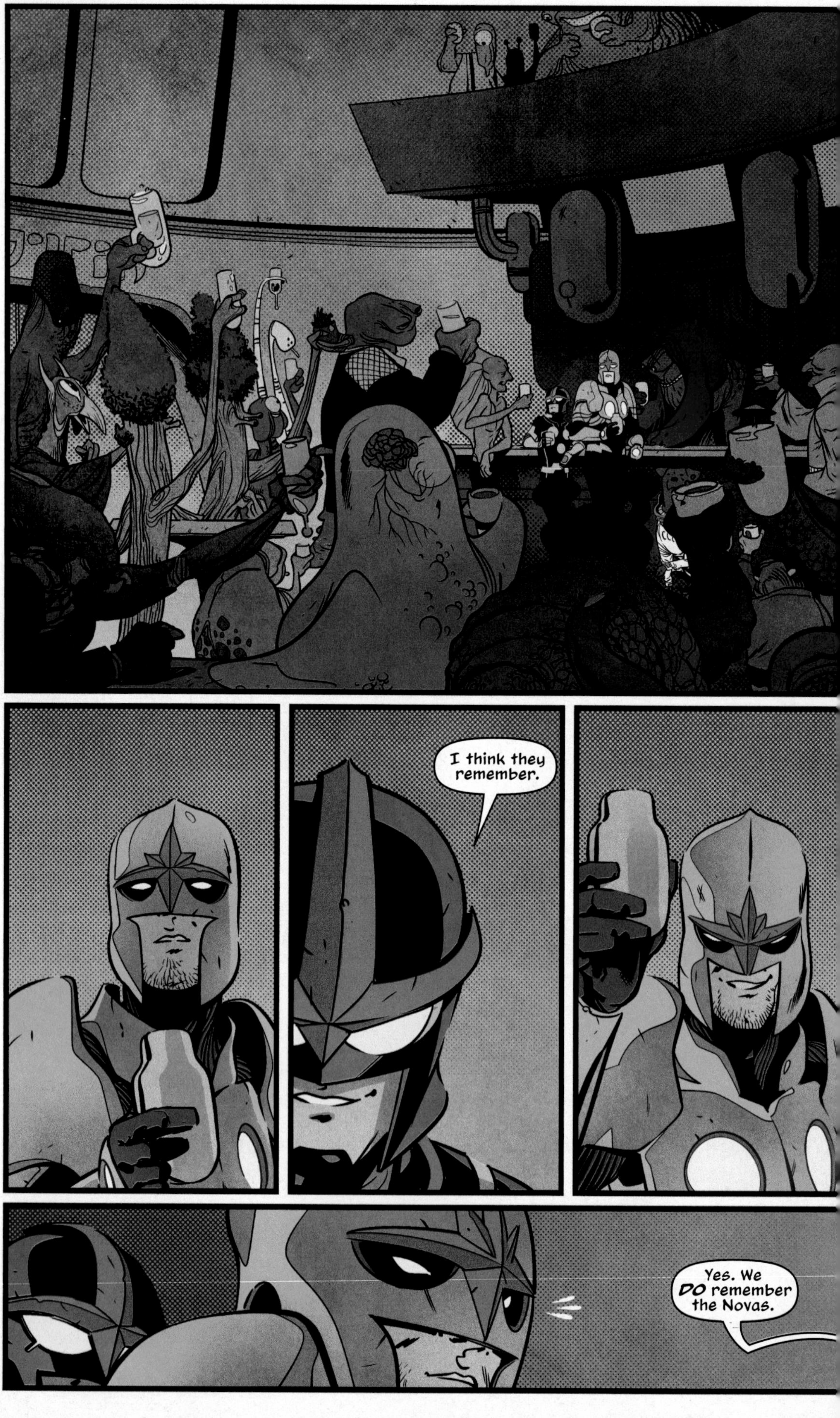
I think they remember.
Yes. We DO remember the Novas.

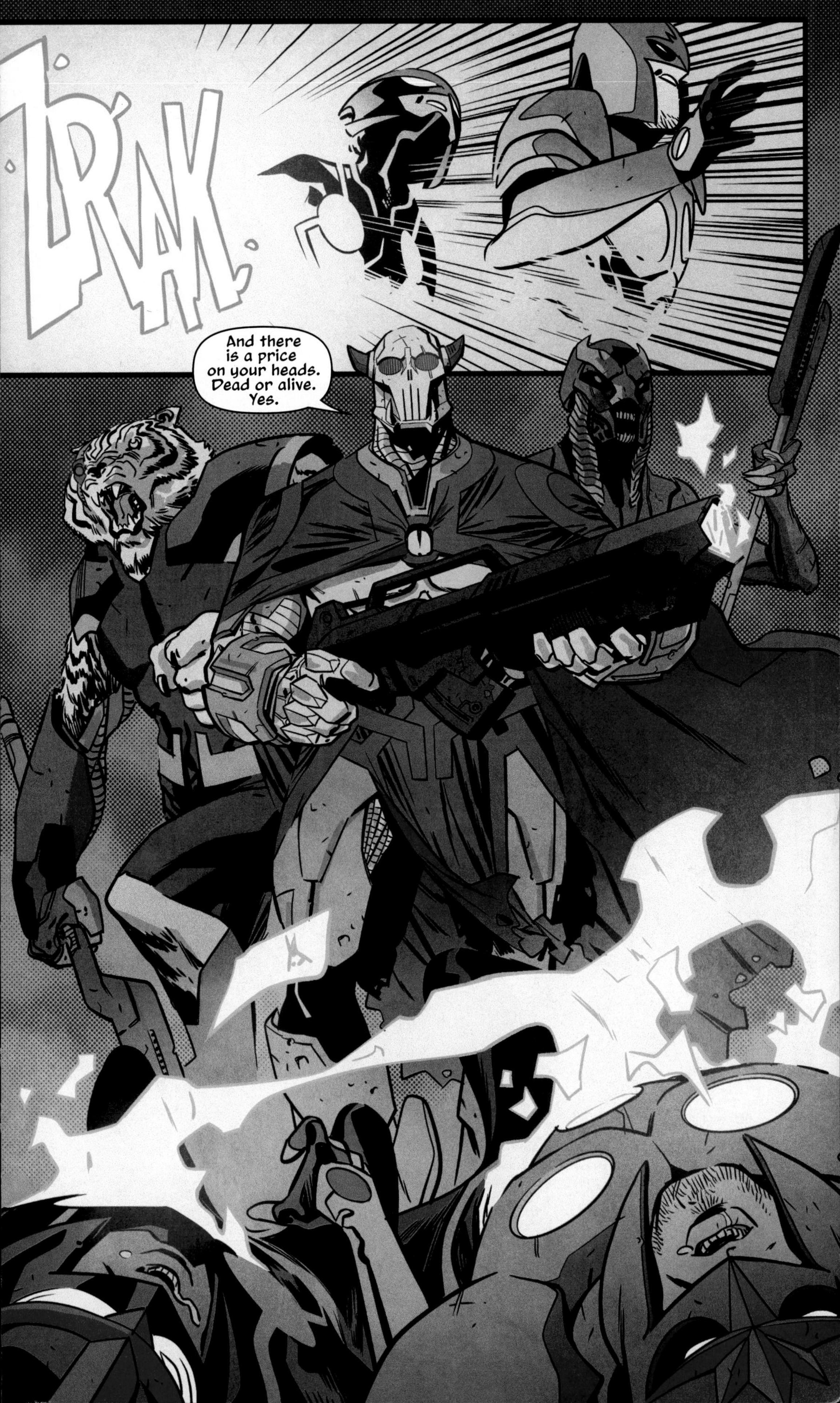
ZRAK
And there is a price on your heads. Dead or alive. Yes.

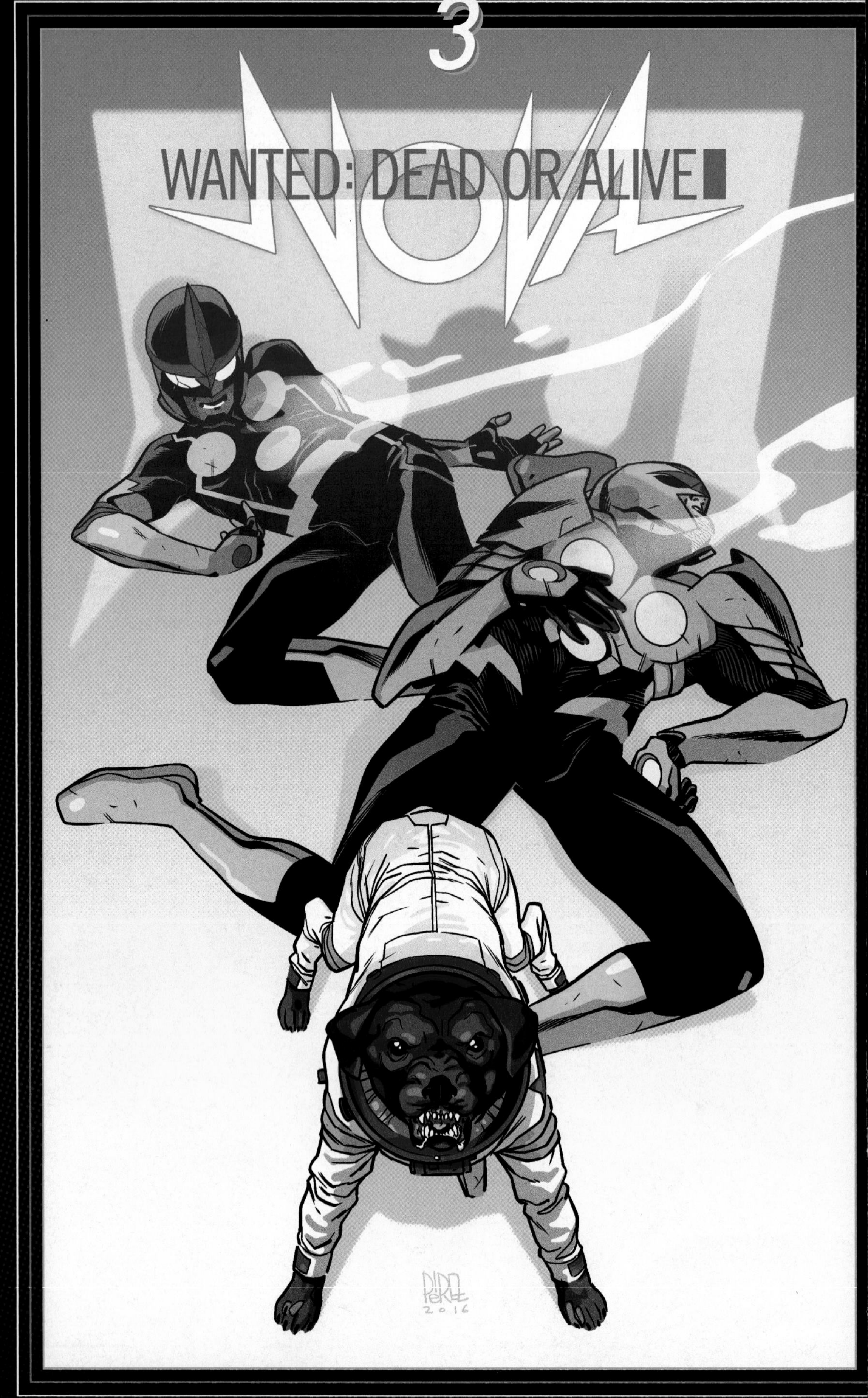
3
NOVA
WANTED: DEAD OR ALIVE
2016

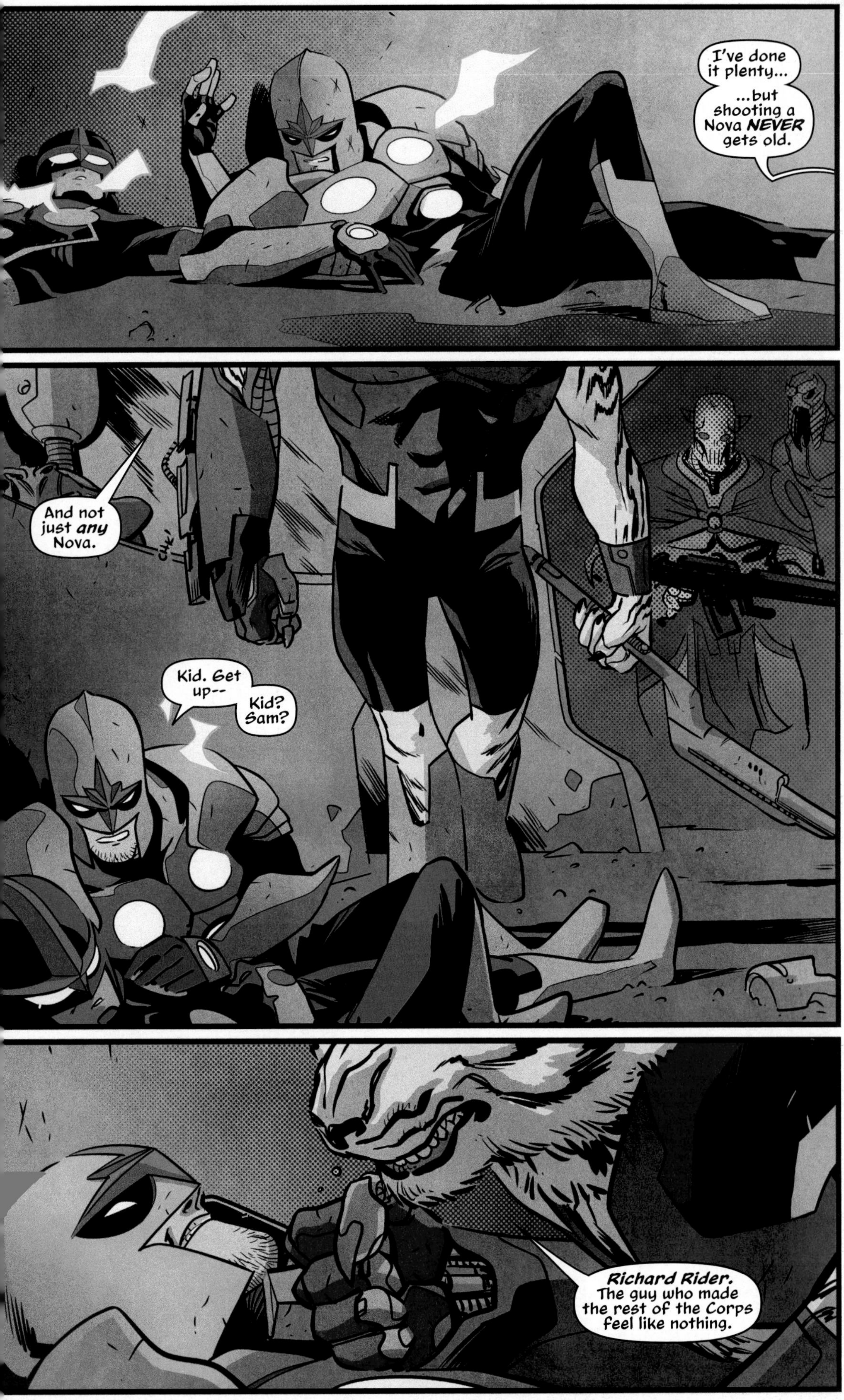
I've done it plenty...
...but shooting a Nova **NEVER** gets old.
And not just *any* Nova.
CHK!
Kid. Get up--
Kid? Sam?
Richard Rider. The guy who made the rest of the Corps feel like nothing.

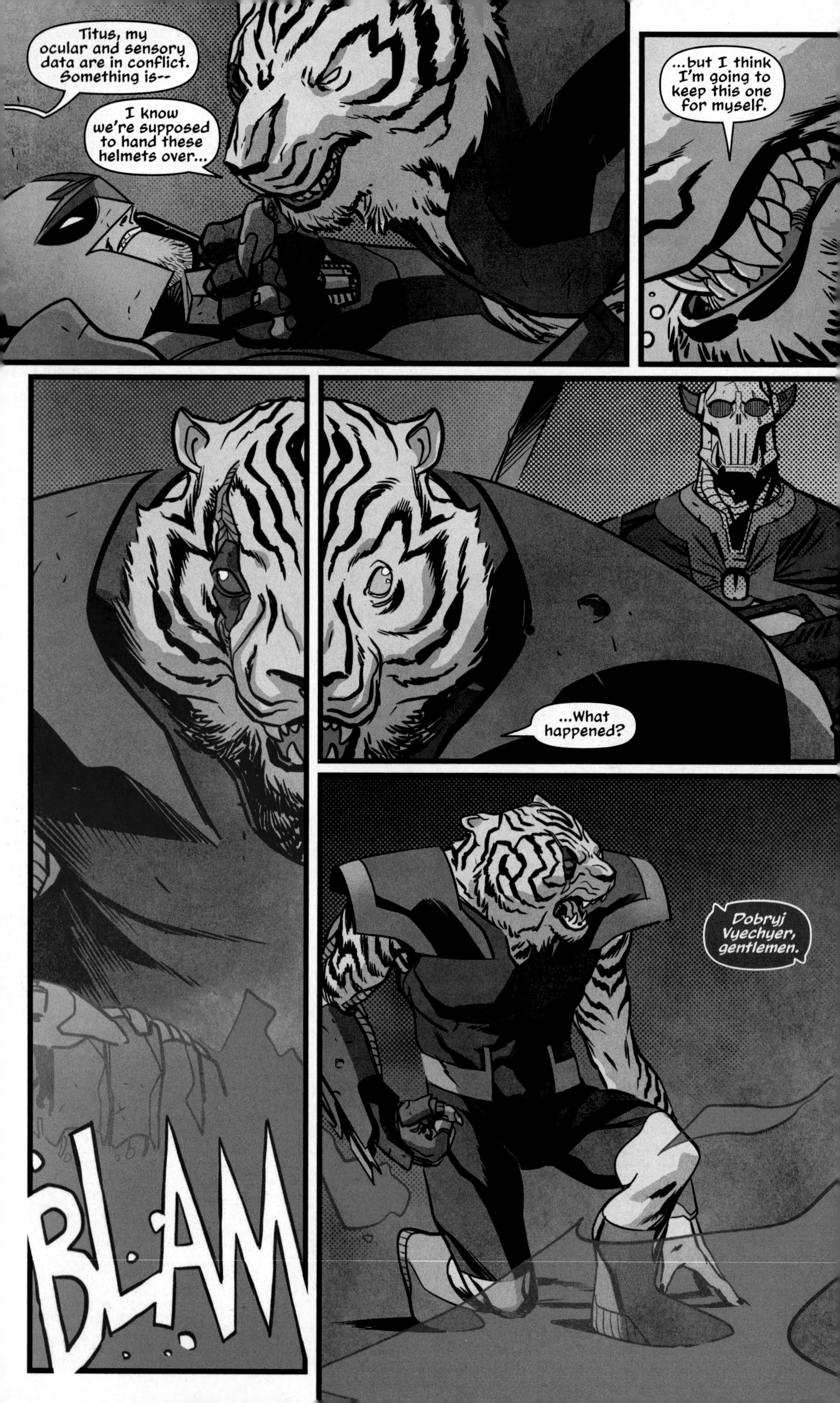

Titus, my ocular and sensory data are in conflict. Something is--
I know we're supposed to hand these helmets over...
...but I think I'm going to keep this one for myself.
...What happened?
BLAM
Dobryj Vyechyer, gentlemen.

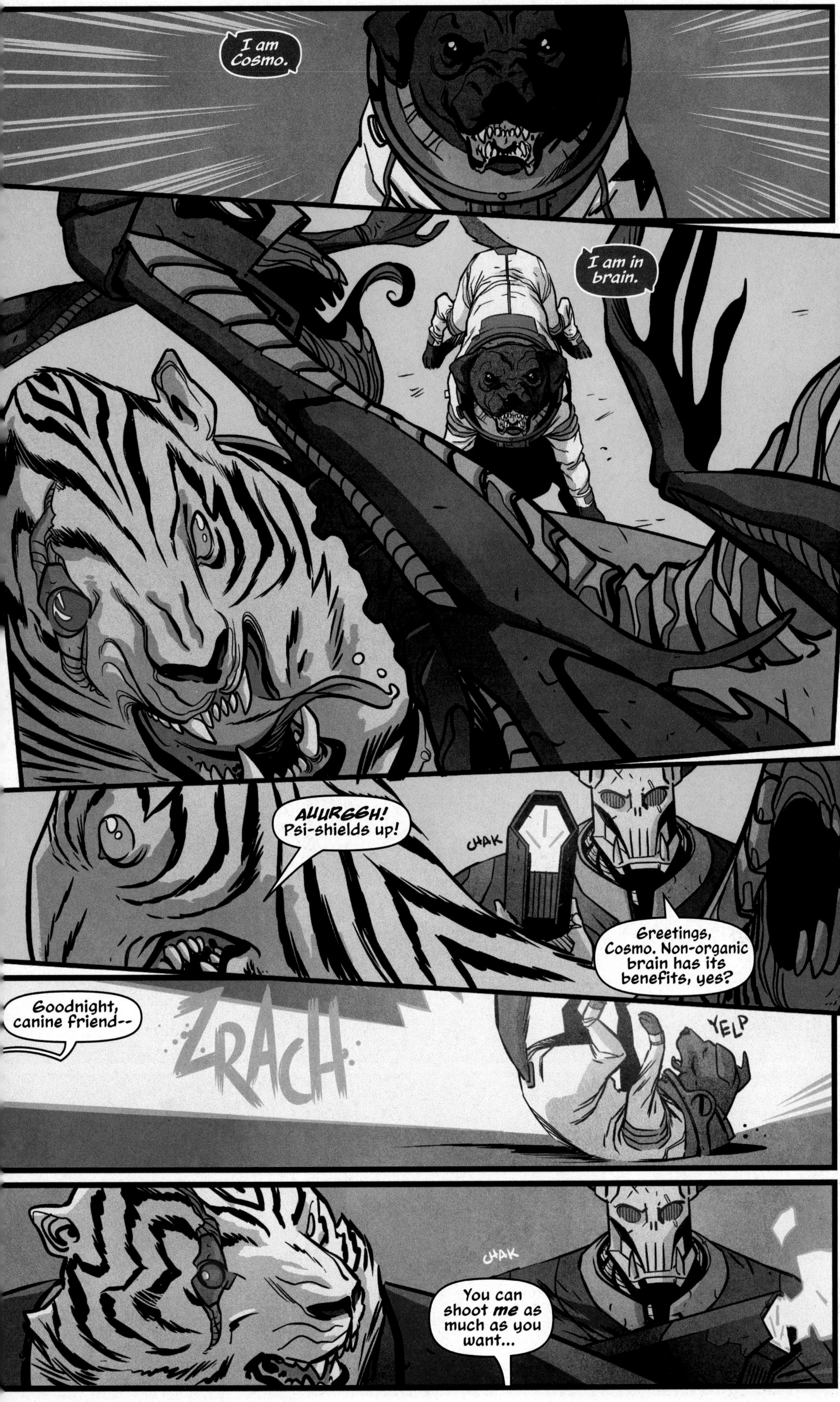
I am Cosmo.
I am in brain.
AUURGGH! Psi-shields up!
CHAK
Greetings, Cosmo. Non-organic brain has its benefits, yes?
Goodnight, canine friend--
ZRACH
YELP
CHAK
You can shoot *me* as much as you want...

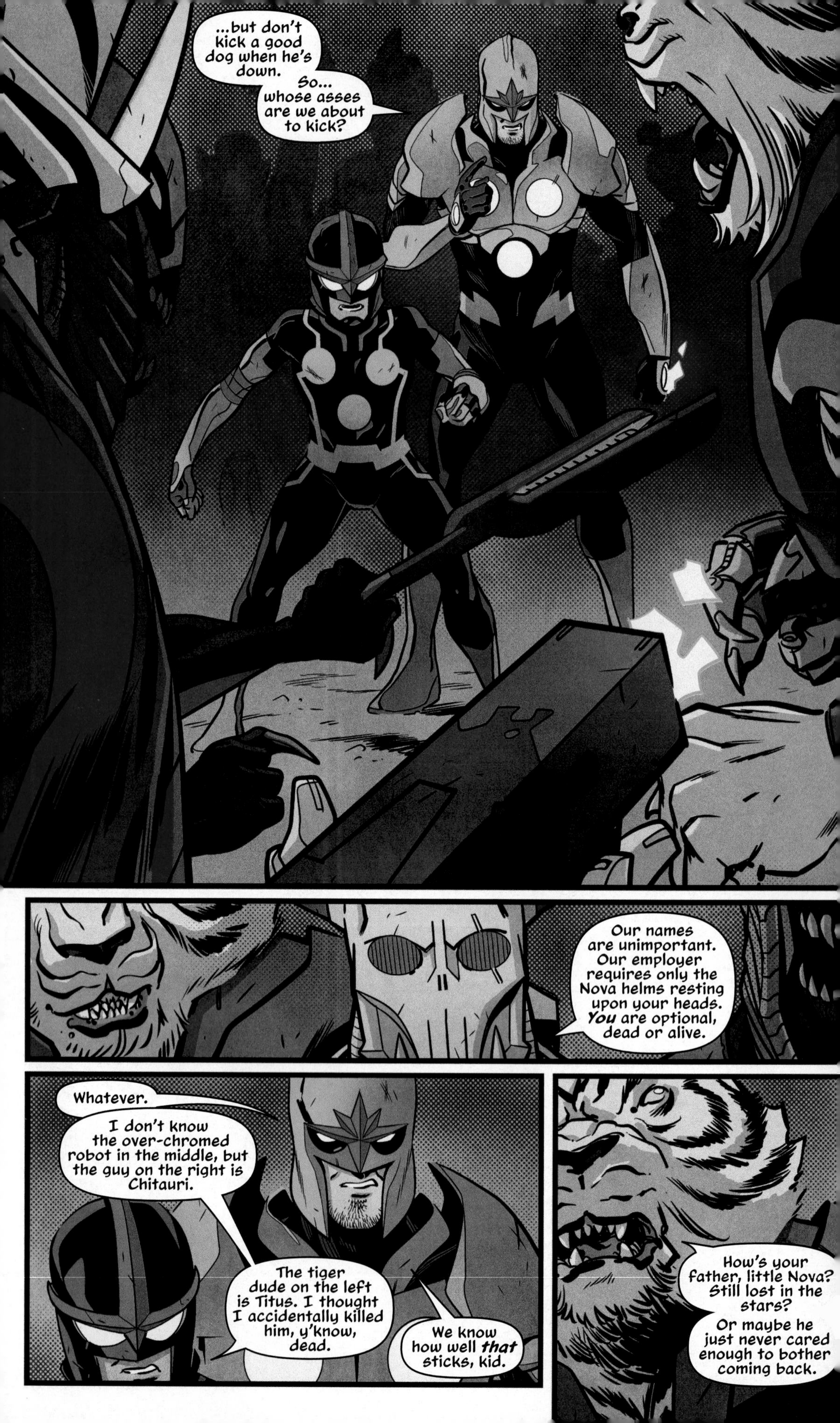
...but don't kick a good dog when he's down.
So... whose asses are we about to kick?
Our names are unimportant. Our employer requires only the Nova helms resting upon your heads. *You* are optional, dead or alive.
Whatever.
I don't know the over-chromed robot in the middle, but the guy on the right is Chitauri.
The tiger dude on the left is Titus. I thought I accidentally killed him, y'know, dead.
We know how well *that* sticks, kid.
How's your father, little Nova? Still lost in the stars?
Or maybe he just never cared enough to bother coming back.

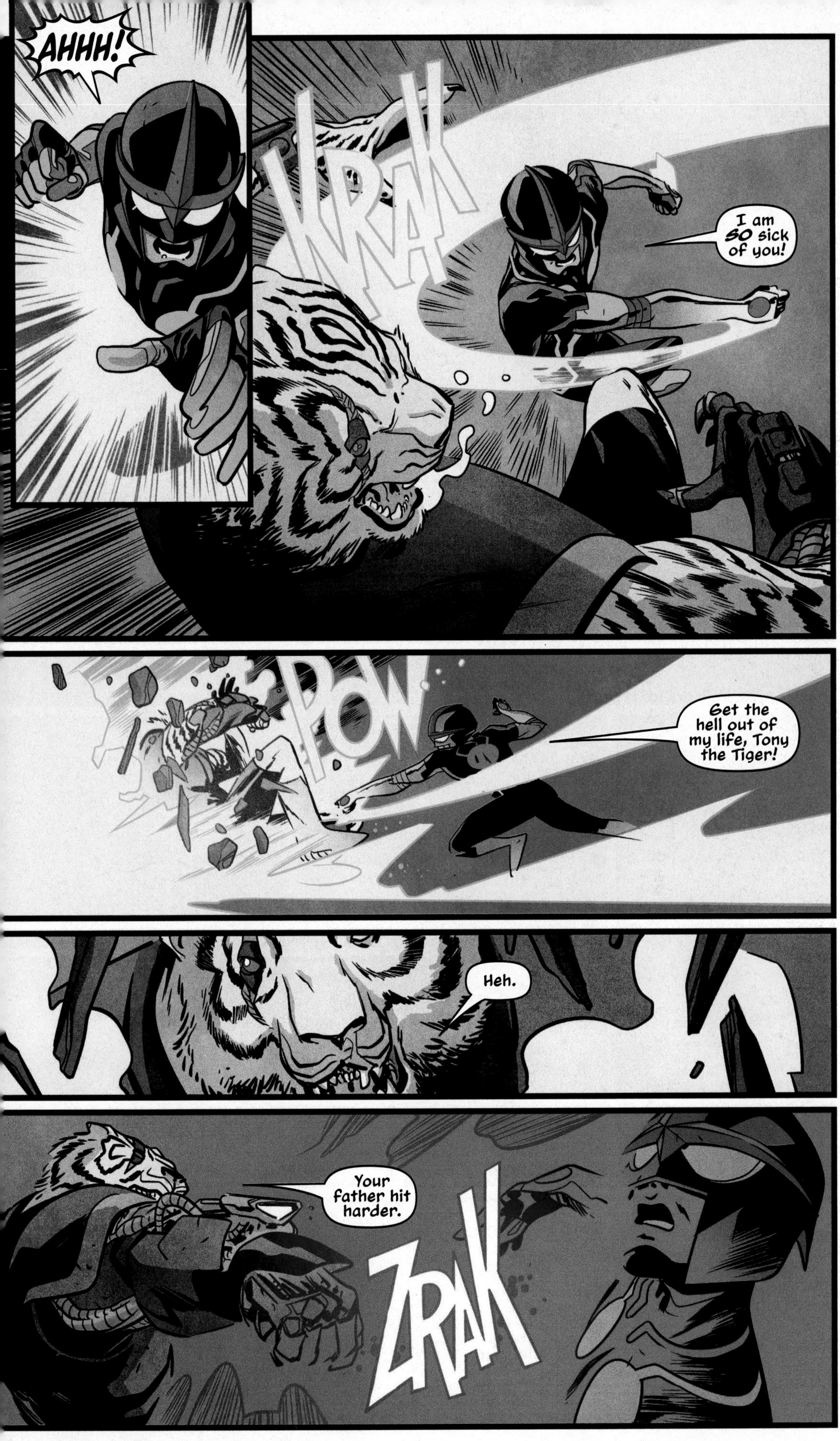
AHHH!
KRAK
I am SO sick of you!
POW
Get the hell out of my life, Tony the Tiger!
Heh.
Your father hit harder.
ZRAK

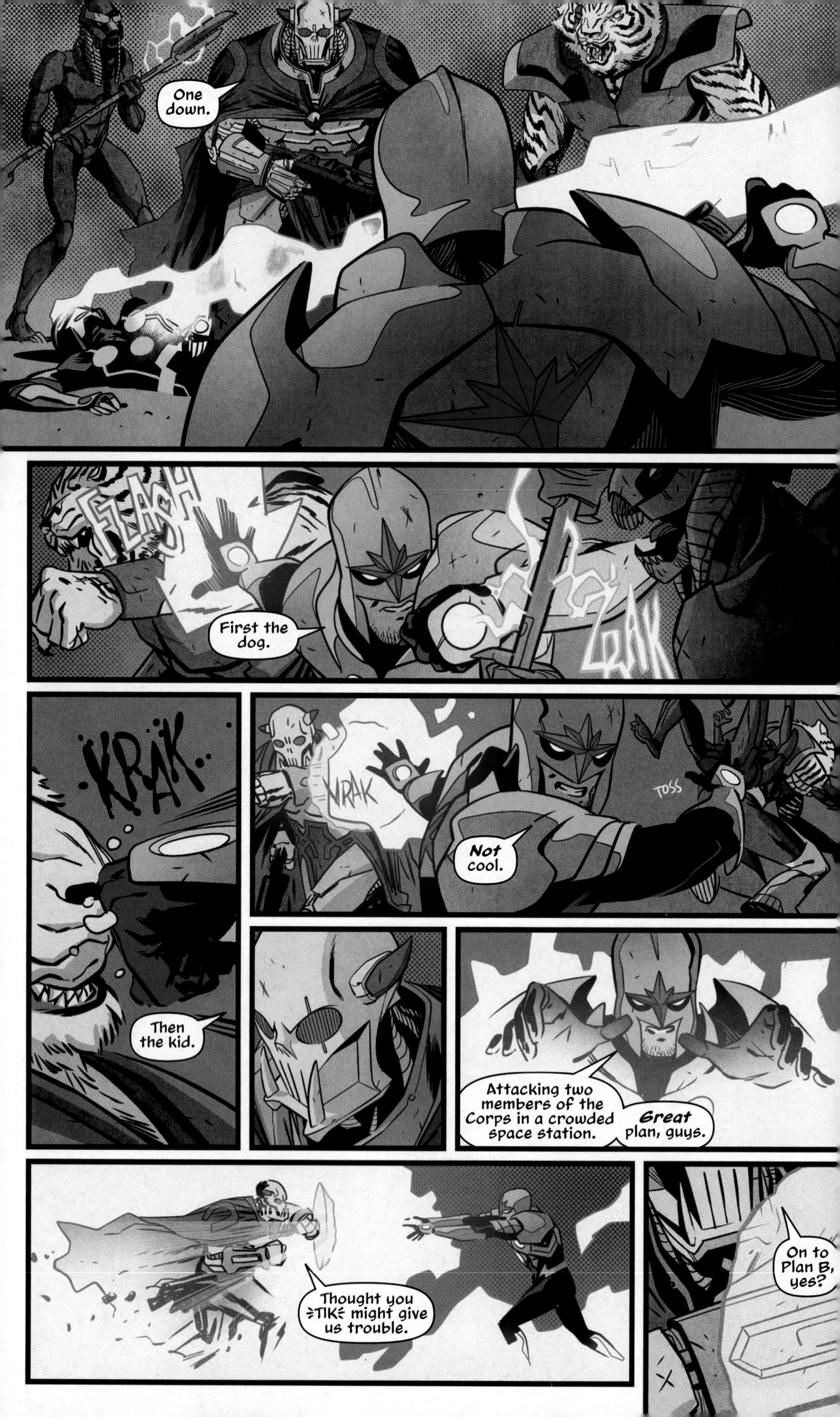
One down.
FLASH
First the dog.
ZRAK
KRAK
Then the kid.
VRAK
TOSS
Not cool.
Attacking two members of the Corps in a crowded space station.
Great plan, guys.
Thought you ≥TIK≤ might give us trouble.
On to Plan B, yes?

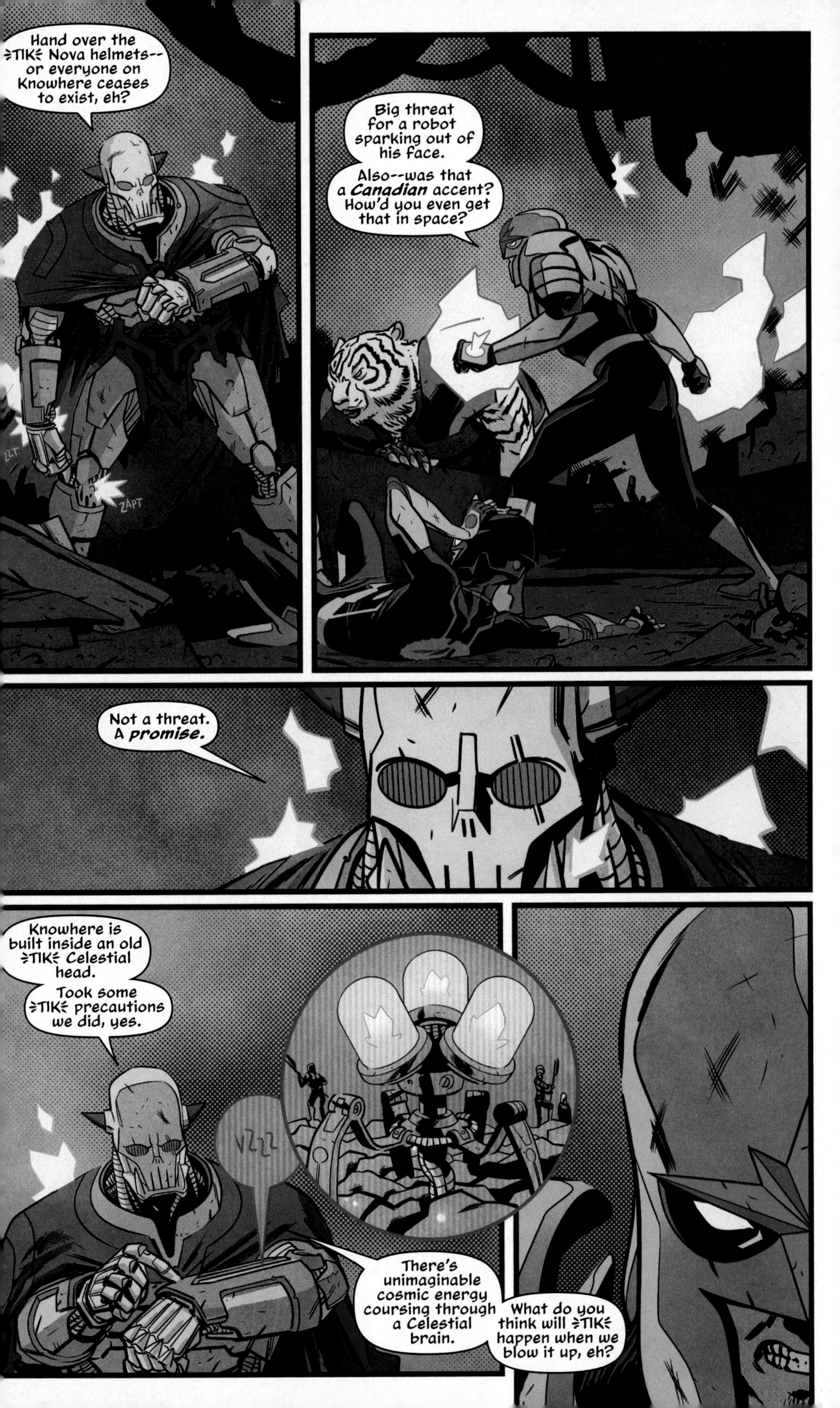

Hand over the ≑TIK≑ Nova helmets--or everyone on Knowhere ceases to exist, eh?
ZLT
ZAPT
Big threat for a robot sparking out of his face.
Also--was that a *Canadian* accent? How'd you even get that in space?
Not a threat. A *promise.*
Knowhere is built inside an old ≑TIK≑ Celestial head.
Took some ≑TIK≑ precautions we did, yes.
VZZZ
There's unimaginable cosmic energy coursing through a Celestial brain.
What do you think will ≑TIK≑ happen when we blow it up, eh?

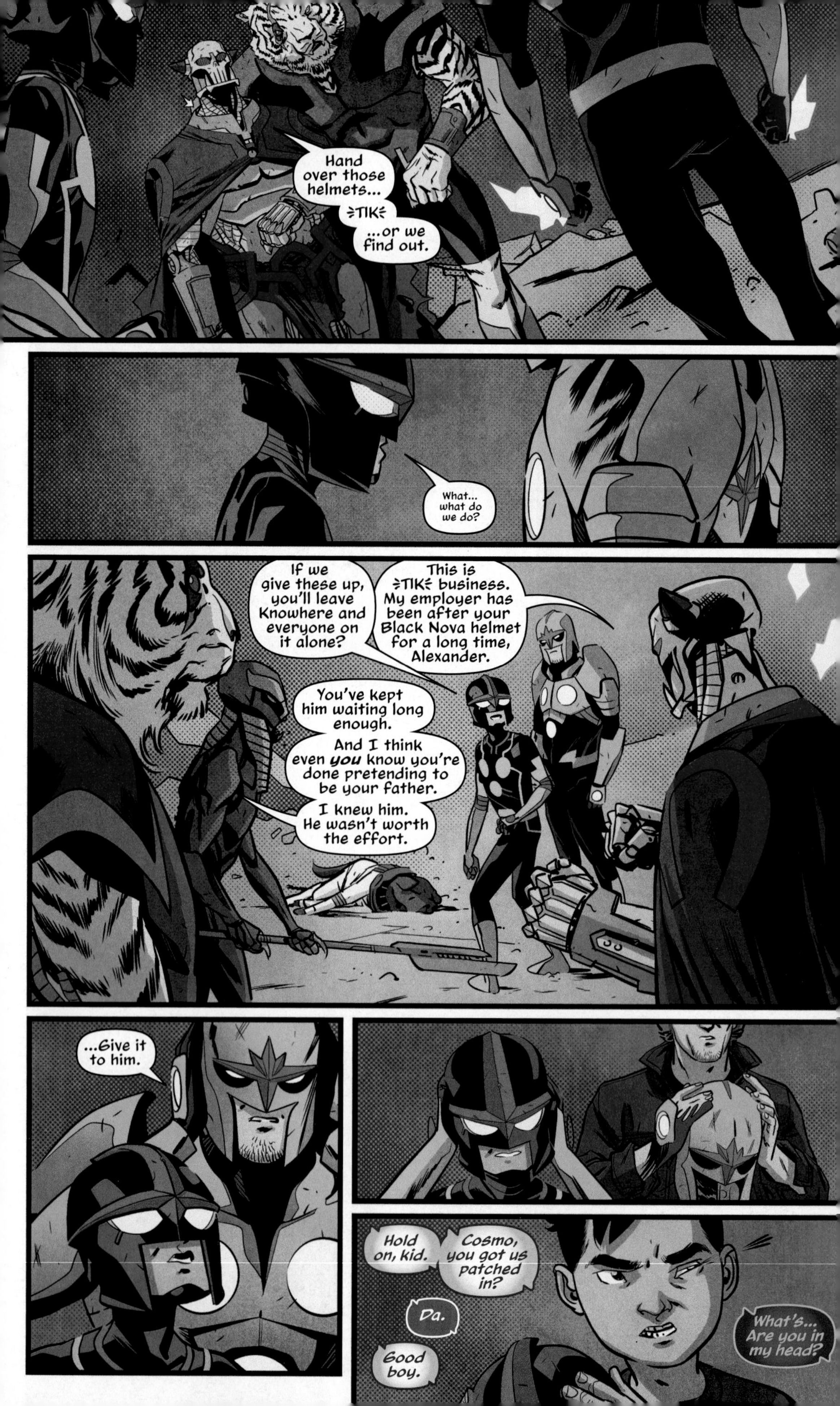

Hand over those helmets...
⋛TIK⋚
...or we find out.
What... what do we do?
If we give these up, you'll leave Knowhere and everyone on it alone?
This is ⋛TIK⋚ business. My employer has been after your Black Nova helmet for a long time, Alexander.
You've kept him waiting long enough.
And I think even *you* know you're done pretending to be your father.
I knew him. He wasn't worth the effort.
...Give it to him.
Hold on, kid.
Cosmo, you got us patched in?
Da.
Good boy.
What's... Are you in my head?

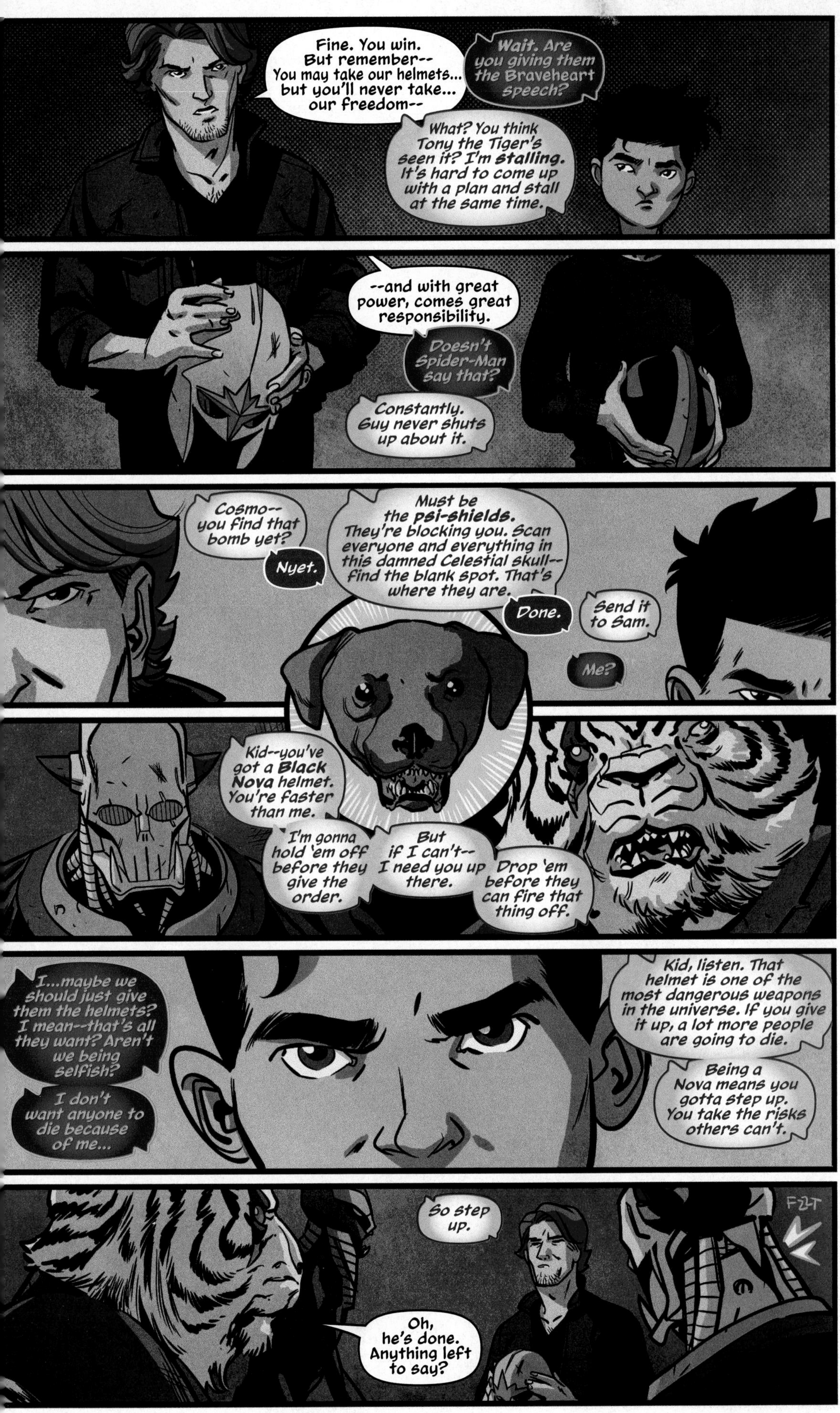

Fine. You win. But remember-- You may take our helmets... but you'll never take... our freedom--
Wait. Are you giving them the Braveheart speech?
What? You think Tony the Tiger's seen it? I'm stalling. It's hard to come up with a plan and stall at the same time.
--and with great power, comes great responsibility.
Doesn't Spider-Man say that?
Constantly. Guy never shuts up about it.
Cosmo-- you find that bomb yet?
Nyet.
Must be the psi-shields. They're blocking you. Scan everyone and everything in this damned Celestial skull-- find the blank spot. That's where they are.
Done.
Send it to Sam.
Me?
Kid--you've got a Black Nova helmet. You're faster than me.
I'm gonna hold 'em off before they give the order.
But if I can't-- I need you up there.
Drop 'em before they can fire that thing off.
I...maybe we should just give them the helmets? I mean--that's all they want? Aren't we being selfish?
I don't want anyone to die because of me...
Kid, listen. That helmet is one of the most dangerous weapons in the universe. If you give it up, a lot more people are going to die.
Being a Nova means you gotta step up. You take the risks others can't.
So step up.
FZZT
Oh, he's done. Anything left to say?

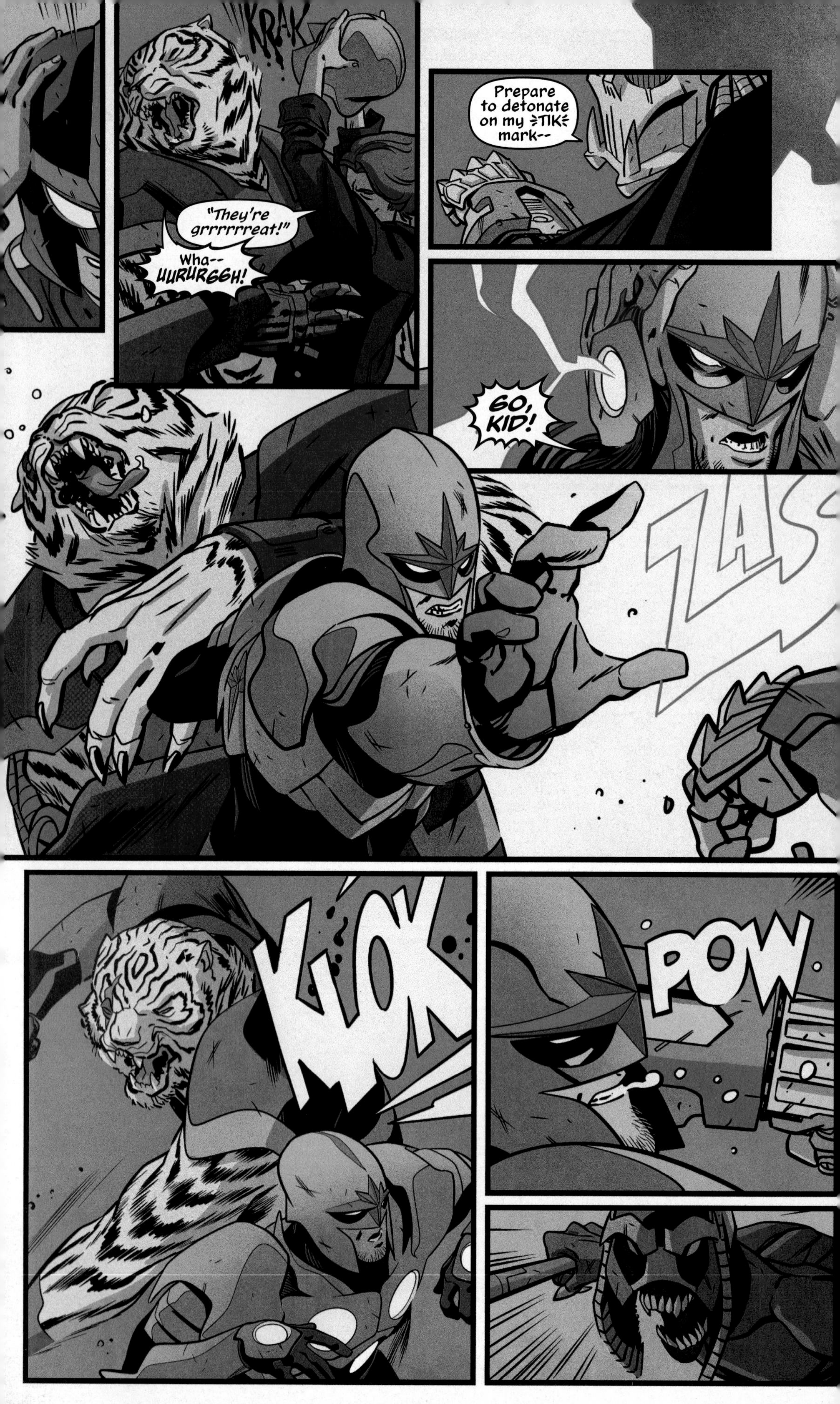
KRAK
"They're grrrrrreat!"
Wha-- UURURGGH!
Prepare to detonate on my ≠TIK≠ mark--
GO, KID!
ZAS
KLOK
POW

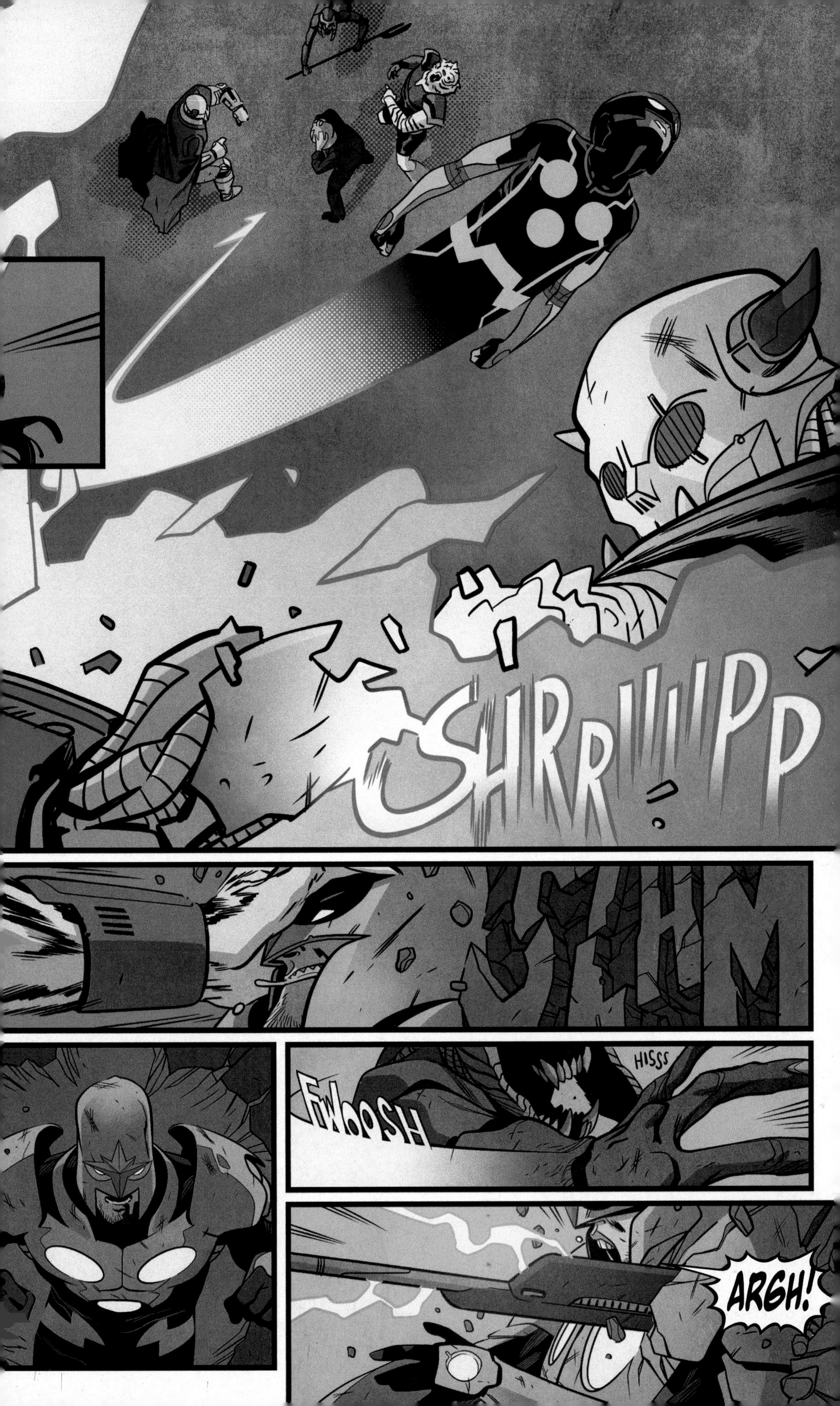
SHRRIIIIPP
FWOOSH
HISSS
ARGH!

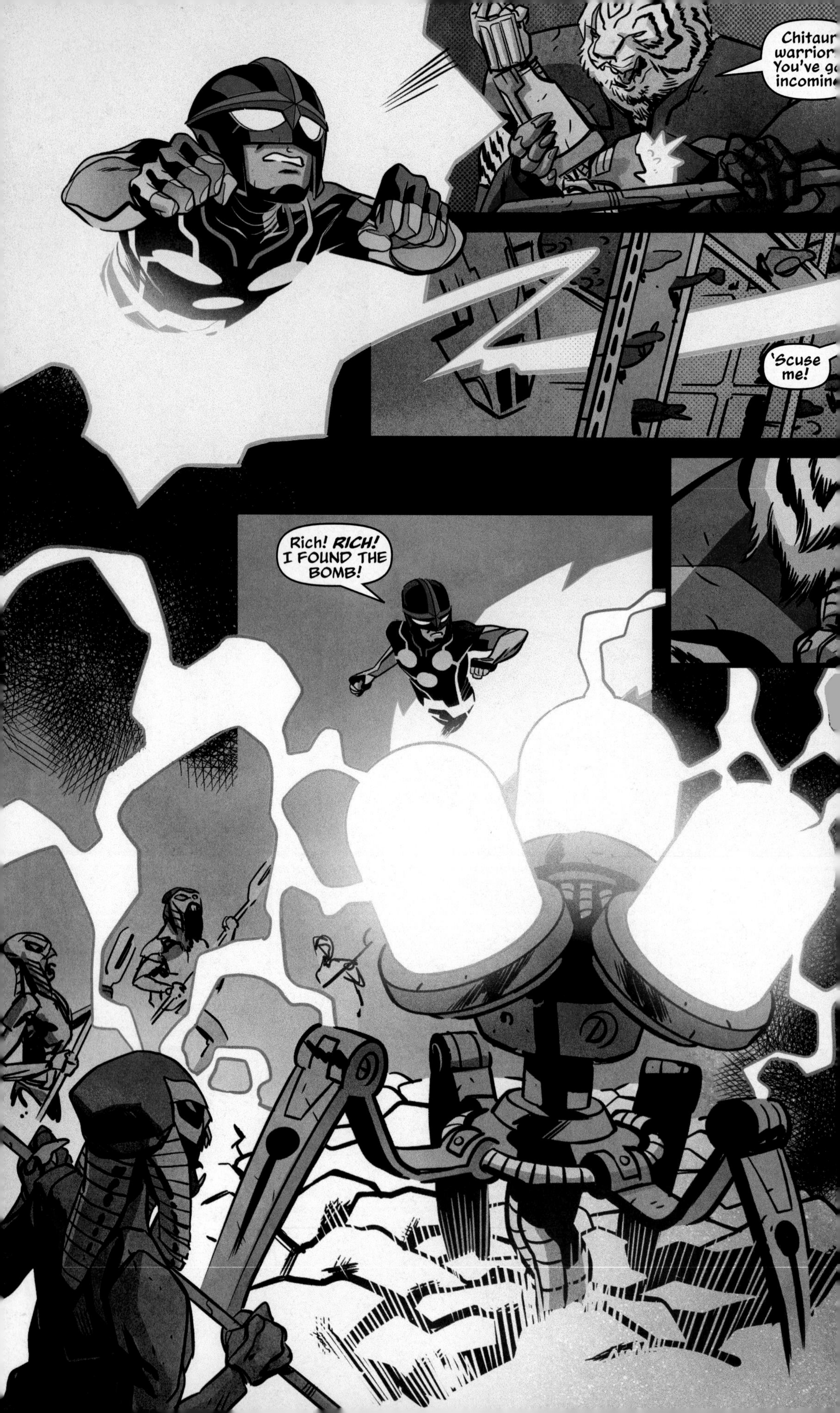
Chitaur
warrior
You've g
incomin
'Scuse me!
Rich! RICH! I FOUND THE BOMB!

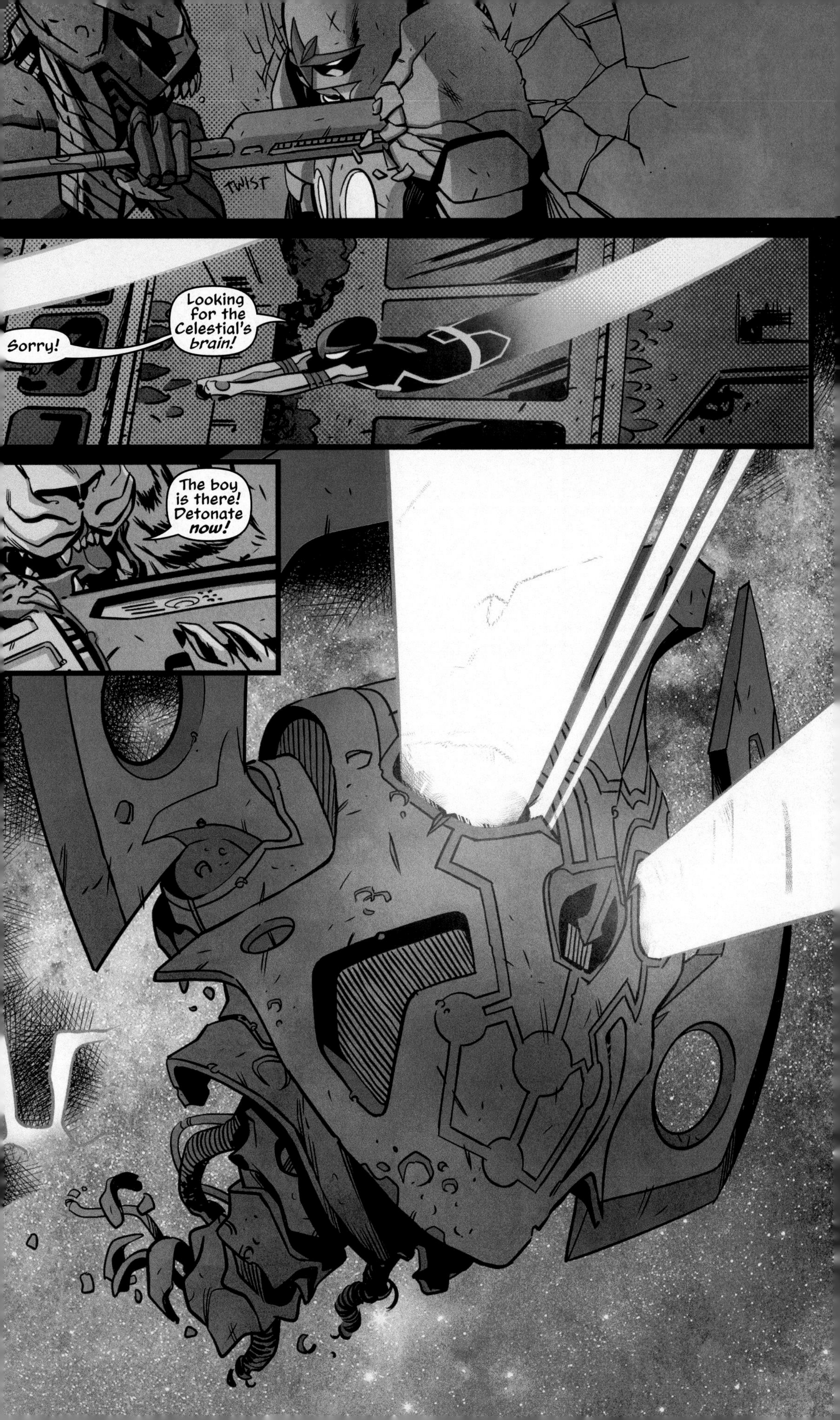
TWIST
Looking for the Celestial's brain!
Sorry!
The boy is there! Detonate now!

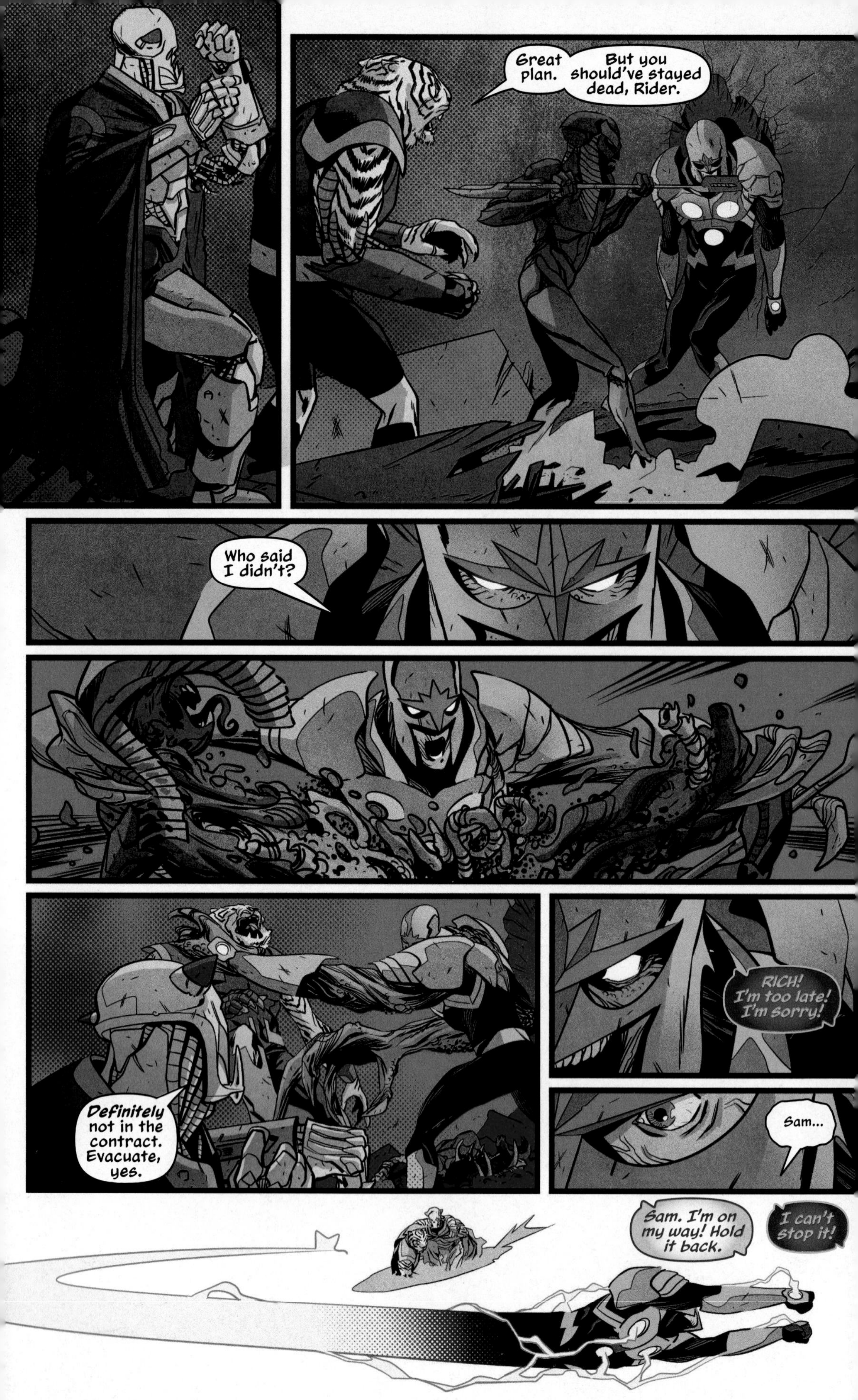
Great plan.
But you should've stayed dead, Rider.
Who said I didn't?
RICH! I'm too late! I'm sorry!
Definitely not in the contract. Evacuate, yes.
Sam...
Sam. I'm on my way! Hold it back.
I can't stop it!

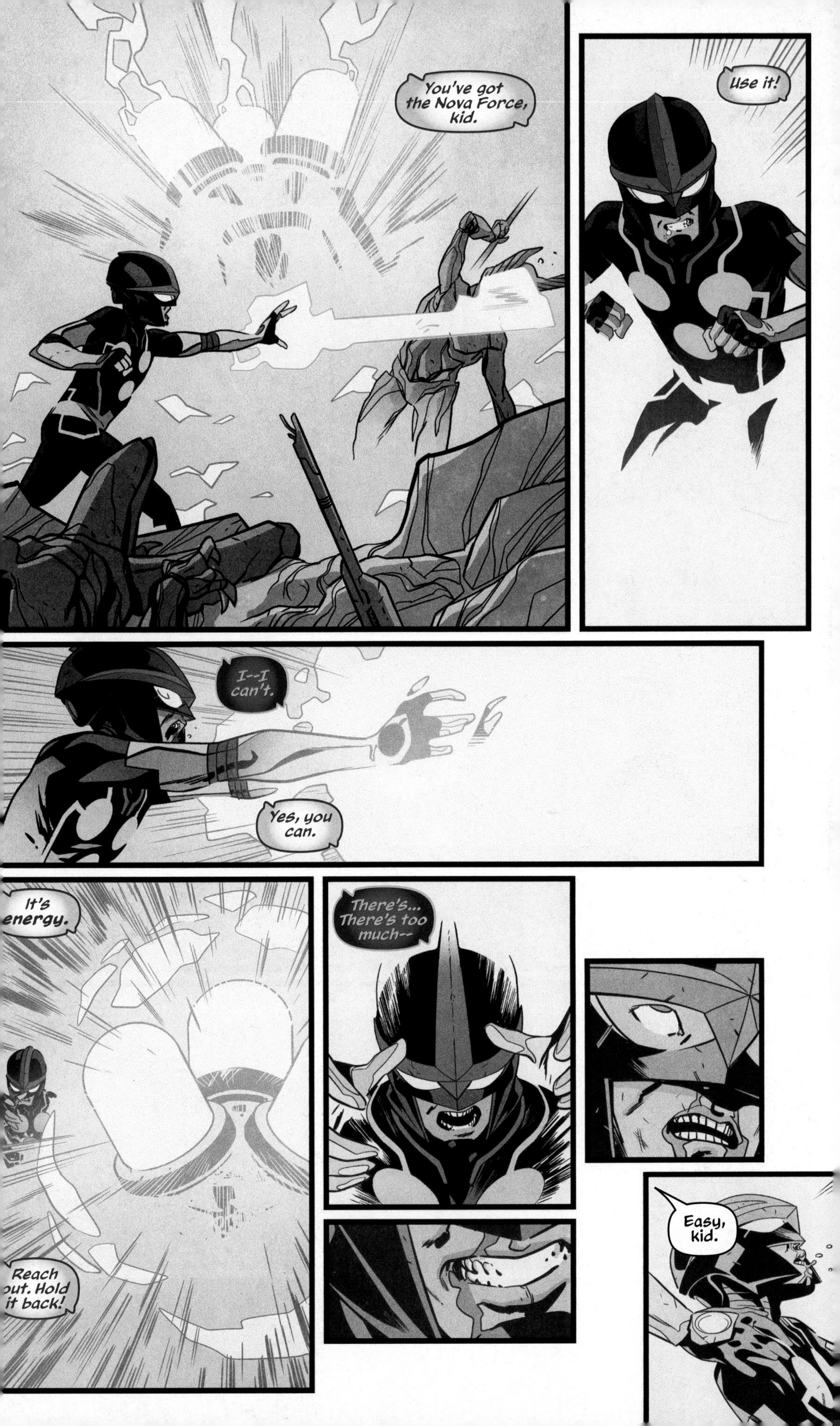
You've got the Nova Force, kid.
Use it!
I--I can't.
Yes, you can.
It's energy.
Reach out. Hold it back!
There's... There's too much--
Easy, kid.

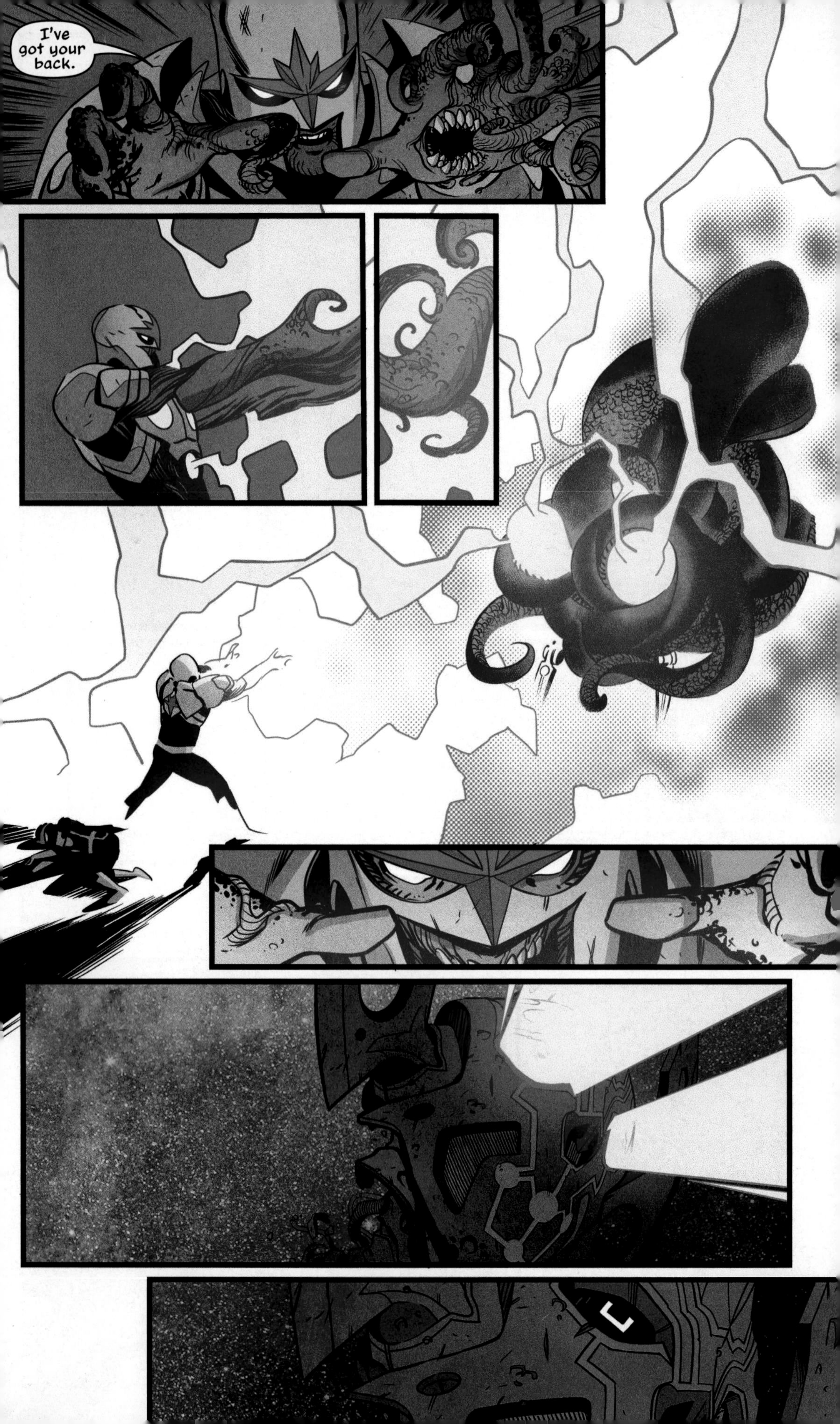
I've got your back.

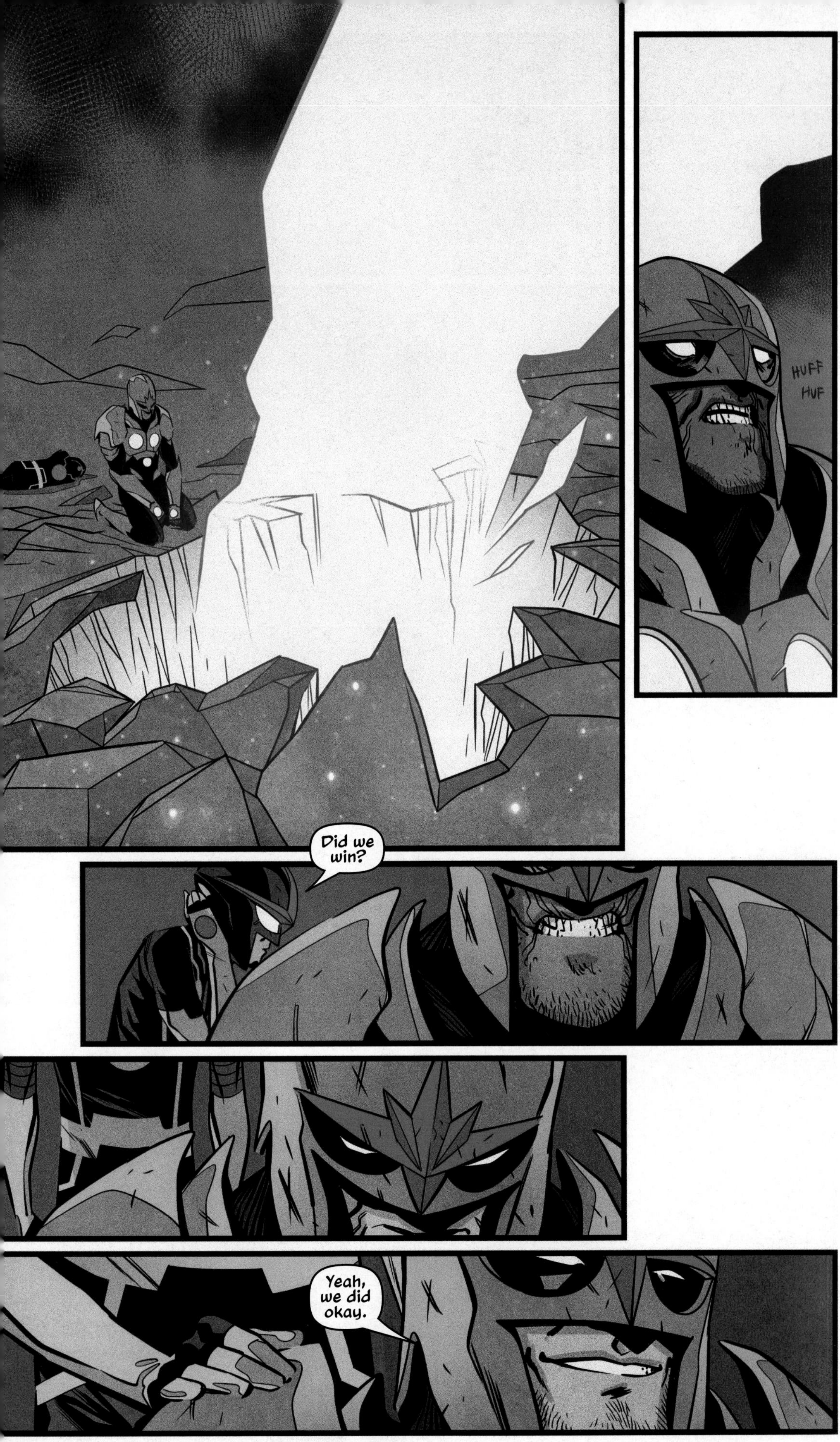
HUFF
HUF
Did we win?
Yeah, we did okay.

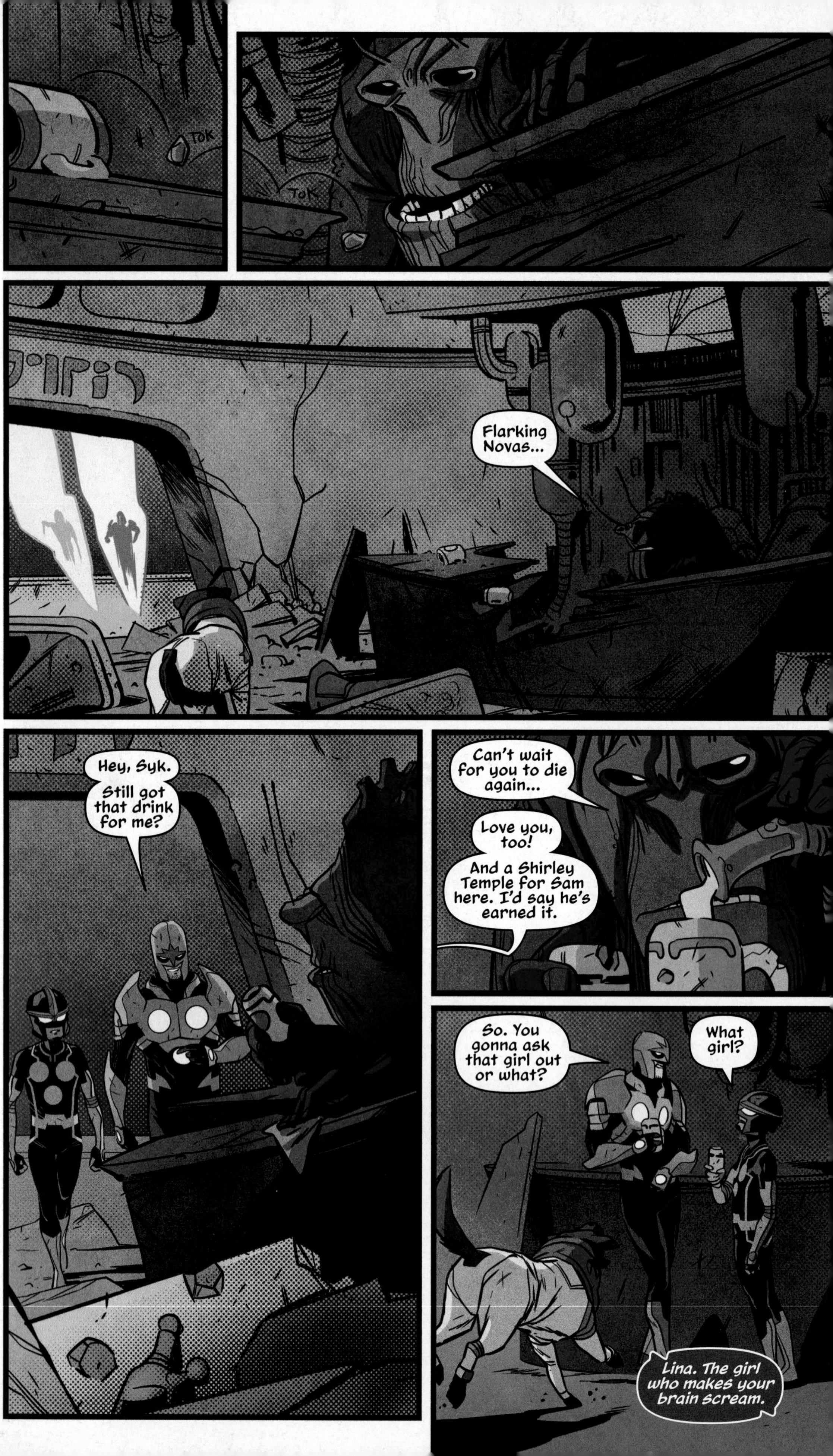
TOK
TOK
Flarking Novas...
Hey, Syk. Still got that drink for me?
Can't wait for you to die again...
Love you, too!
And a Shirley Temple for Sam here. I'd say he's earned it.
So. You gonna ask that girl out or what?
What girl?
Lina. The girl who makes your brain scream.

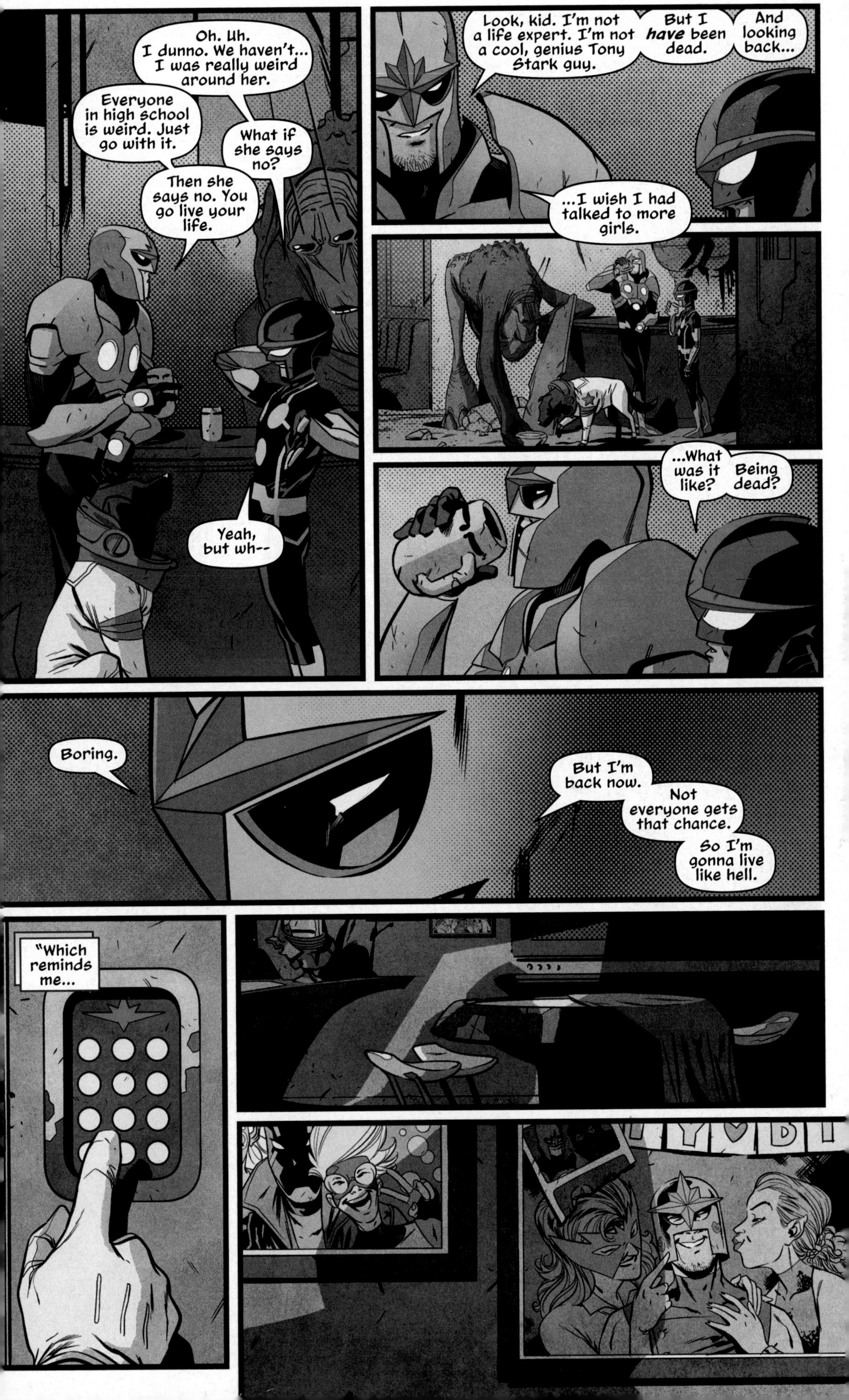

Oh. Uh. I dunno. We haven't... I was really weird around her.
Everyone in high school is weird. Just go with it.
What if she says no?
Then she says no. You go live your life.
Yeah, but wh--
Look, kid. I'm not a life expert. I'm not a cool, genius Tony Stark guy.
But I *have* been dead.
And looking back...
...I wish I had talked to more girls.
...What was it like?
Being dead?
Boring.
But I'm back now.
Not everyone gets that chance.
So I'm gonna live like hell.
"Which reminds me...

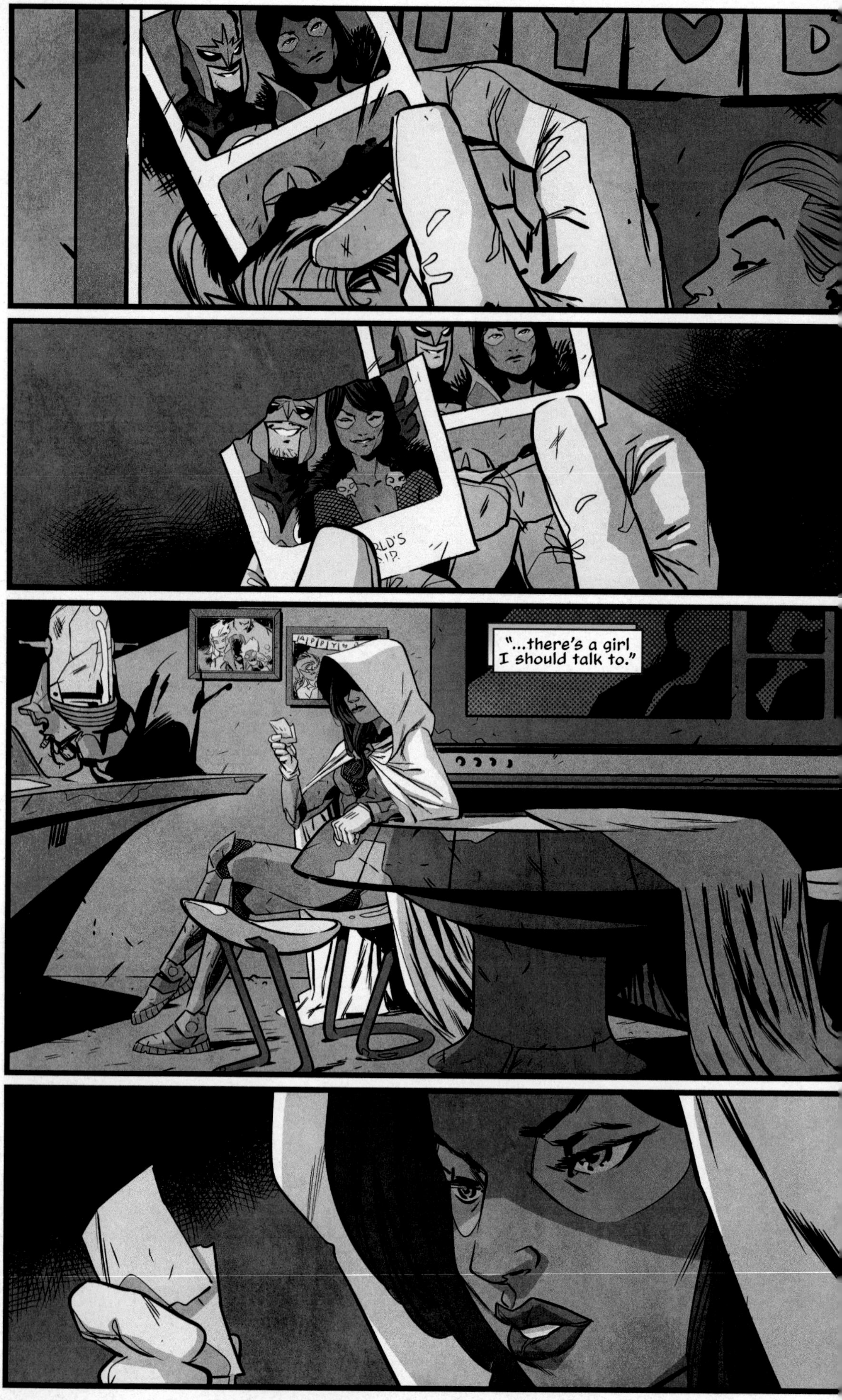
"...there's a girl I should talk to."

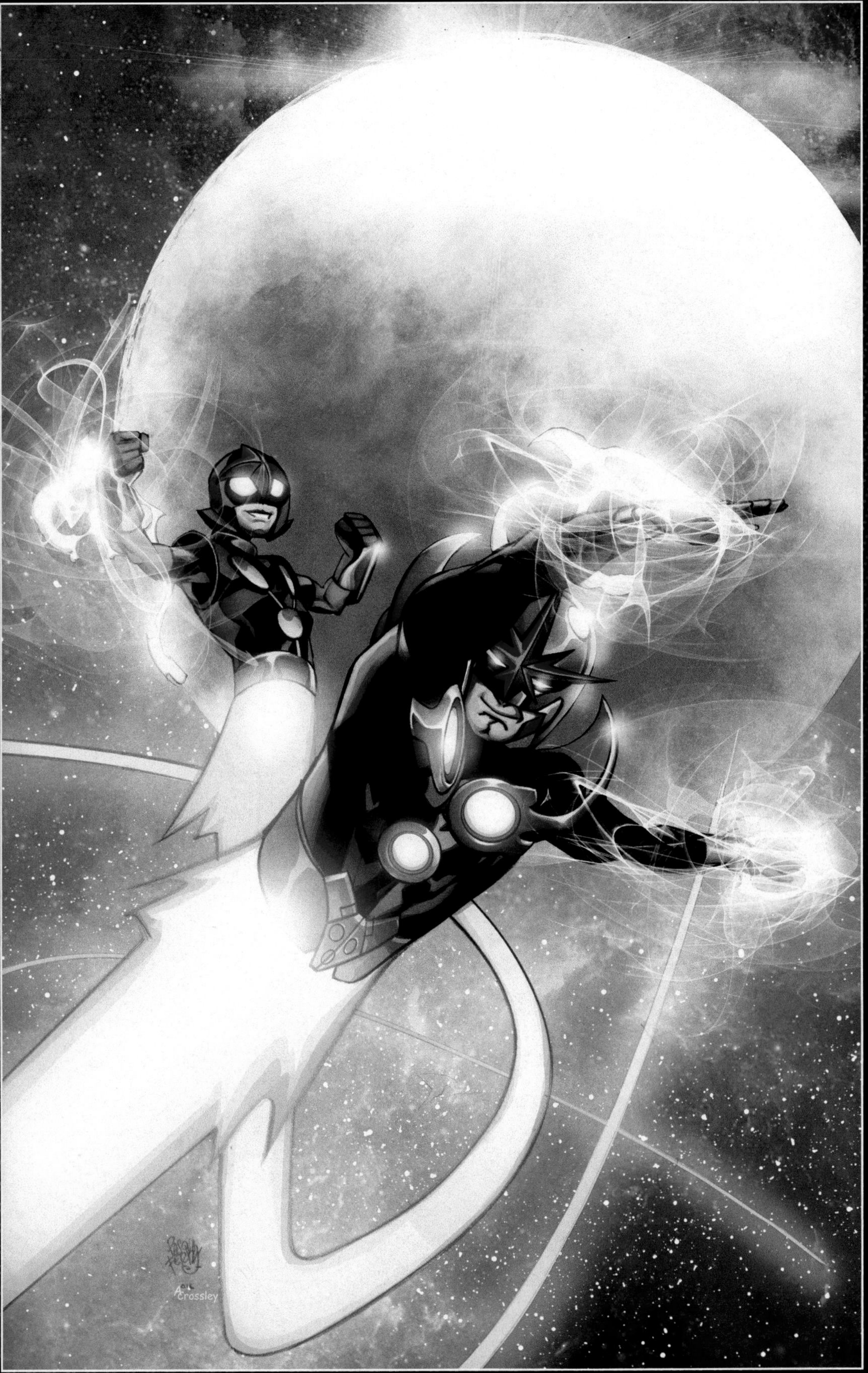
A. Crossley

PASQUAL FERRY & ANDREW CROSSLEY

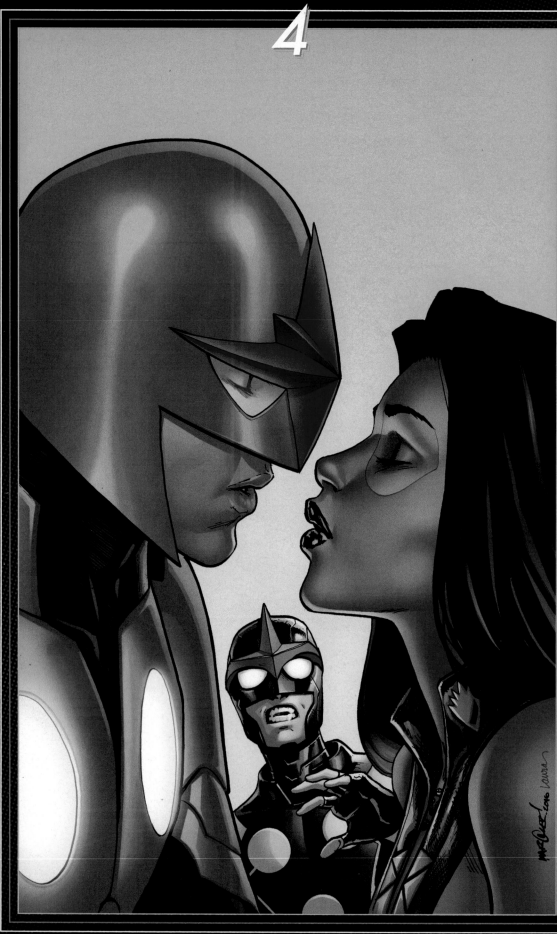

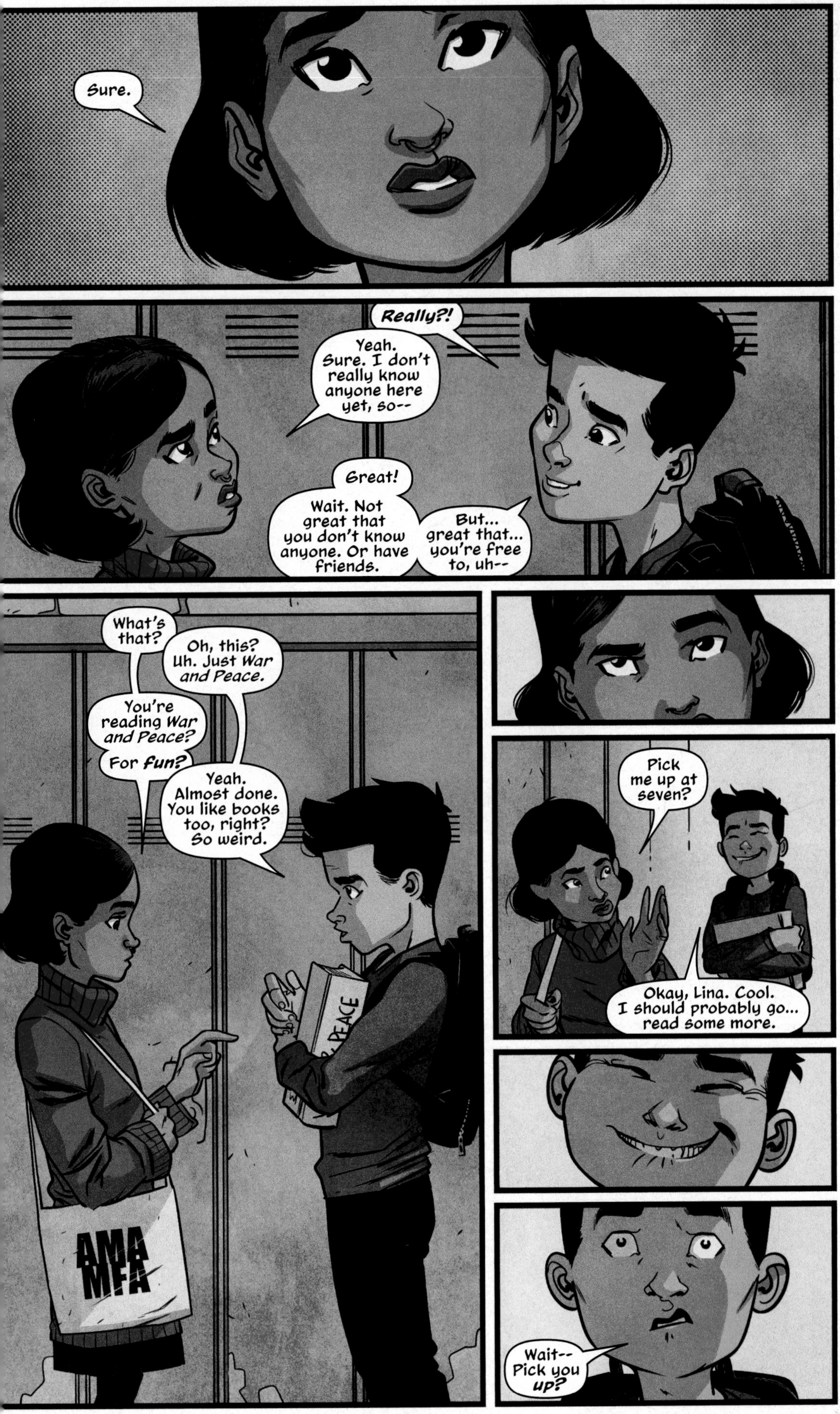
Sure.
Really?!
Yeah. Sure. I don't really know anyone here yet, so--
Great!
Wait. Not great that you don't know anyone. Or have friends.
But... great that... you're free to, uh--
What's that?
Oh, this? Uh. Just War and Peace.
You're reading War and Peace?
For fun?
Yeah. Almost done. You like books too, right? So weird.
PEACE
AMA MFA
Pick me up at seven?
Okay, Lina. Cool. I should probably go... read some more.
Wait-- Pick you up?

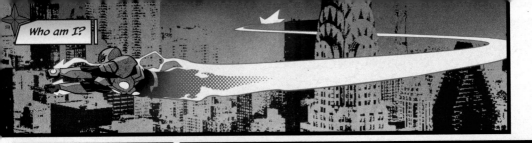

Who am I?

I'm Rich.

Richard Rider.

A New Warrior, a Defender, a Champion of Xandar.

Nova.

I know who I am.

I guess now the better question is...

...What am I?

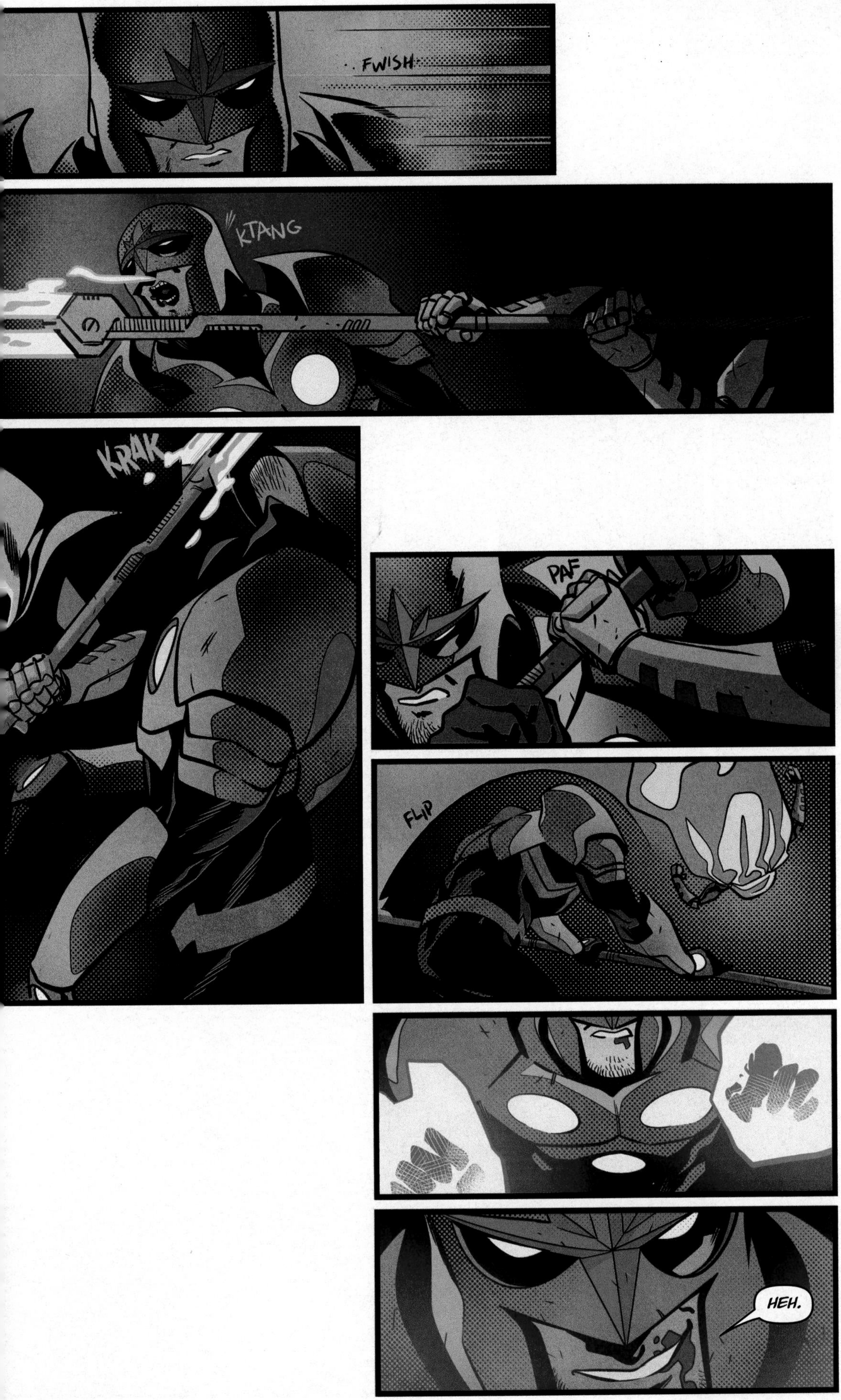
FWISH
KTANG
KRAK
PAF
FLIP
HEH.

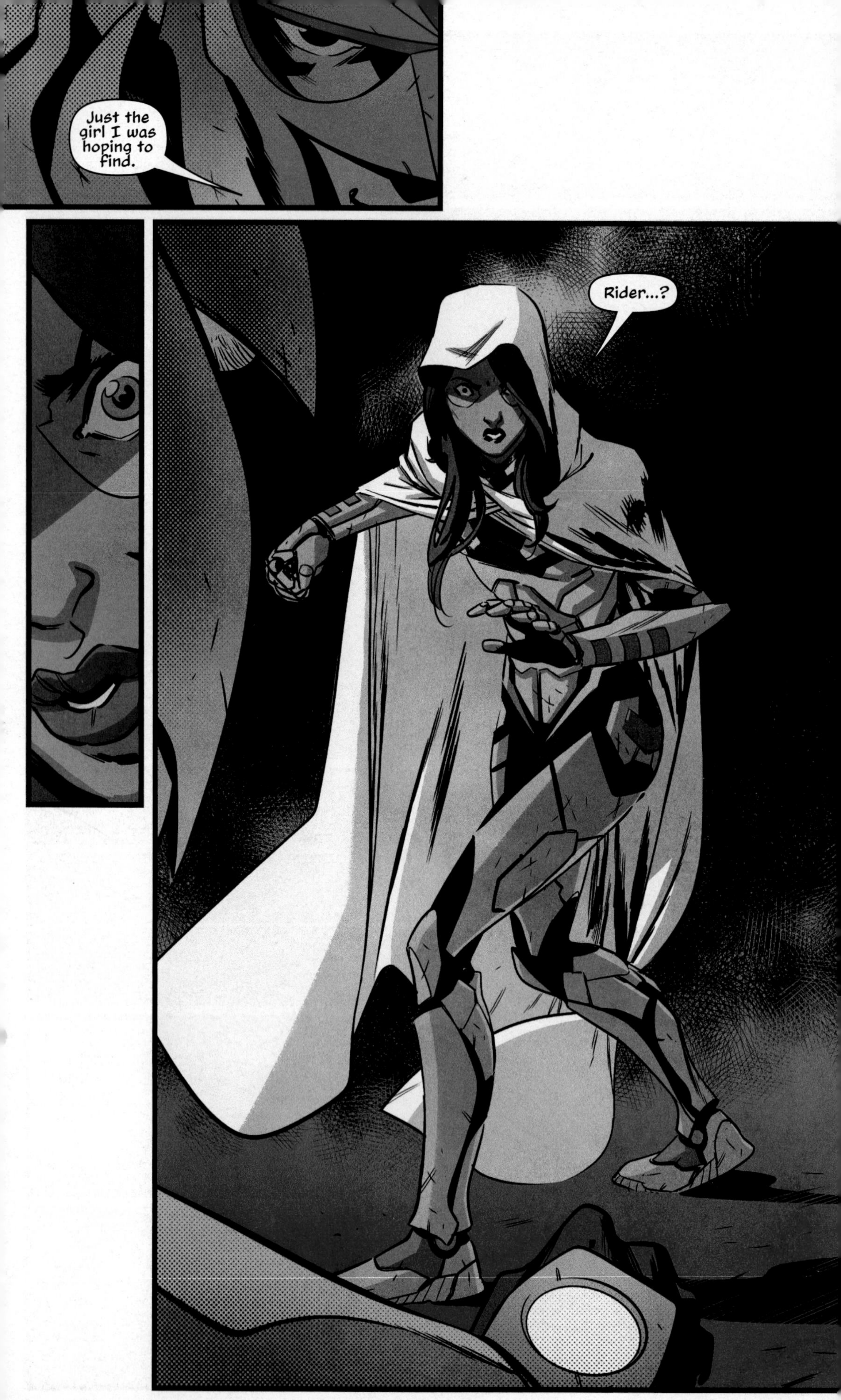
Just the girl I was hoping to find.
Rider...?

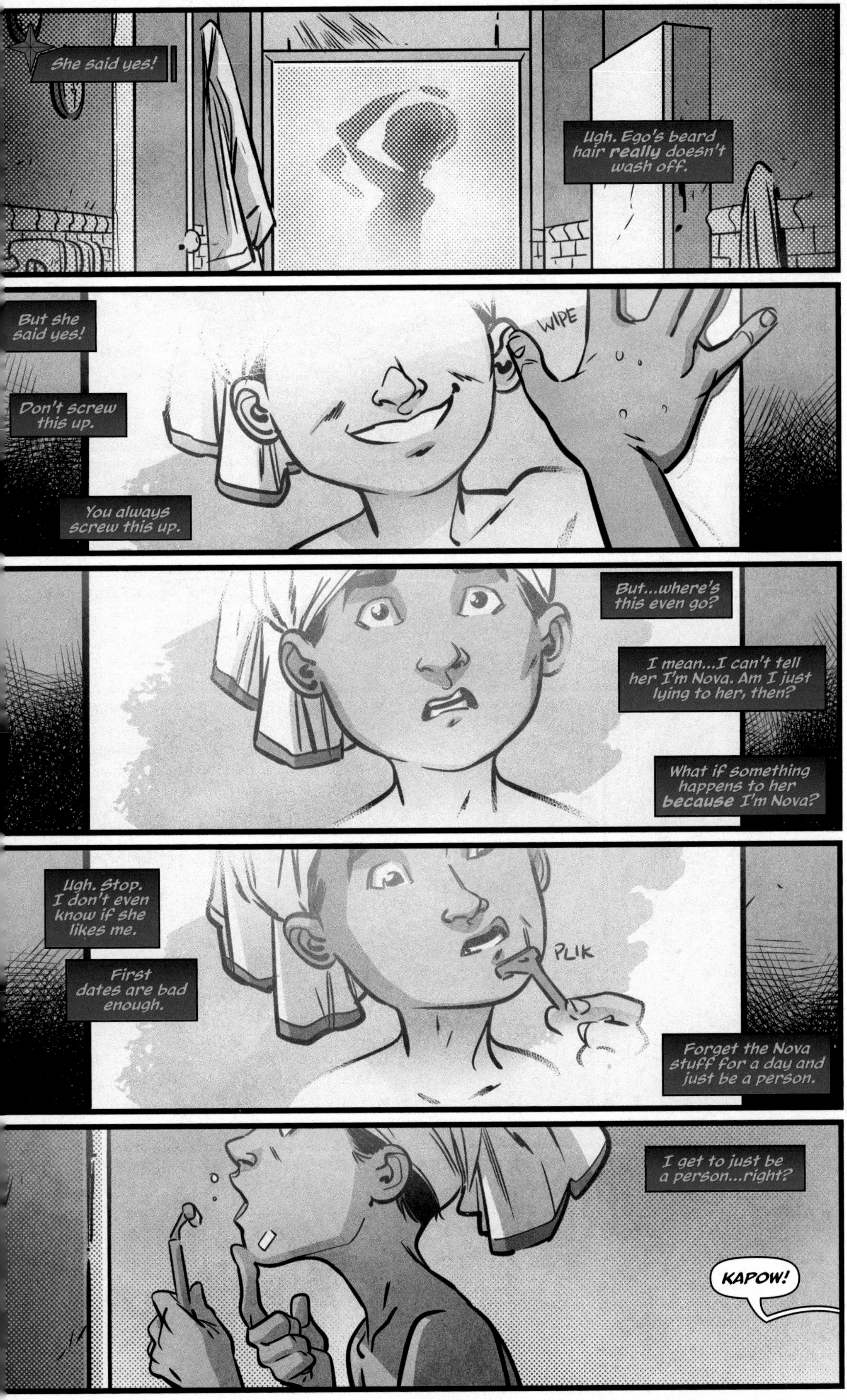
She said yes!
Ugh. Ego's beard hair really doesn't wash off.
But she said yes!
WIPE
Don't screw this up.
You always screw this up.
But...where's this even go?
I mean...I can't tell her I'm Nova. Am I just lying to her, then?
What if something happens to her because I'm Nova?
Ugh. Stop. I don't even know if she likes me.
PLIK
First dates are bad enough.
Forget the Nova stuff for a day and just be a person.
I get to just be a person...right?
KAPOW!

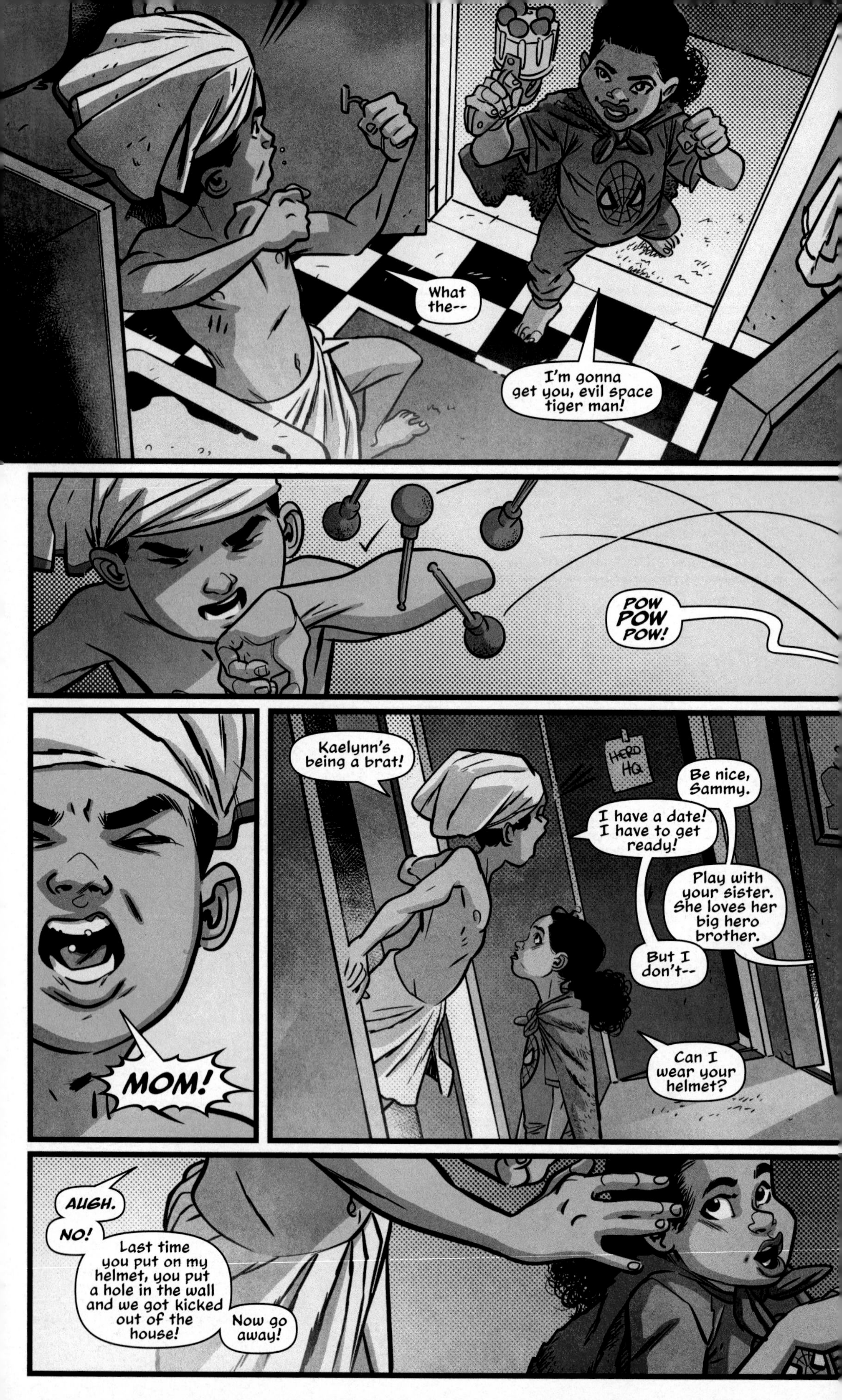
What the--
I'm gonna get you, evil space tiger man!
POW POW POW!
MOM!
Kaelynn's being a brat!
HERO HQ
Be nice, Sammy.
I have a date! I have to get ready!
Play with your sister. She loves her big hero brother.
But I don't--
Can I wear your helmet?
AUGH.
NO!
Last time you put on my helmet, you put a hole in the wall and we got kicked out of the house!
Now go away!

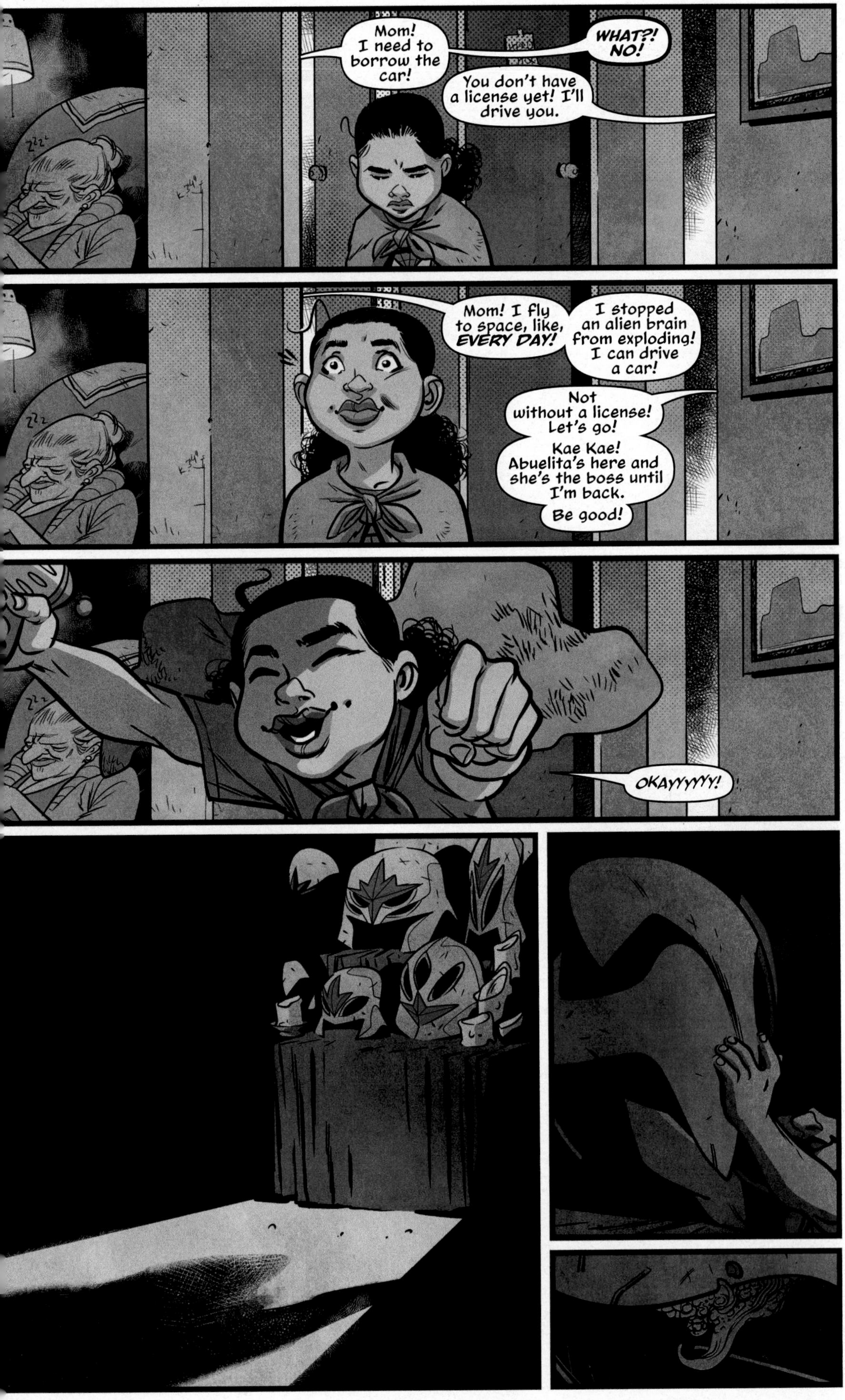

Mom! I need to borrow the car!
WHAT?! NO!
You don't have a license yet! I'll drive you.
Mom! I fly to space, like, EVERY DAY!
I stopped an alien brain from exploding! I can drive a car!
Not without a license! Let's go!
Kae Kae! Abuelita's here and she's the boss until I'm back.
Be good!
OKAYYYYYY!

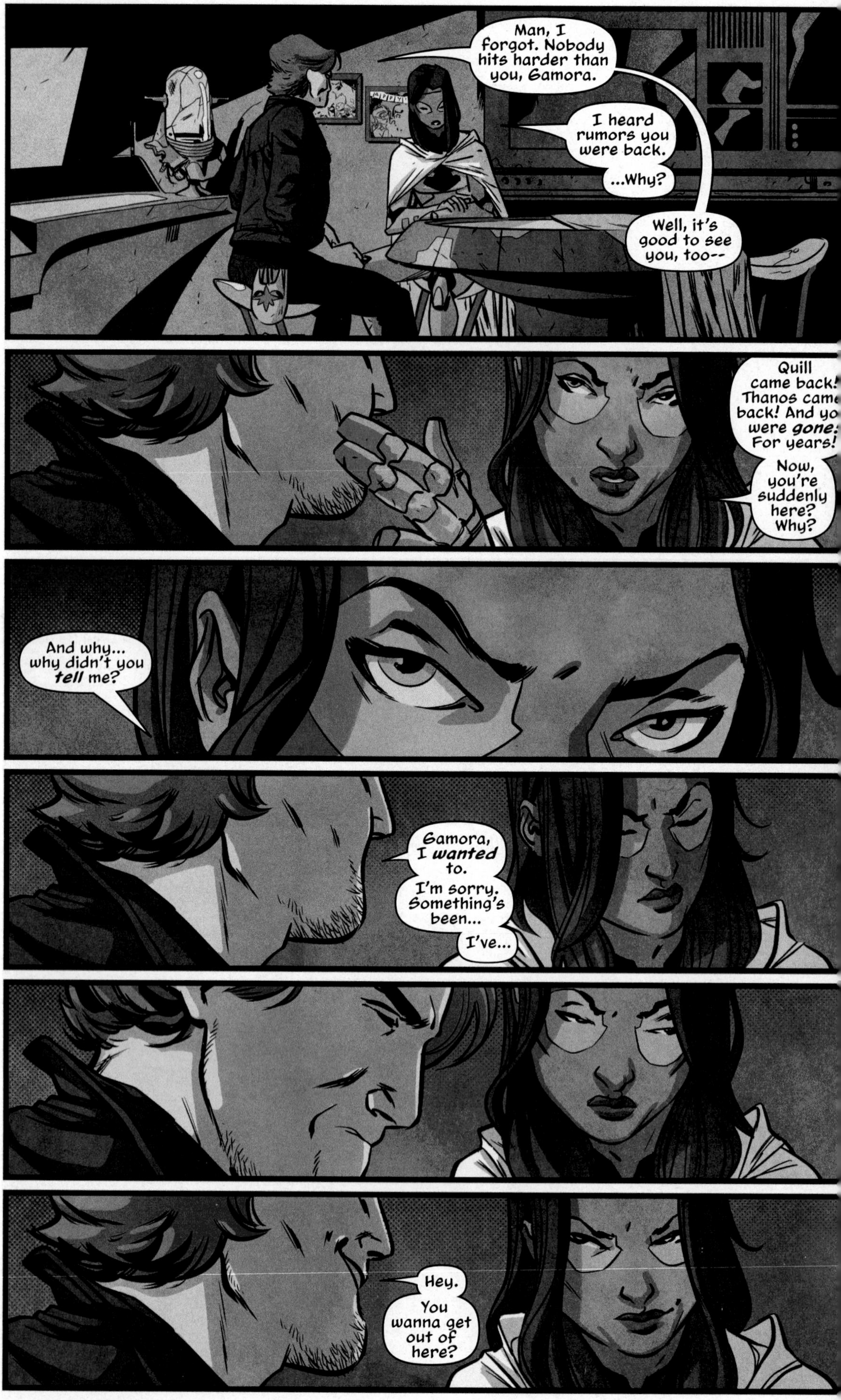
Man, I forgot. Nobody hits harder than you, Gamora.
I heard rumors you were back.
...Why?
Well, it's good to see you, too--
Quill came back! Thanos came back! And you were *gone!* For years!
Now, you're suddenly here? Why?
And why... why didn't you *tell* me?
Gamora, I *wanted* to.
I'm sorry. Something's been...
I've...
Hey.
You wanna get out of here?

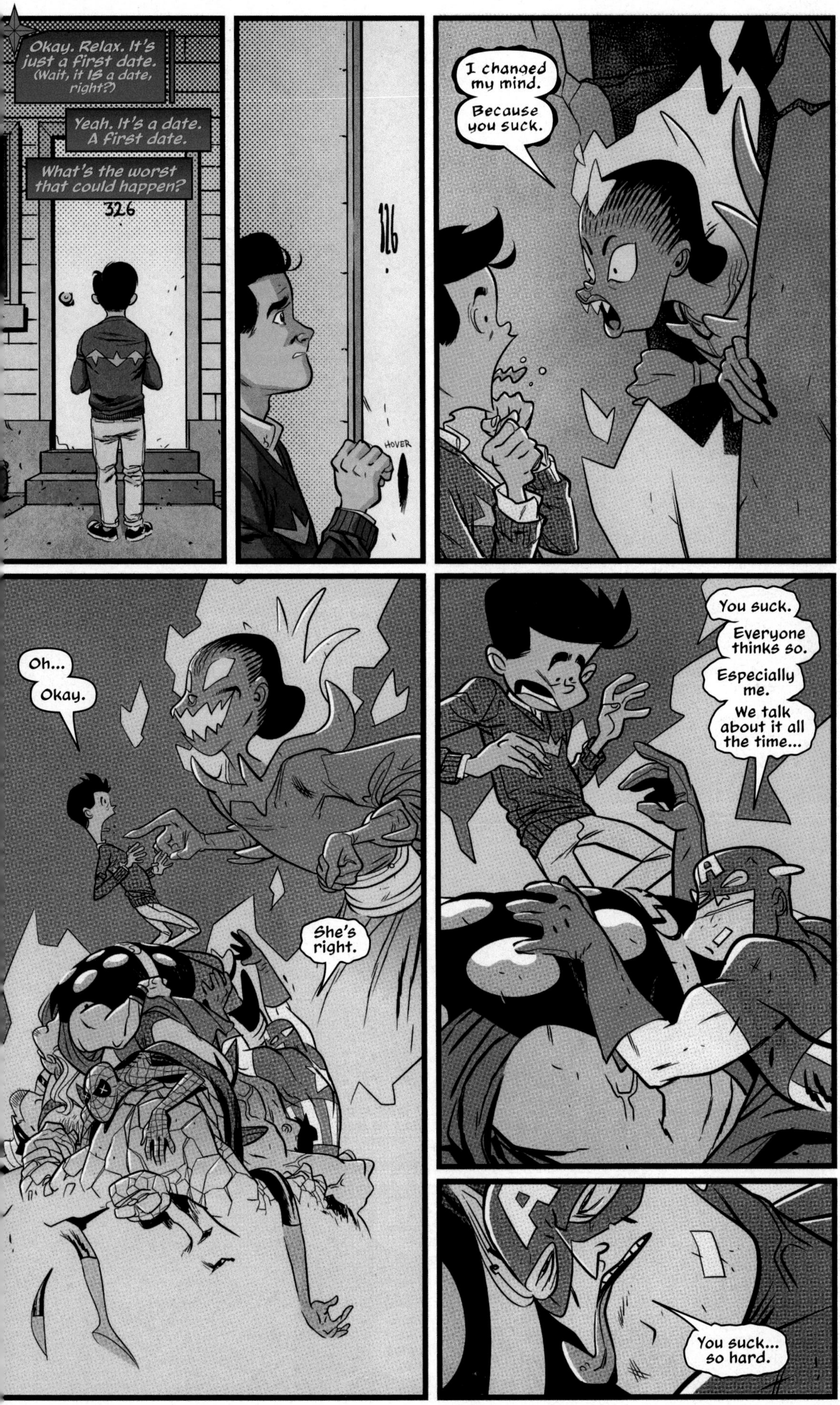

Okay. Relax. It's just a first date. (Wait, it IS a date, right?)
Yeah. It's a date. A first date.
What's the worst that could happen?
326
326
HOVER
I changed my mind.
Because you suck.
Oh...
Okay.
She's right.
You suck.
Everyone thinks so.
Especially me.
We talk about it all the time...
You suck... so hard.

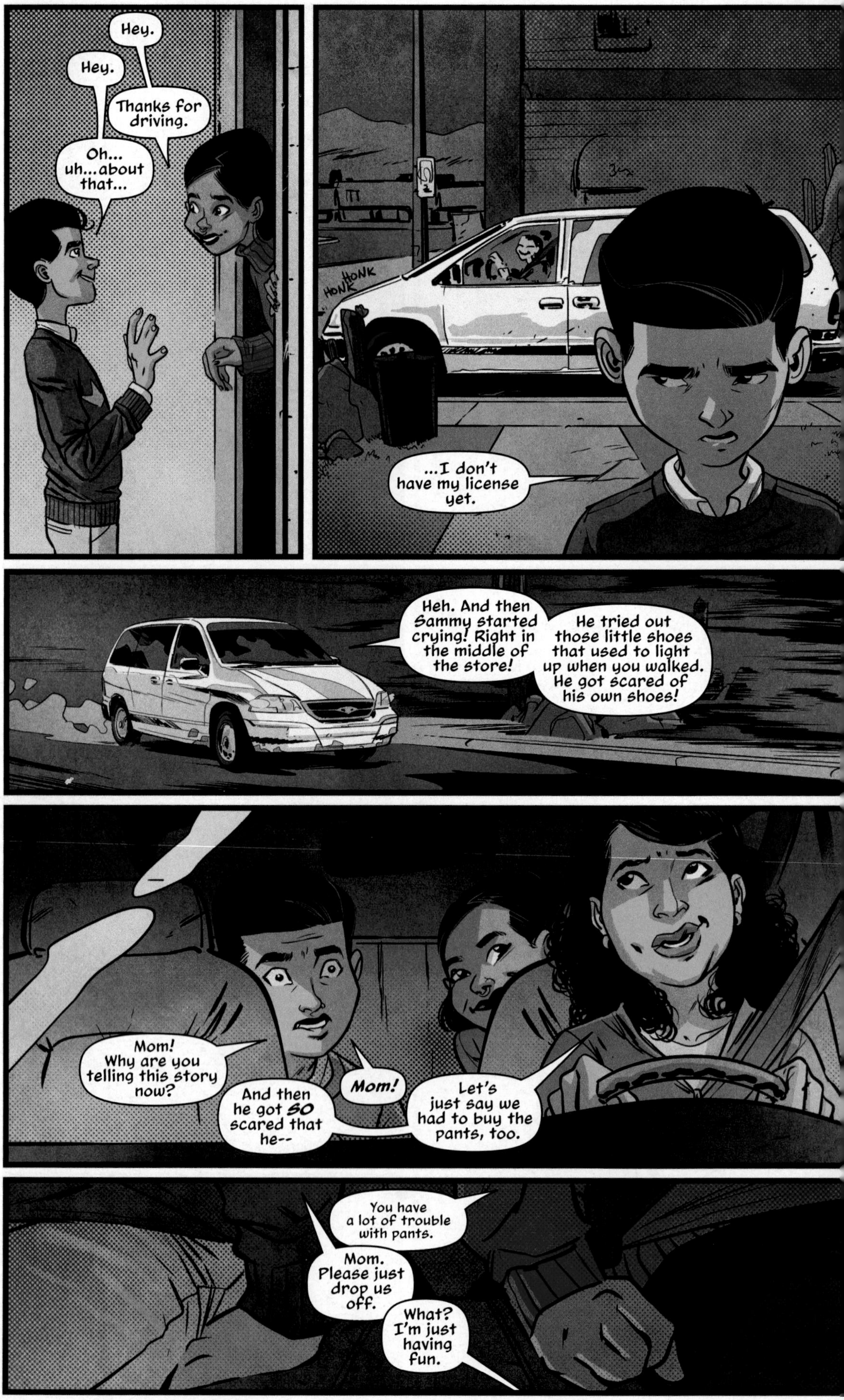
Hey.
Hey.
Thanks for driving.
Oh... uh...about that...
HONK HONK
...I don't have my license yet.
Heh. And then Sammy started crying! Right in the middle of the store!
He tried out those little shoes that used to light up when you walked. He got scared of his own shoes!
Mom! Why are you telling this story now?
And then he got SO scared that he--
Mom!
Let's just say we had to buy the pants, too.
You have a lot of trouble with pants.
Mom. Please just drop us off.
What? I'm just having fun.

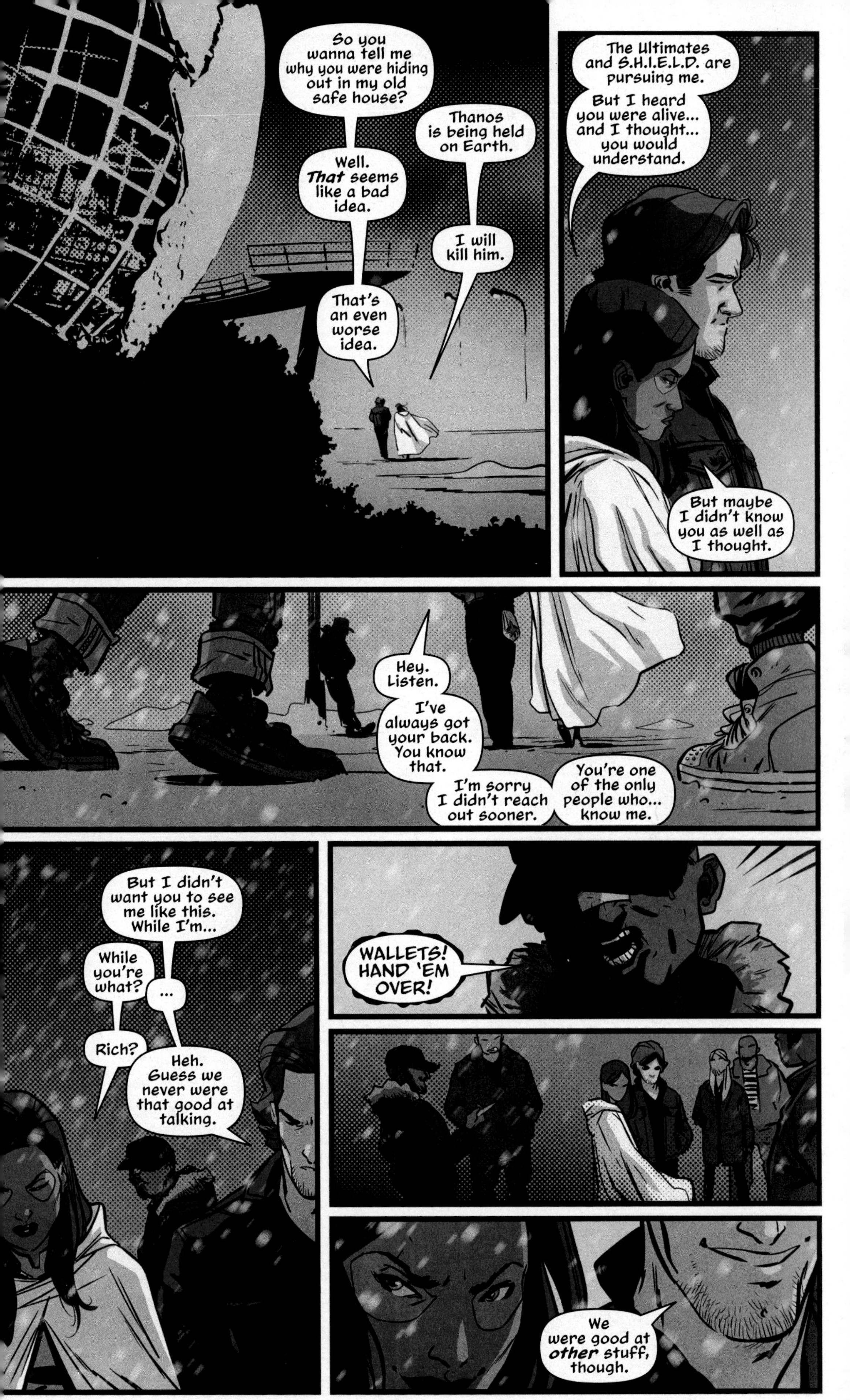
So you wanna tell me why you were hiding out in my old safe house?
Thanos is being held on Earth.
Well. *That* seems like a bad idea.
I will kill him.
That's an even worse idea.
The Ultimates and S.H.I.E.L.D. are pursuing me.
But I heard you were alive... and I thought... you would understand.
But maybe I didn't know you as well as I thought.
Hey. Listen.
I've always got your back. You know that.
I'm sorry I didn't reach out sooner.
You're one of the only people who... know me.
But I didn't want you to see me like this. While I'm...
While you're what?
...
Rich?
Heh. Guess we never were that good at talking.
WALLETS! HAND 'EM OVER!
We were good at *other* stuff, though.

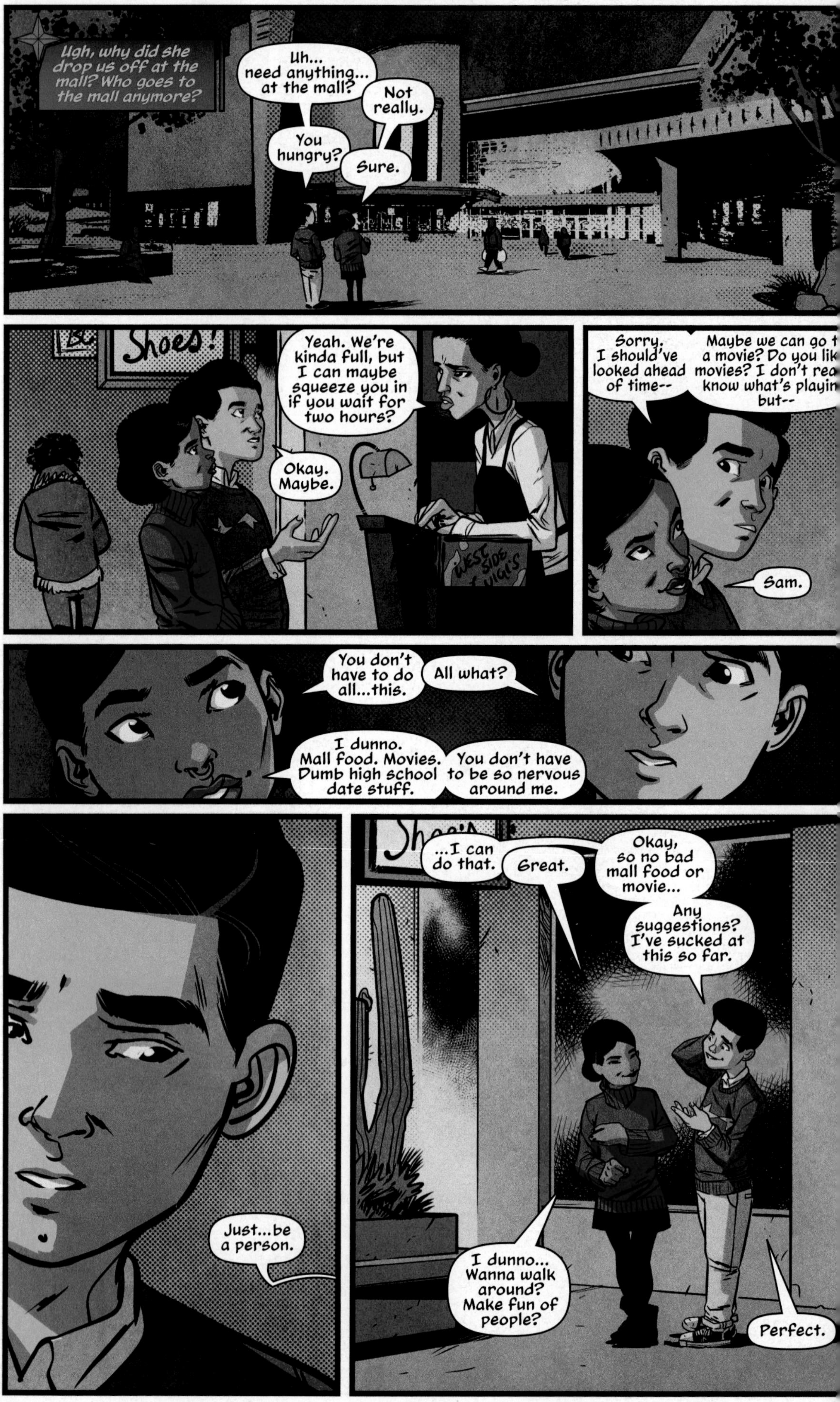
Ugh, why did she drop us off at the mall? Who goes to the mall anymore?
Uh... need anything... at the mall?
Not really.
You hungry?
Sure.
Shoes!
Yeah. We're kinda full, but I can maybe squeeze you in if you wait for two hours?
Okay. Maybe.
WEST SIDE LUIGI'S
Sorry. I should've looked ahead of time--
Maybe we can go t a movie? Do you lik movies? I don't rea know what's playin but--
Sam.
You don't have to do all...this.
All what?
I dunno. Mall food. Movies. Dumb high school date stuff.
You don't have to be so nervous around me.
Just...be a person.
...I can do that.
Great.
Okay, so no bad mall food or movie...
Any suggestions? I've sucked at this so far.
I dunno... Wanna walk around? Make fun of people?
Perfect.

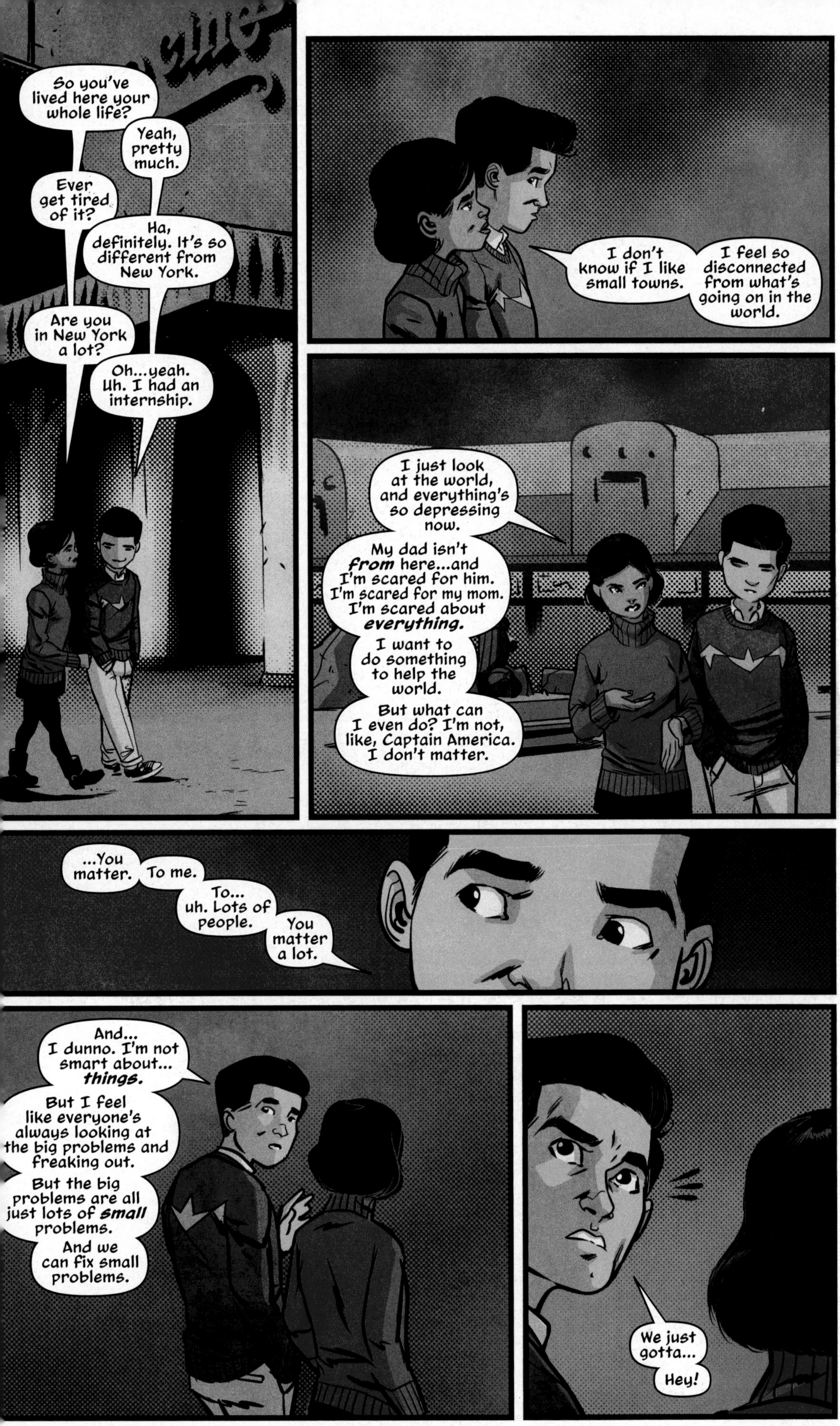
So you've lived here your whole life?
Yeah, pretty much.
Ever get tired of it?
Ha, definitely. It's so different from New York.
Are you in New York a lot?
Oh...yeah. Uh. I had an internship.
I don't know if I like small towns.
I feel so disconnected from what's going on in the world.
I just look at the world, and everything's so depressing now.
My dad isn't *from* here...and I'm scared for him. I'm scared for my mom. I'm scared about *everything.*
I want to do something to help the world.
But what can I even do? I'm not, like, Captain America. I don't matter.
...You matter.
To me.
To... uh. Lots of people.
You matter a lot.
And... I dunno. I'm not smart about... *things.*
But I feel like everyone's always looking at the big problems and freaking out.
But the big problems are all just lots of *small* problems.
And we can fix small problems.
We just gotta...
Hey!

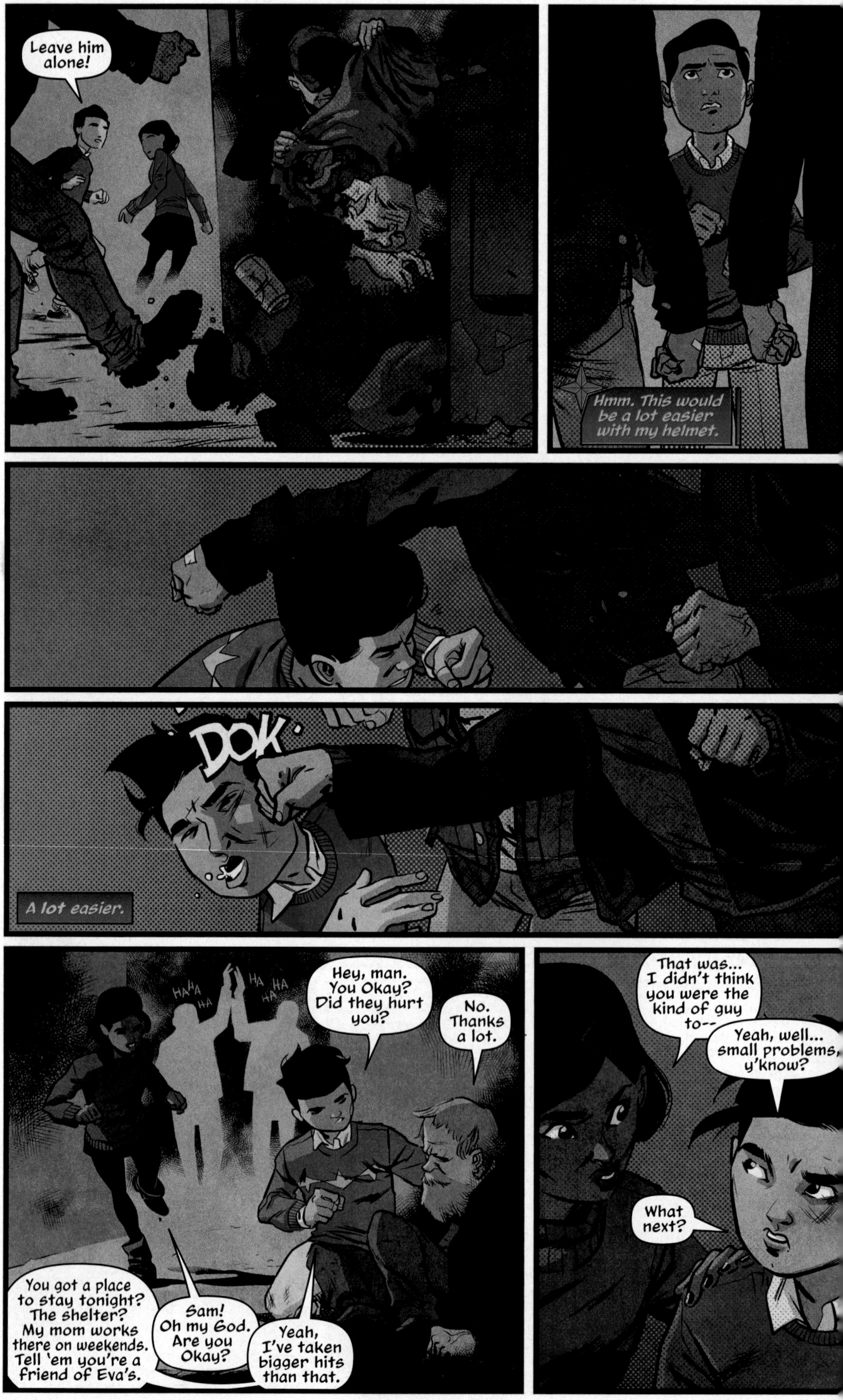

Leave him alone!
Hmm. This would be a lot easier with my helmet.
DOK
A lot easier.
HAHA HA
HA HA HA
Hey, man. You Okay? Did they hurt you?
No. Thanks a lot.
You got a place to stay tonight? The shelter? My mom works there on weekends. Tell 'em you're a friend of Eva's.
Sam! Oh my God. Are you Okay?
Yeah, I've taken bigger hits than that.
That was... I didn't think you were the kind of guy to--
Yeah, well... small problems, y'know?
What next?

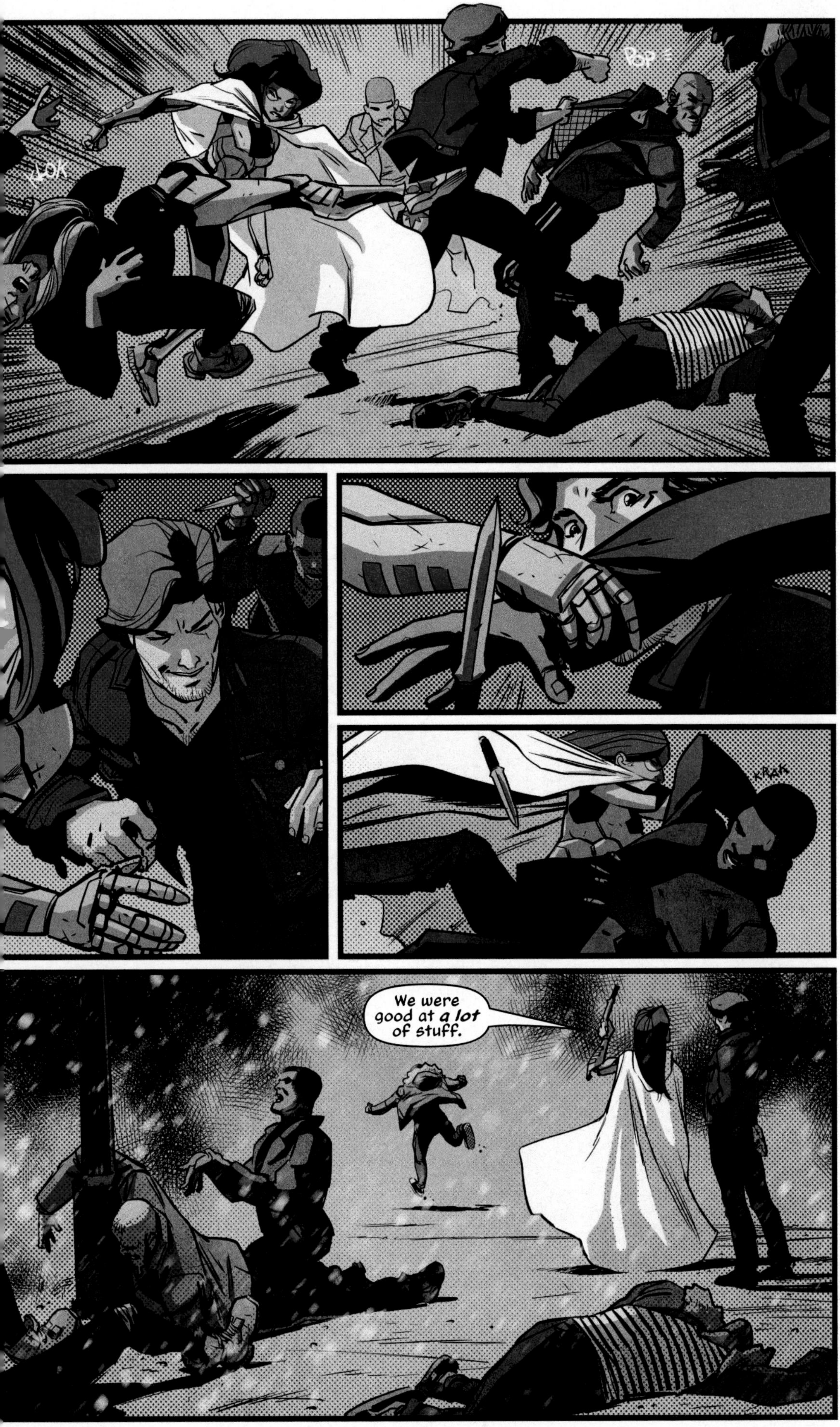
POP
KLOK
KRAK
We were good at *a lot* of stuff.

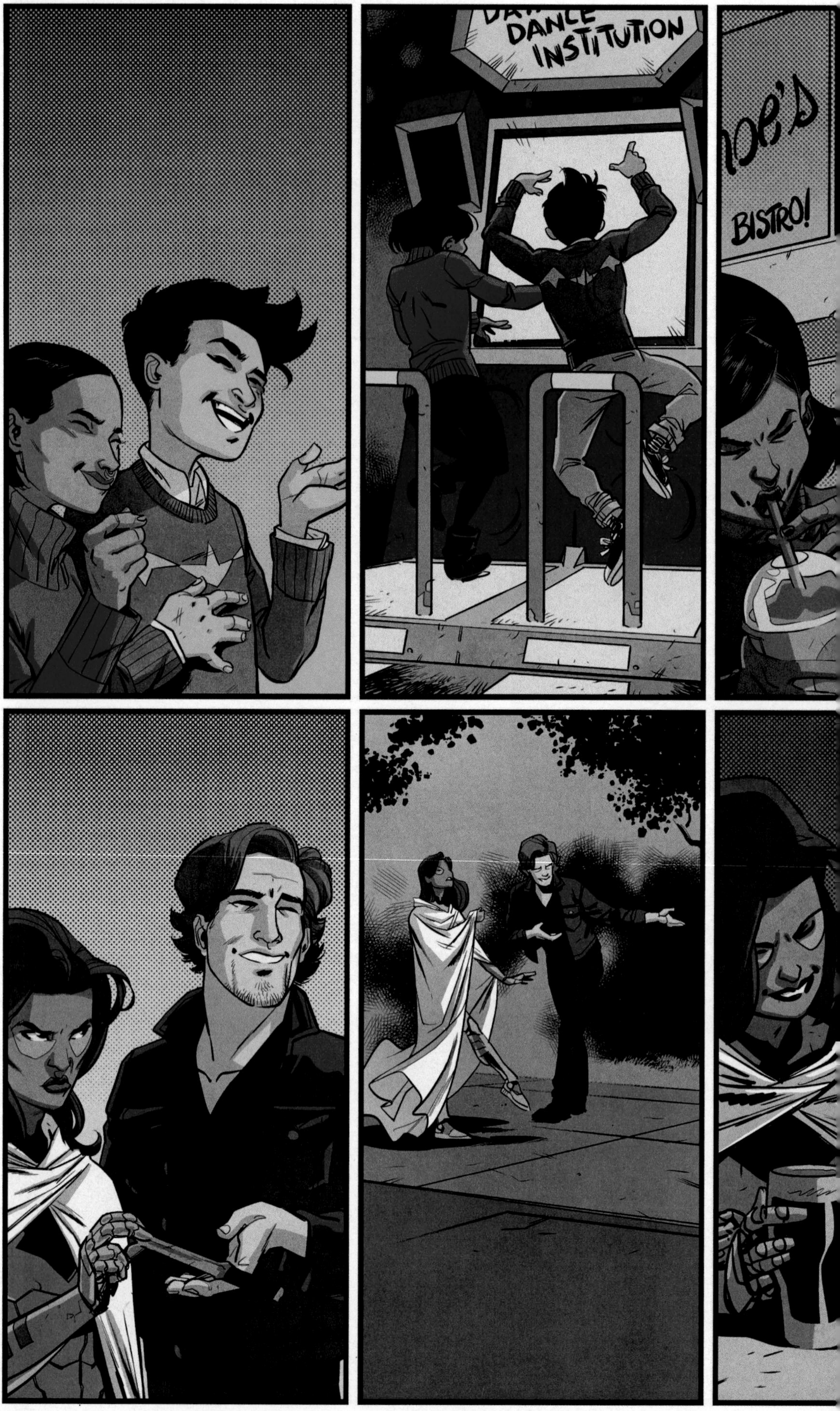
DANCE
INSTITUTION
BISTRO!

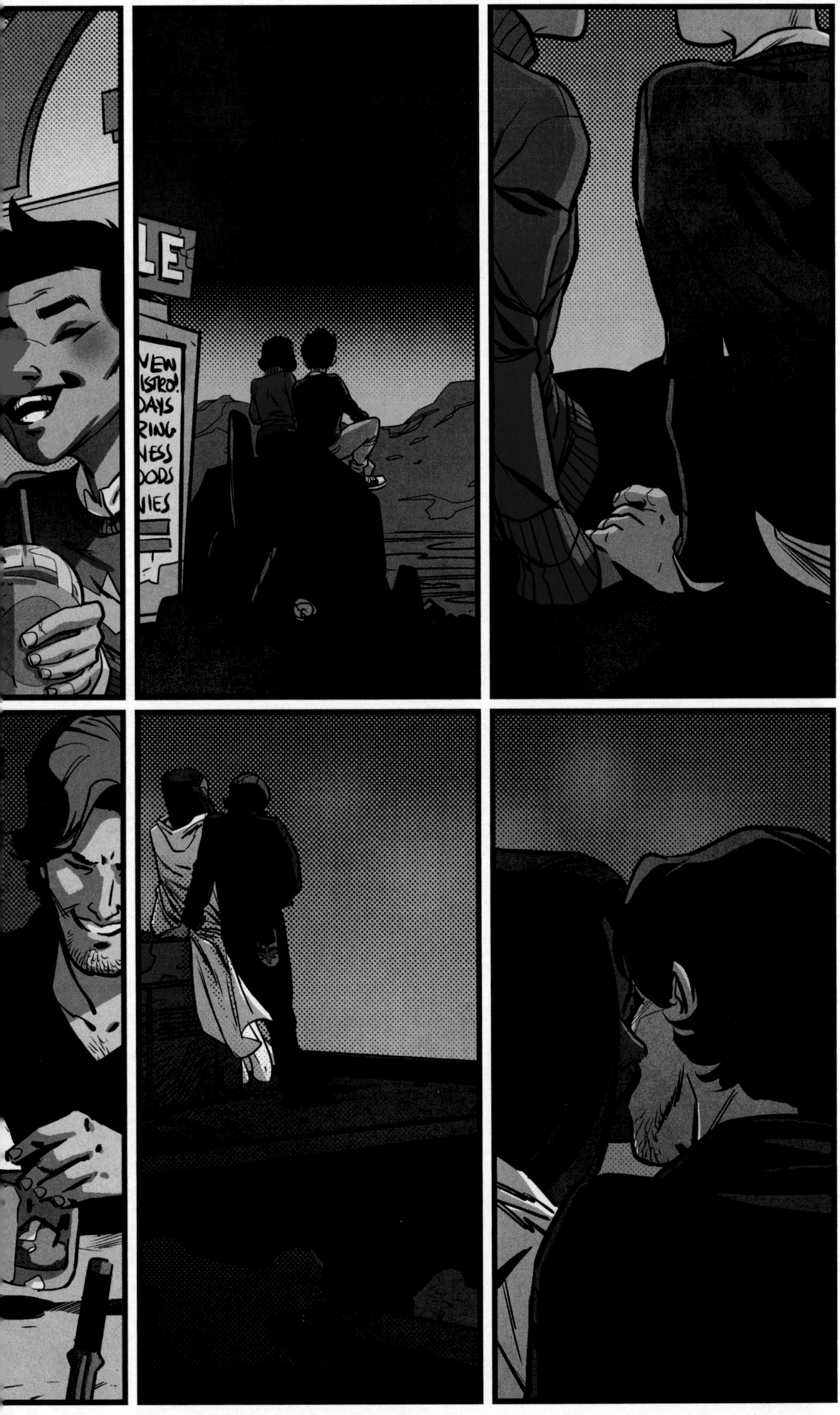
LE
NEW
ISTRO!
DAYS
RING
NESS
OODS
NIES

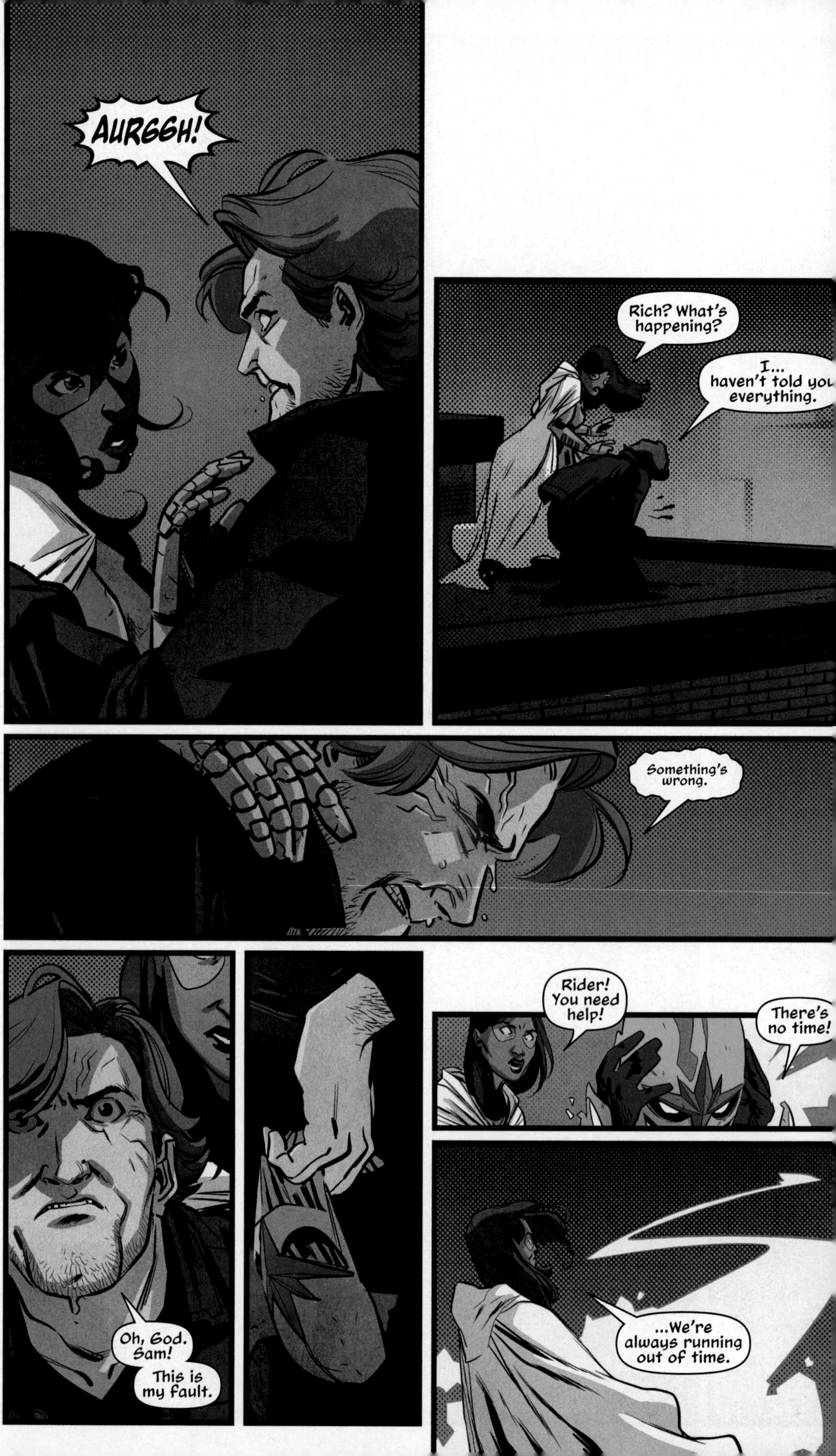
AURGGH!
Rich? What's happening?
I... haven't told you everything.
Something's wrong.
Oh, God. Sam!
This is my fault.
Rider! You need help!
There's no time!
...We're always running out of time.

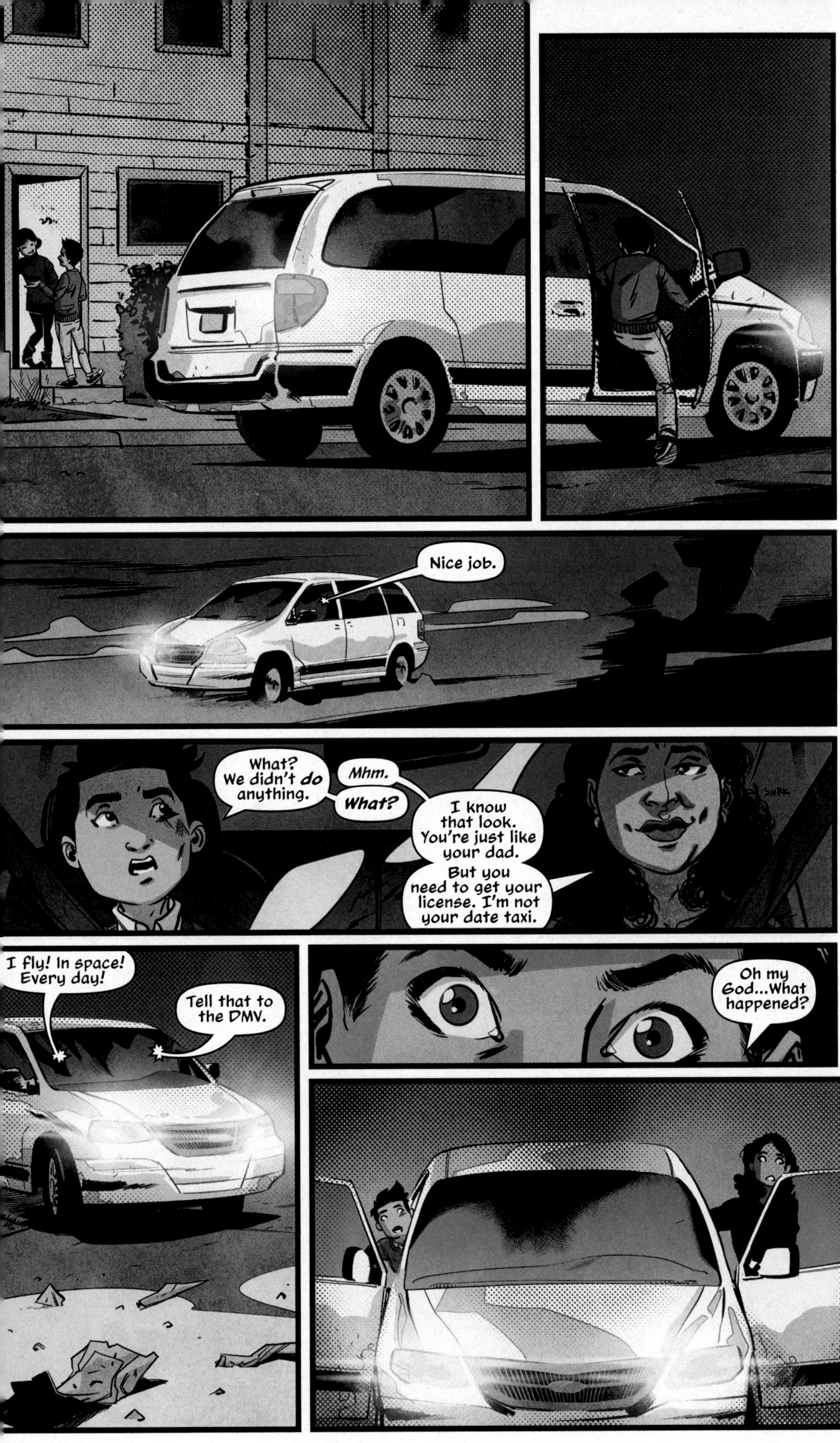
Nice job.
What? We didn't *do* anything.
Mhm.
What?
I know that look. You're just like your dad.
But you need to get your license. I'm not your date taxi.
SNRK
I fly! In space! Every day!
Tell that to the DMV.
Oh my God...What happened?

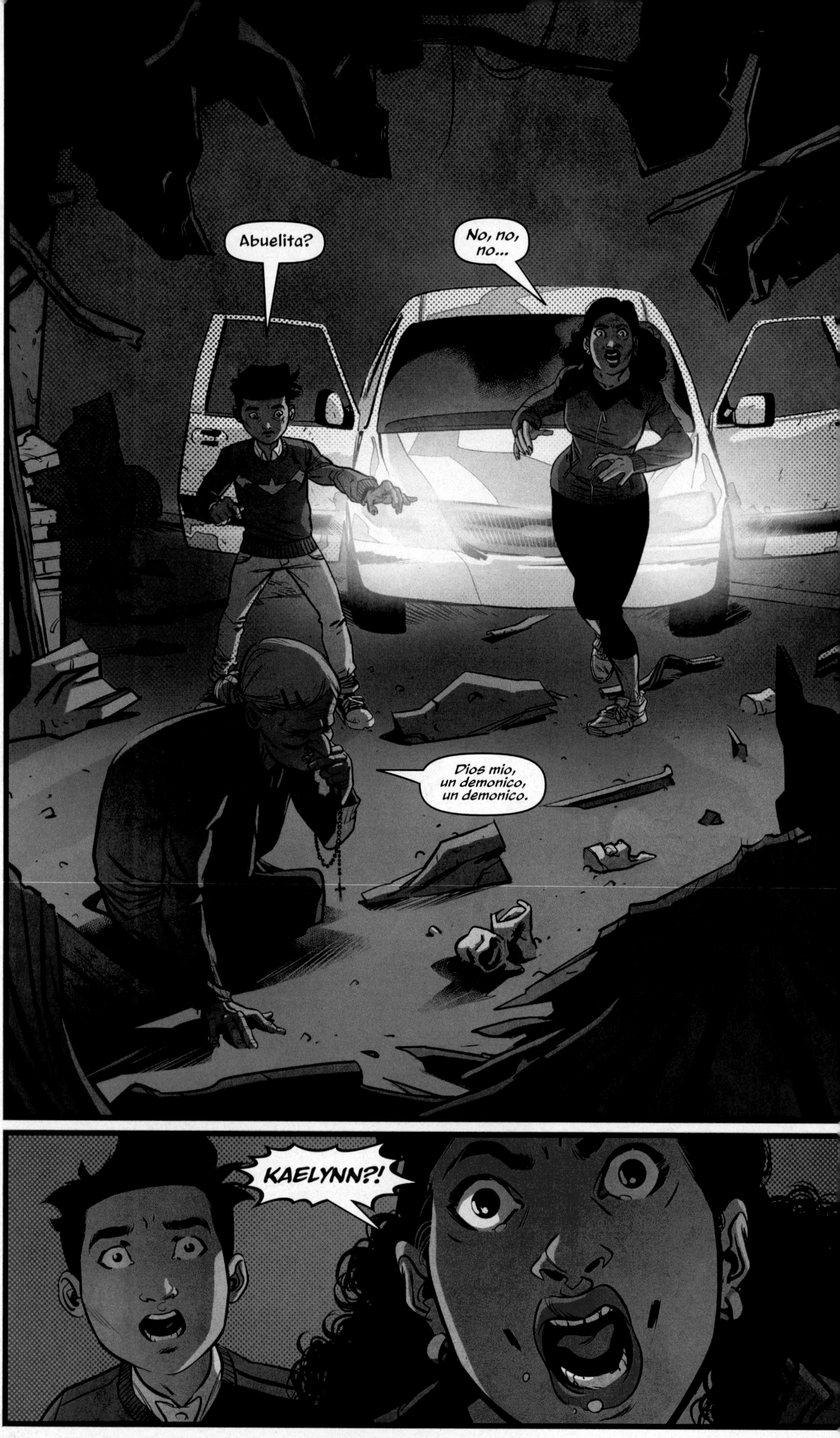
Abuelita?
No, no, no...
Dios mio, un demonico, un demonico.
KAELYNN?!

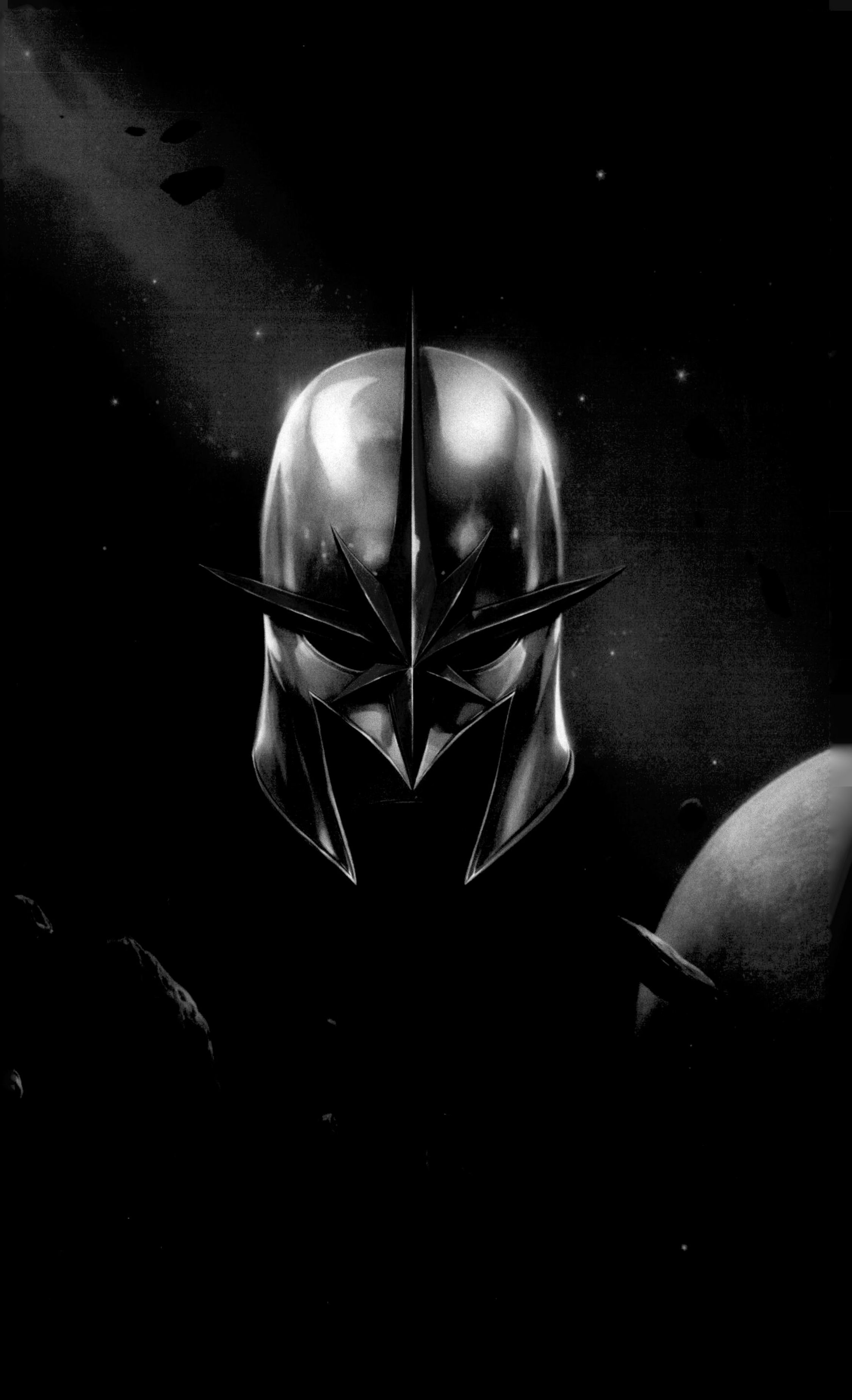

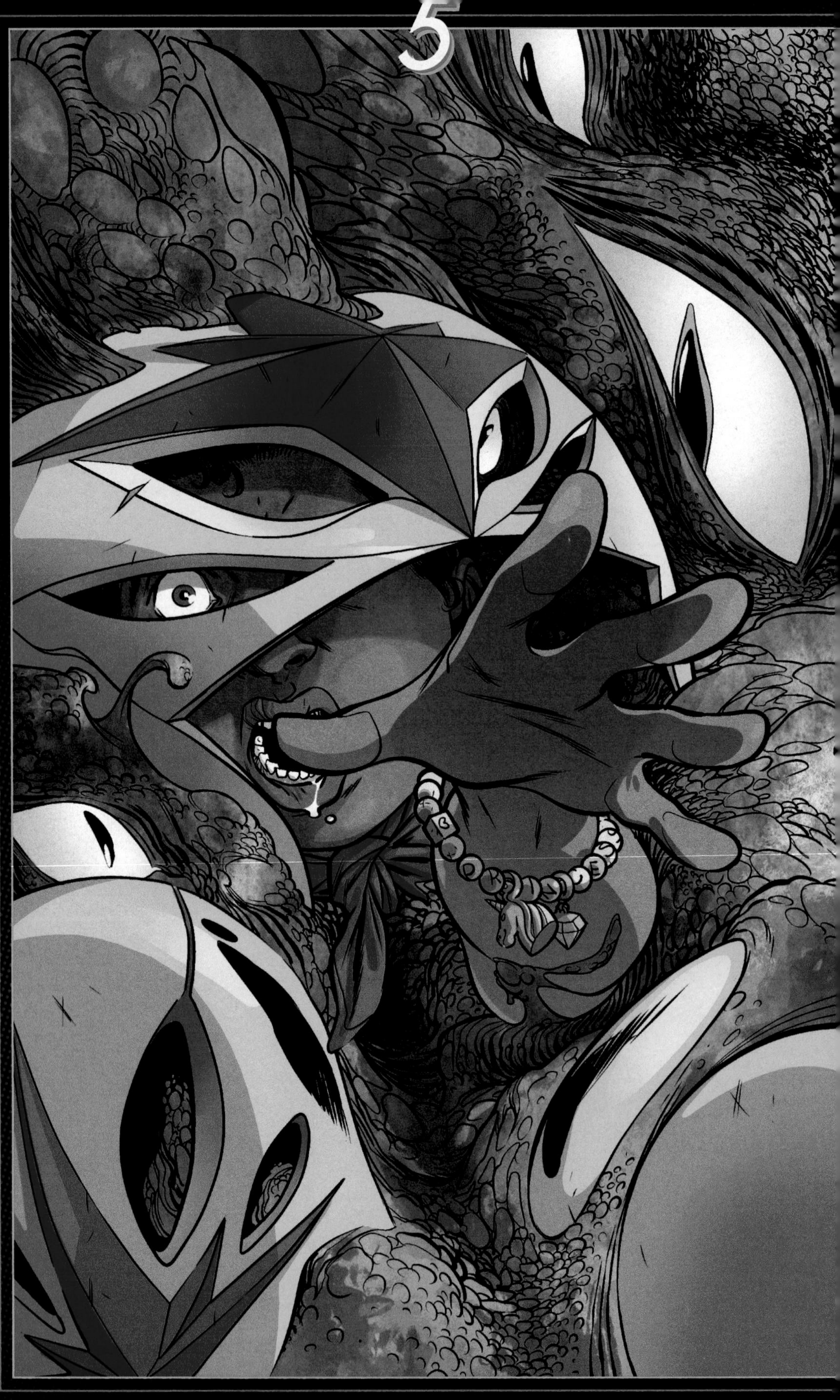
5

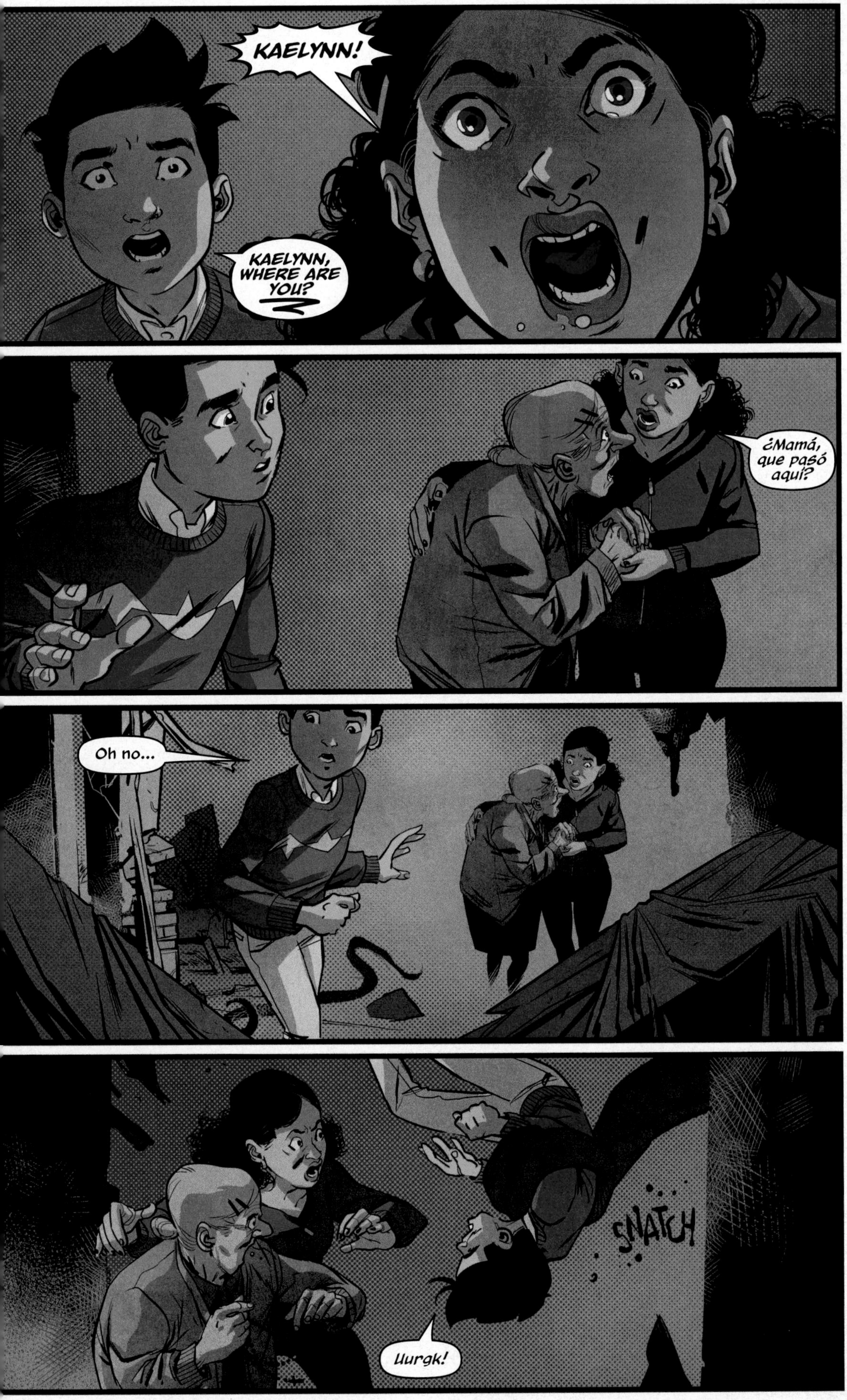

KAELYNN!
KAELYNN, WHERE ARE YOU?
¿Mamá, que pasó aquí?
Oh no...
SNATCH
Uurgk!

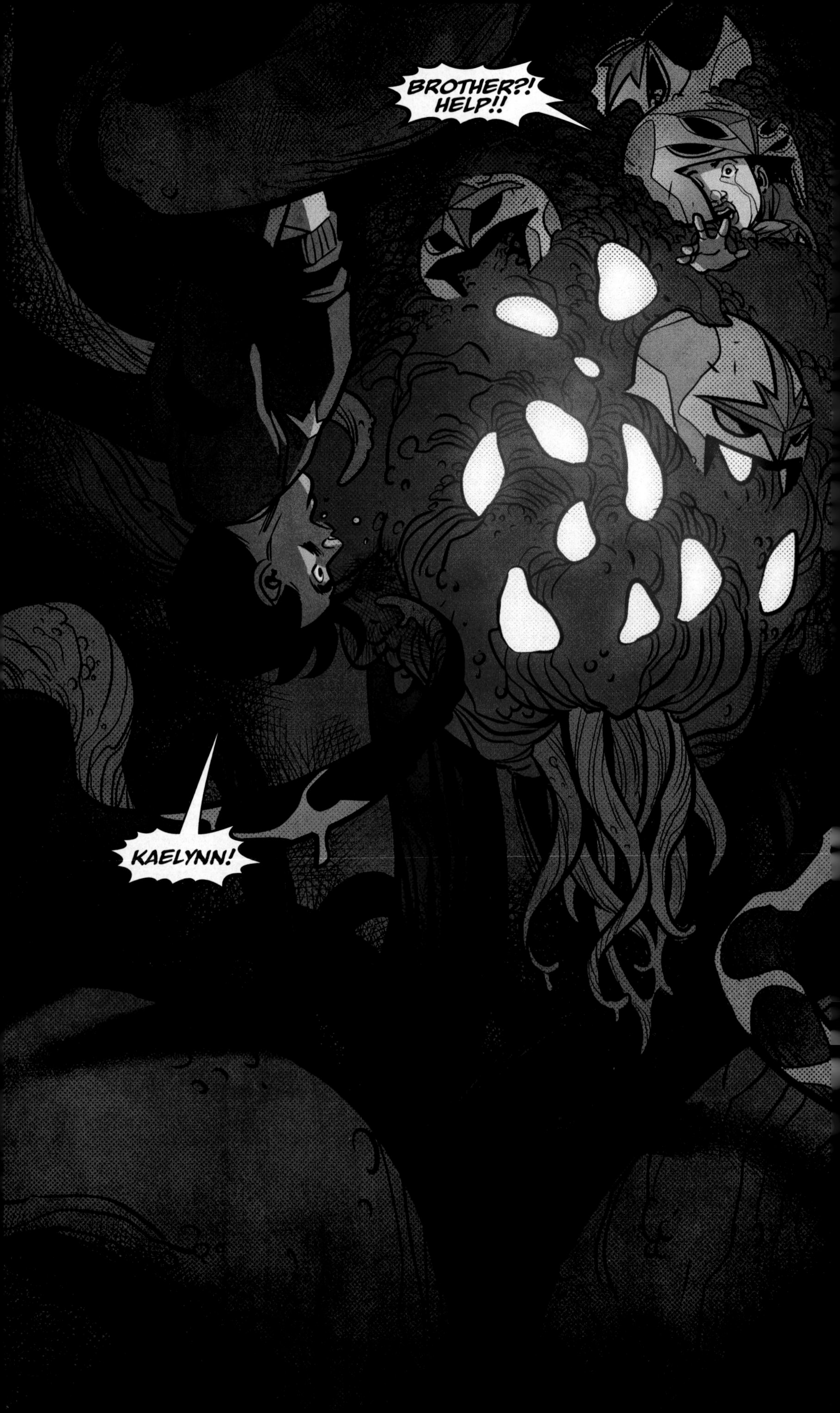
BROTHER?! HELP!!
KAELYNN!

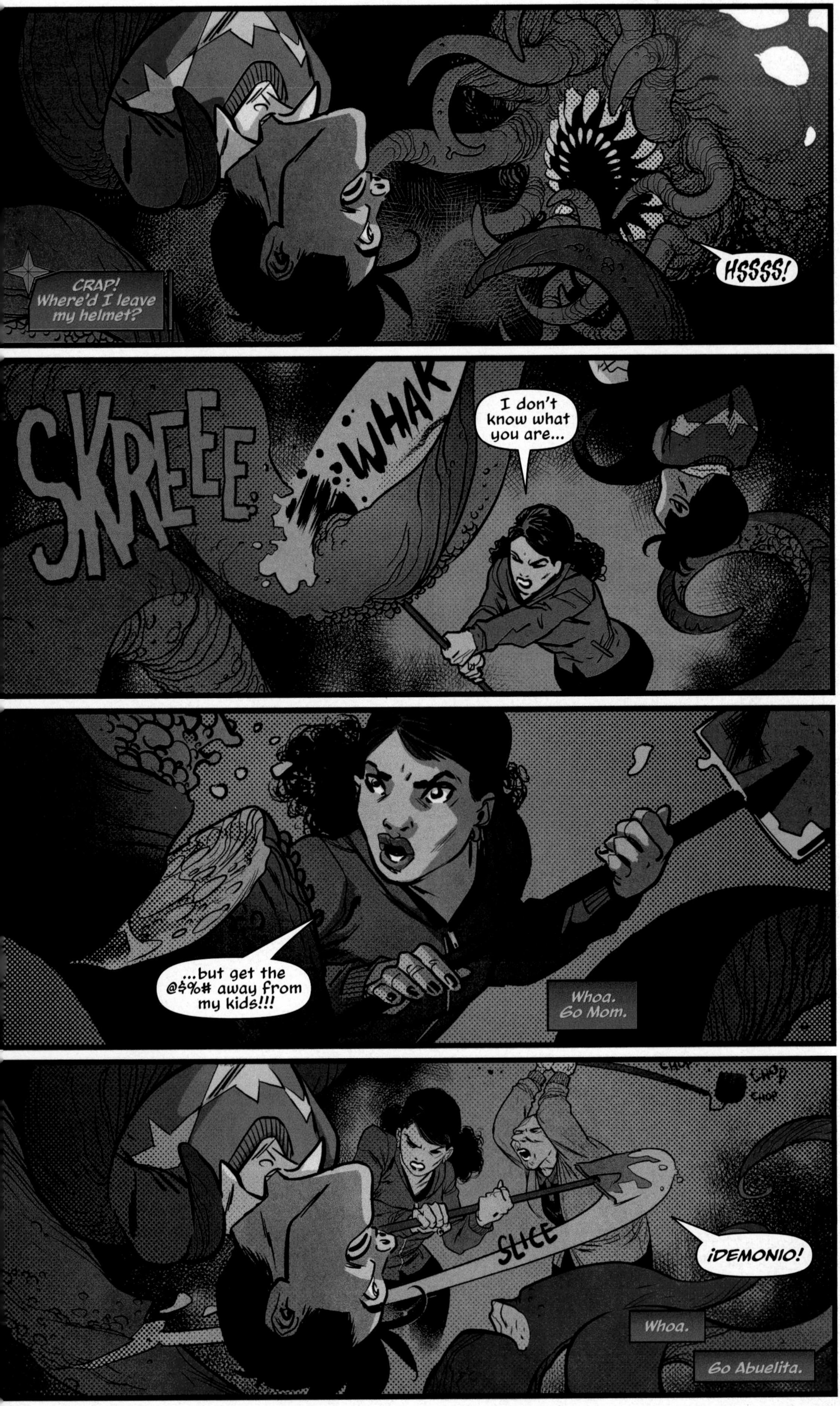
CRAP! Where'd I leave my helmet?
HSSSS!
SKREEEE
WHAK
I don't know what you are...
...but get the @$%# away from my kids!!!
Whoa. Go Mom.
SLICE
¡DEMONIO!
Whoa.
Go Abuelita.

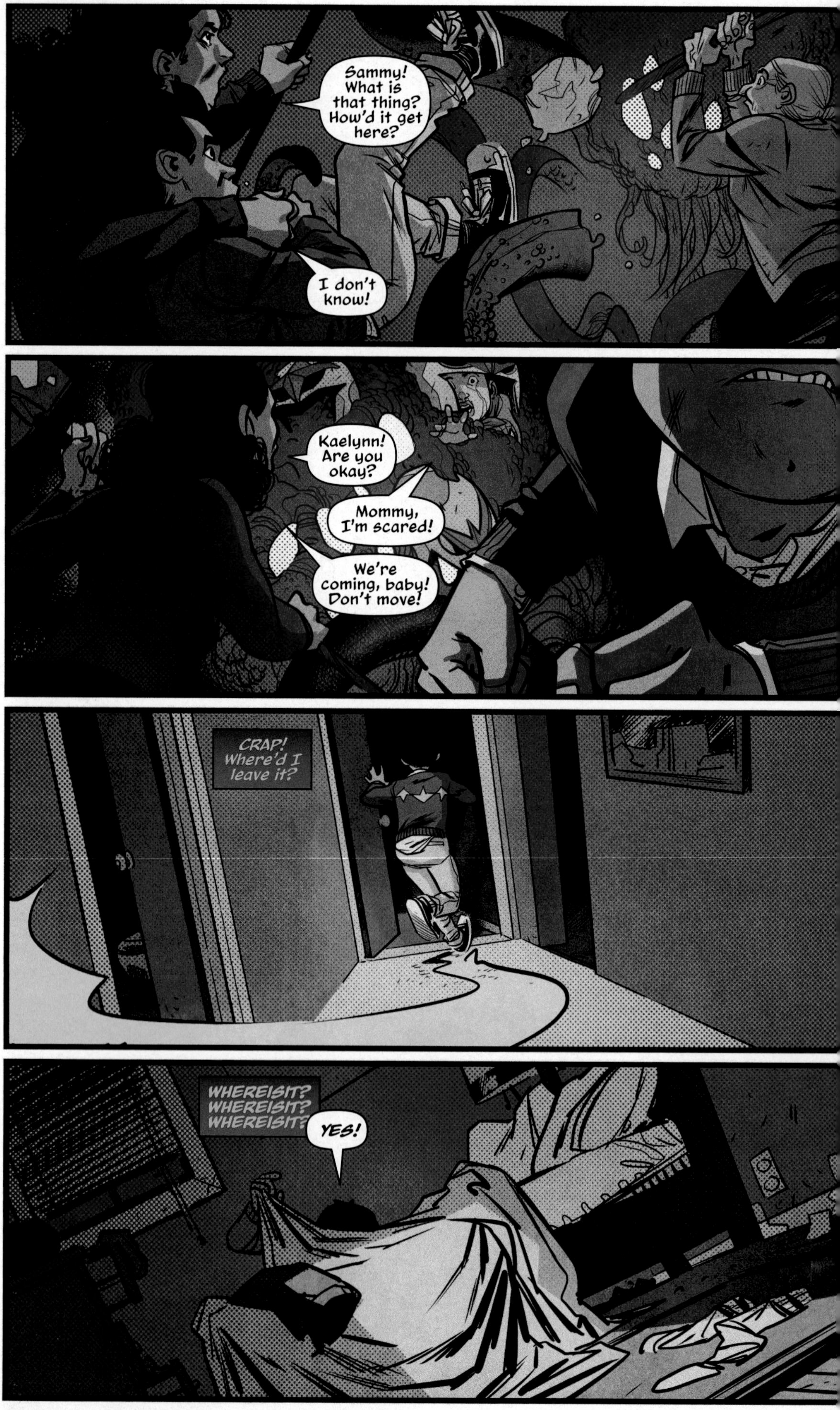
Sammy! What is that thing? How'd it get here?
I don't know!
Kaelynn! Are you okay?
Mommy, I'm scared!
We're coming, baby! Don't move!
CRAP! Where'd I leave it?
WHEREISIT? WHEREISIT? WHEREISIT?
YES!

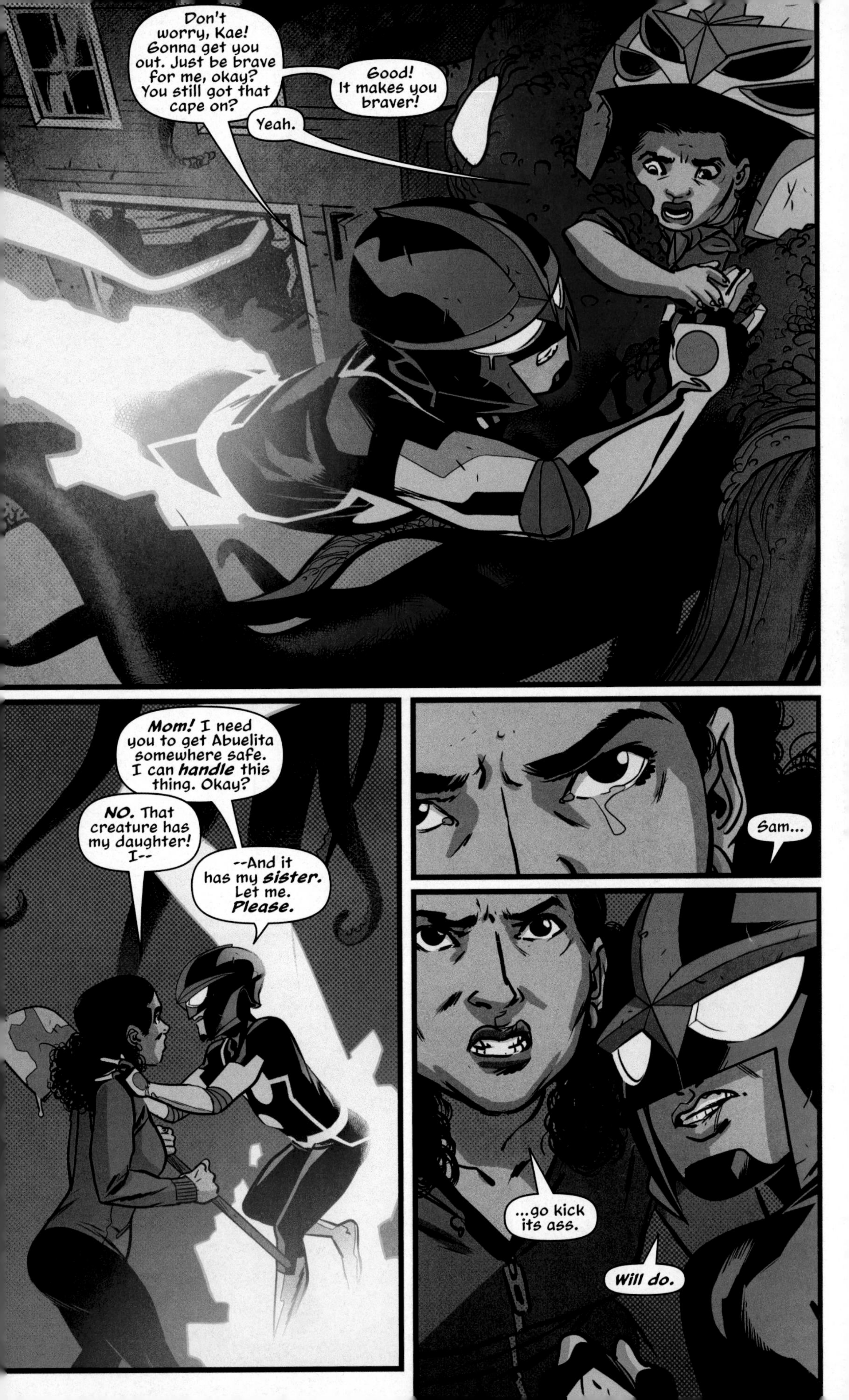
Don't worry, Kae! Gonna get you out. Just be brave for me, okay? You still got that cape on?
Yeah.
Good! It makes you braver!
Mom! I need you to get Abuelita somewhere safe. I can handle this thing. Okay?
NO. That creature has my daughter! I--
--And it has my sister. Let me. Please.
Sam...
...go kick its ass.
Will do.

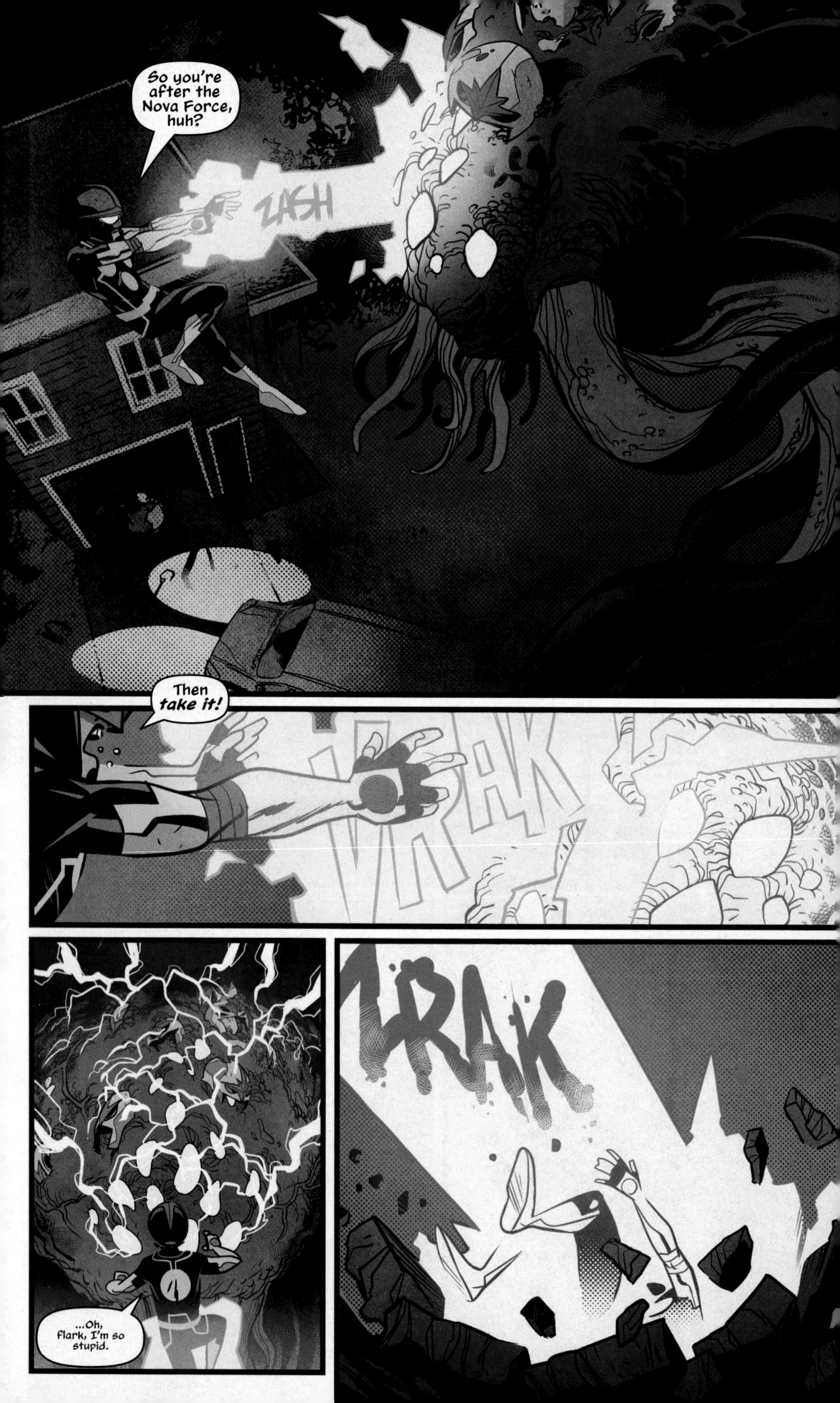
So you're after the Nova Force, huh?
ZASH
Then *take it!*
VRAK
...Oh, flark, I'm so stupid.
ZRAK

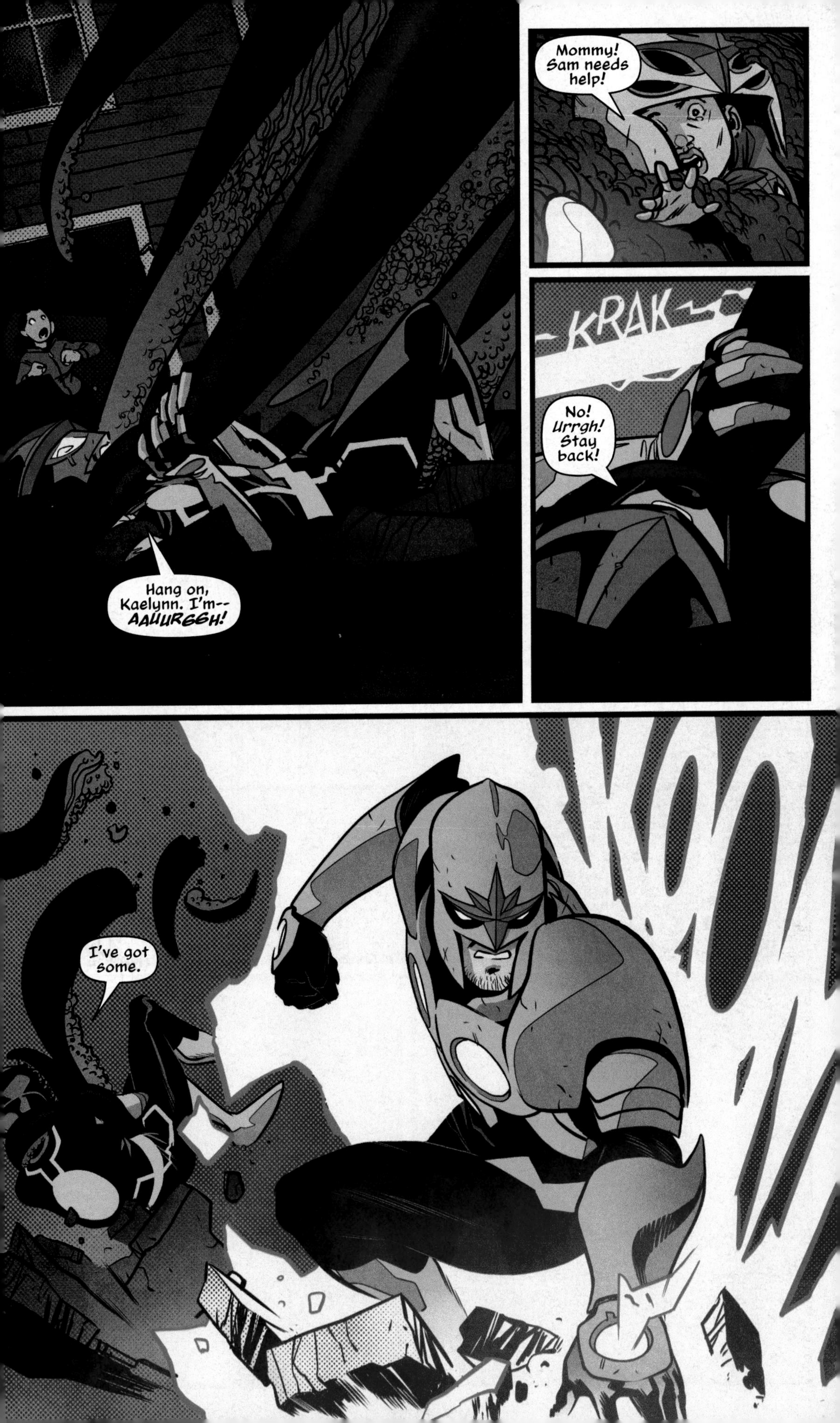
Hang on, Kaelynn. I'm-- AAUURGGH!
Mommy! Sam needs help!
KRAK
No! Urrgh! Stay back!
I've got some.

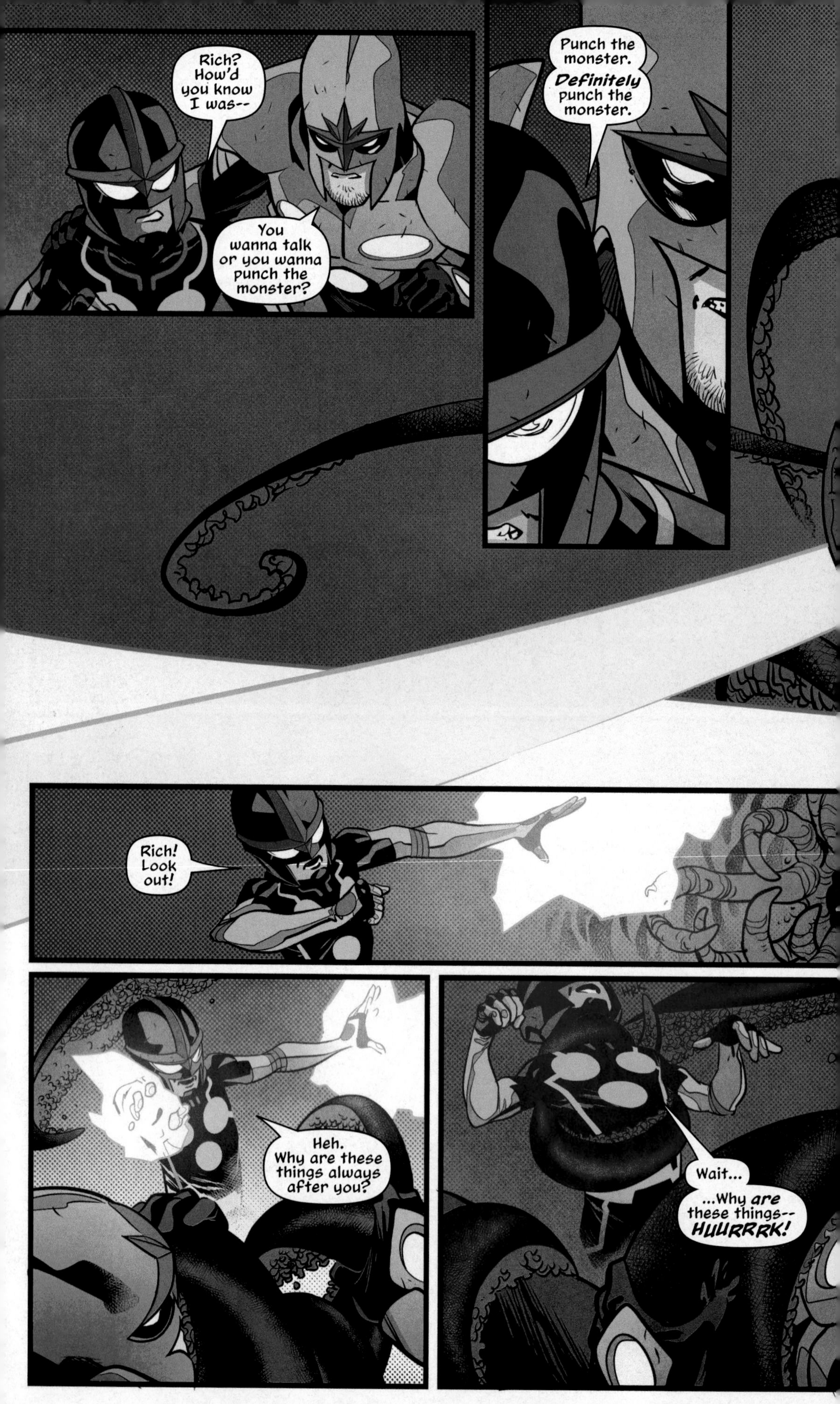
Rich? How'd you know I was--
You wanna talk or you wanna punch the monster?
Punch the monster. *Definitely* punch the monster.
Rich! Look out!
Heh. Why are these things always after you?
Wait...
...Why *are* these things-- ***HUURRRK!***

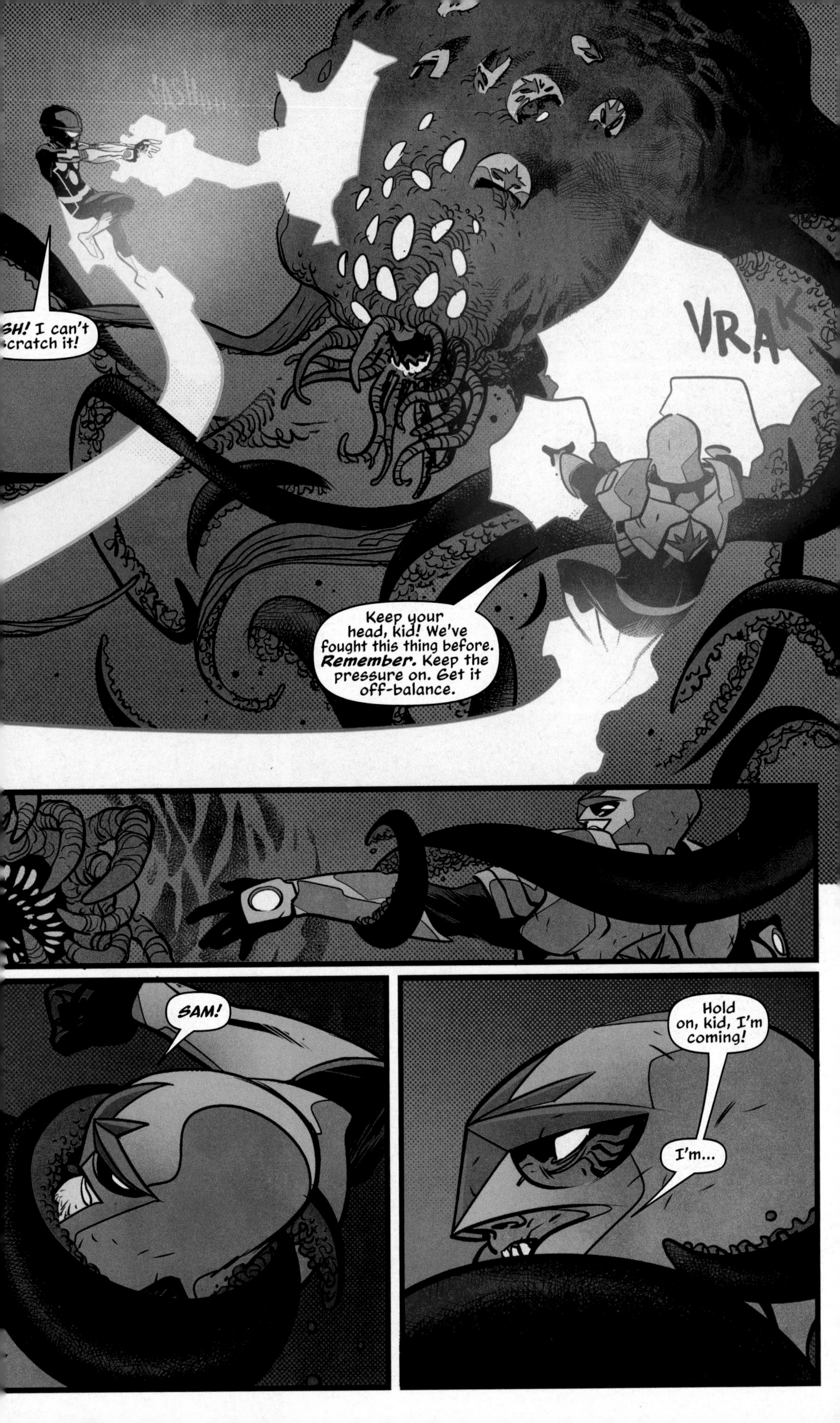

SH! I can't scratch it!
VRAK
Keep your head, kid! We've fought this thing before. *Remember.* Keep the pressure on. Get it off-balance.
SAM!
Hold on, kid, I'm coming!
I'm...

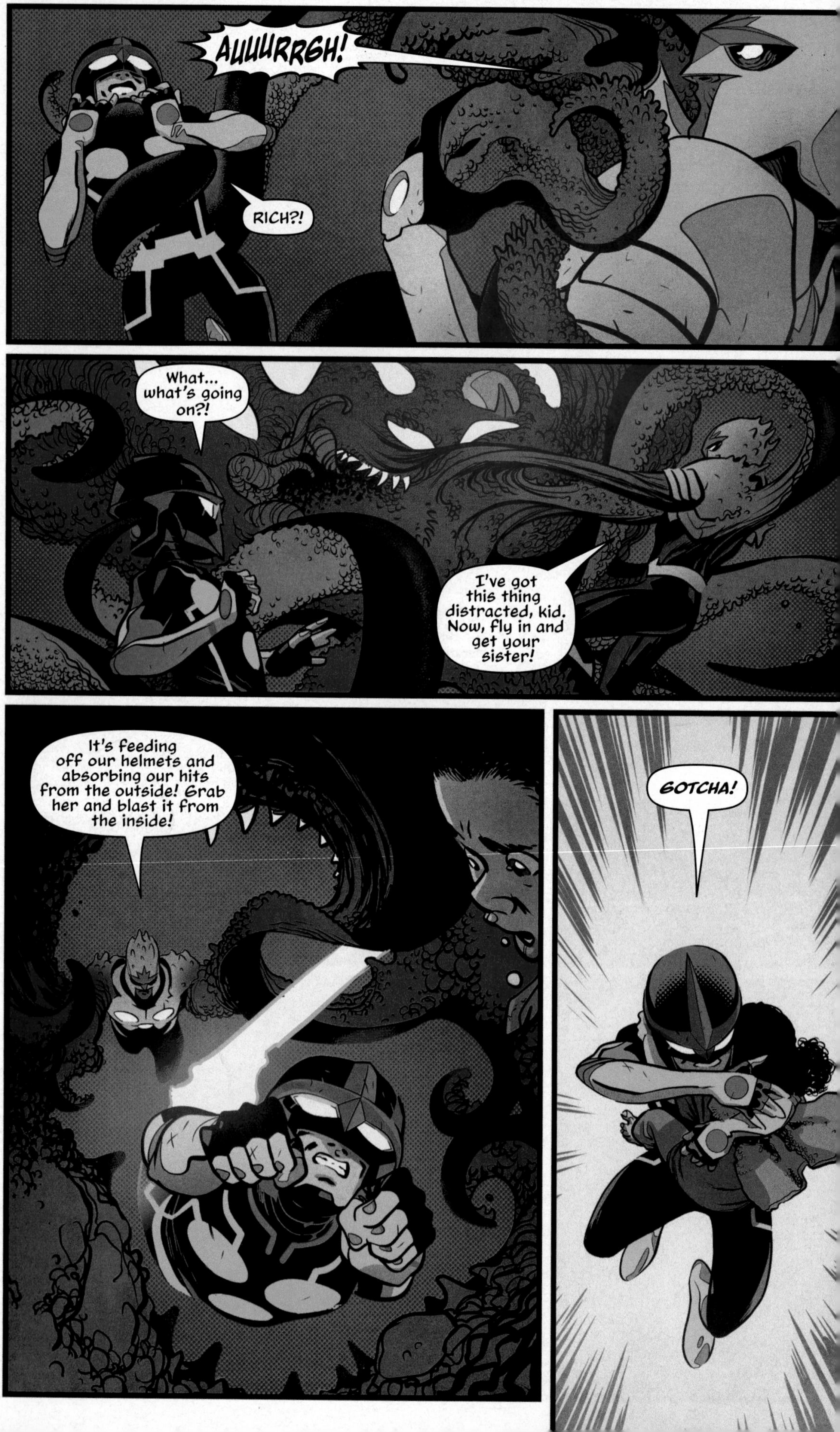
AUUURRGH!
RICH?!
What... what's going on?!
I've got this thing distracted, kid. Now, fly in and get your sister!
It's feeding off our helmets and absorbing our hits from the outside! Grab her and blast it from the inside!
GOTCHA!

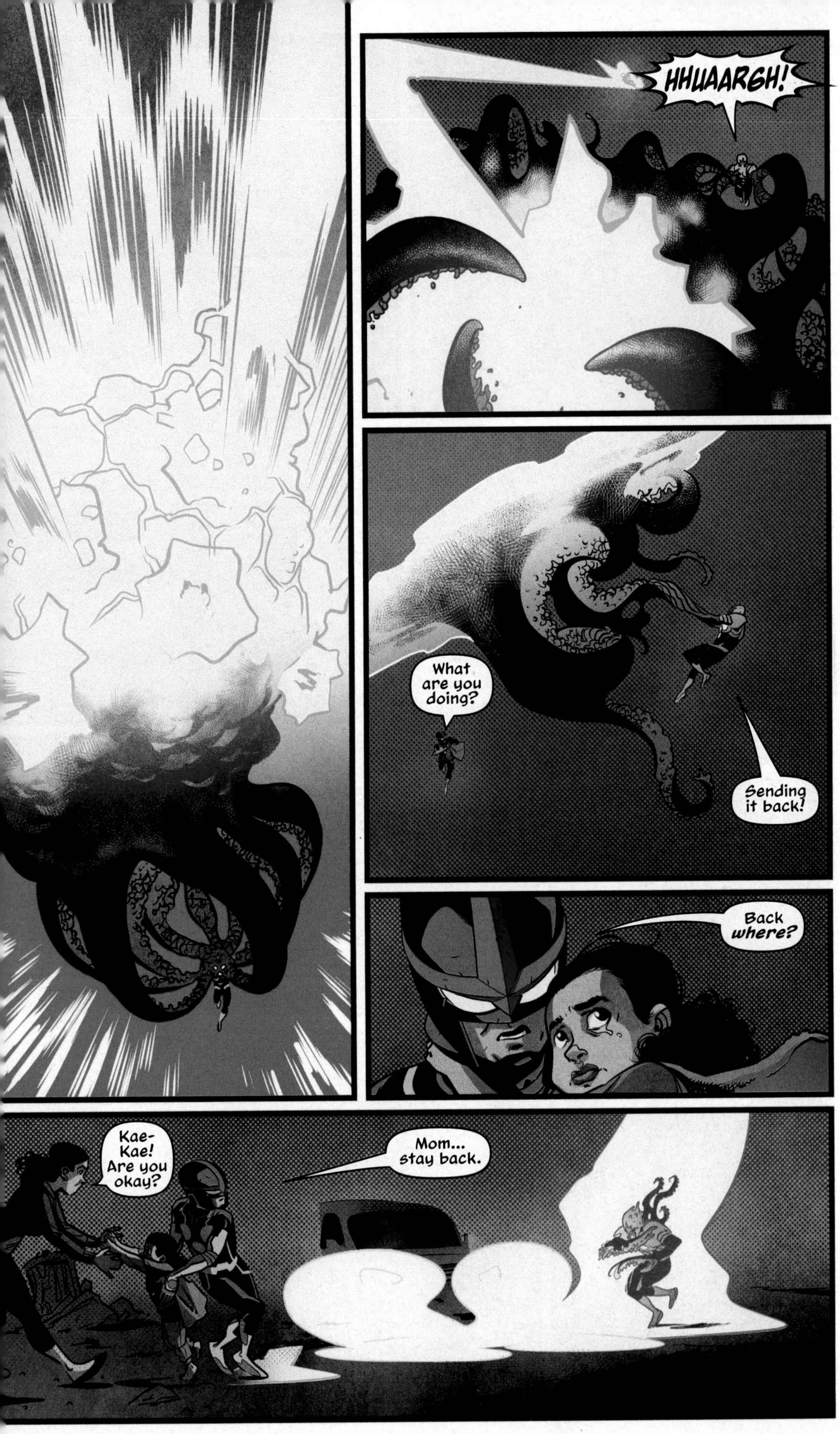
HHUAARGH!
What are you doing?
Sending it back!
Back *where?*
Kae-Kae! Are you okay?
Mom... stay back.

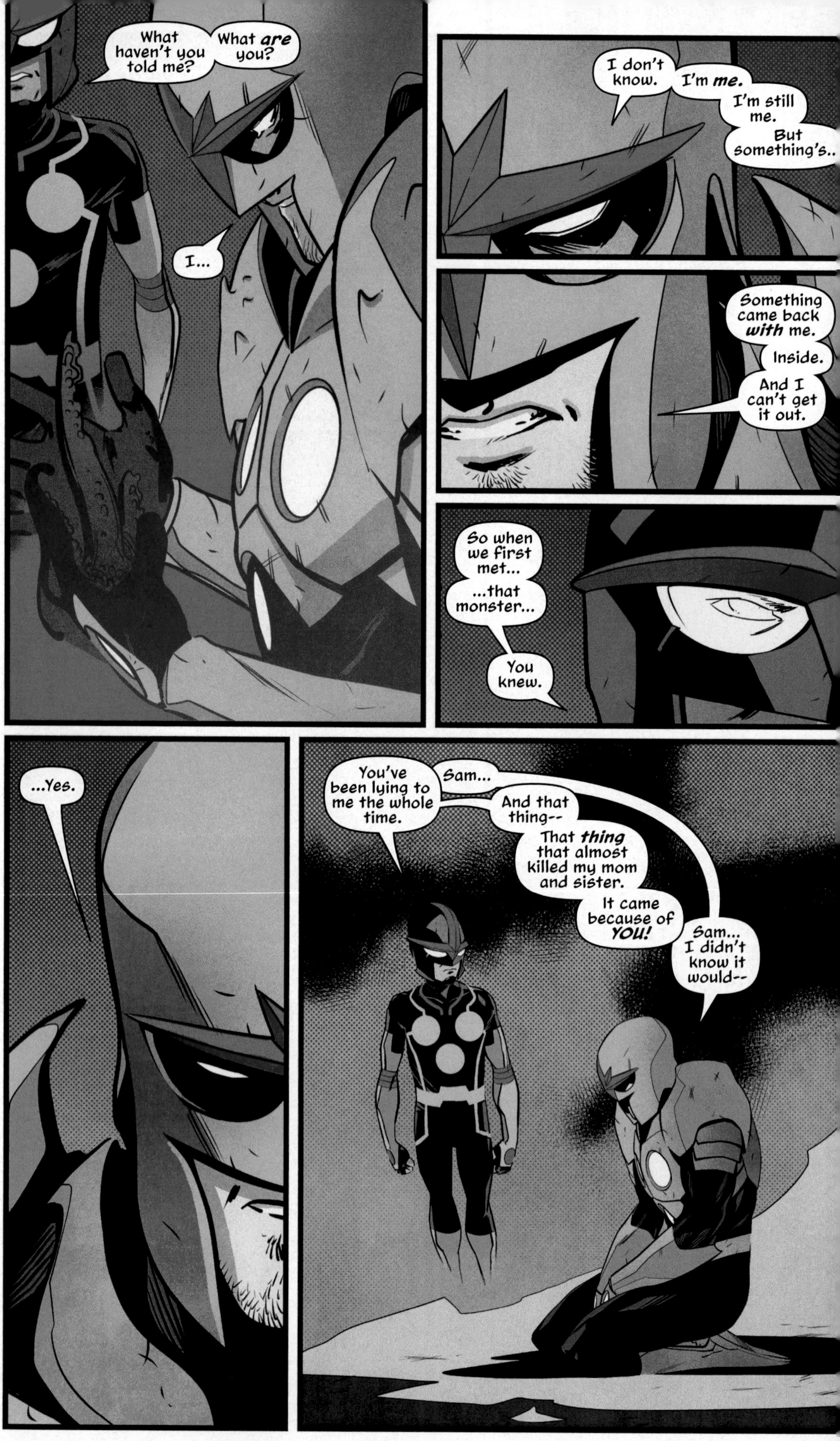

What haven't you told me?
What *are* you?
I...
I don't know.
I'm *me.*
I'm still me.
But something's...
Something came back *with* me.
Inside.
And I can't get it out.
So when we first met...
...that monster...
You knew.
...Yes.
You've been lying to me the whole time.
Sam...
And that thing--
That *thing* that almost killed my mom and sister.
It came because of *YOU!*
Sam... I didn't know it would--

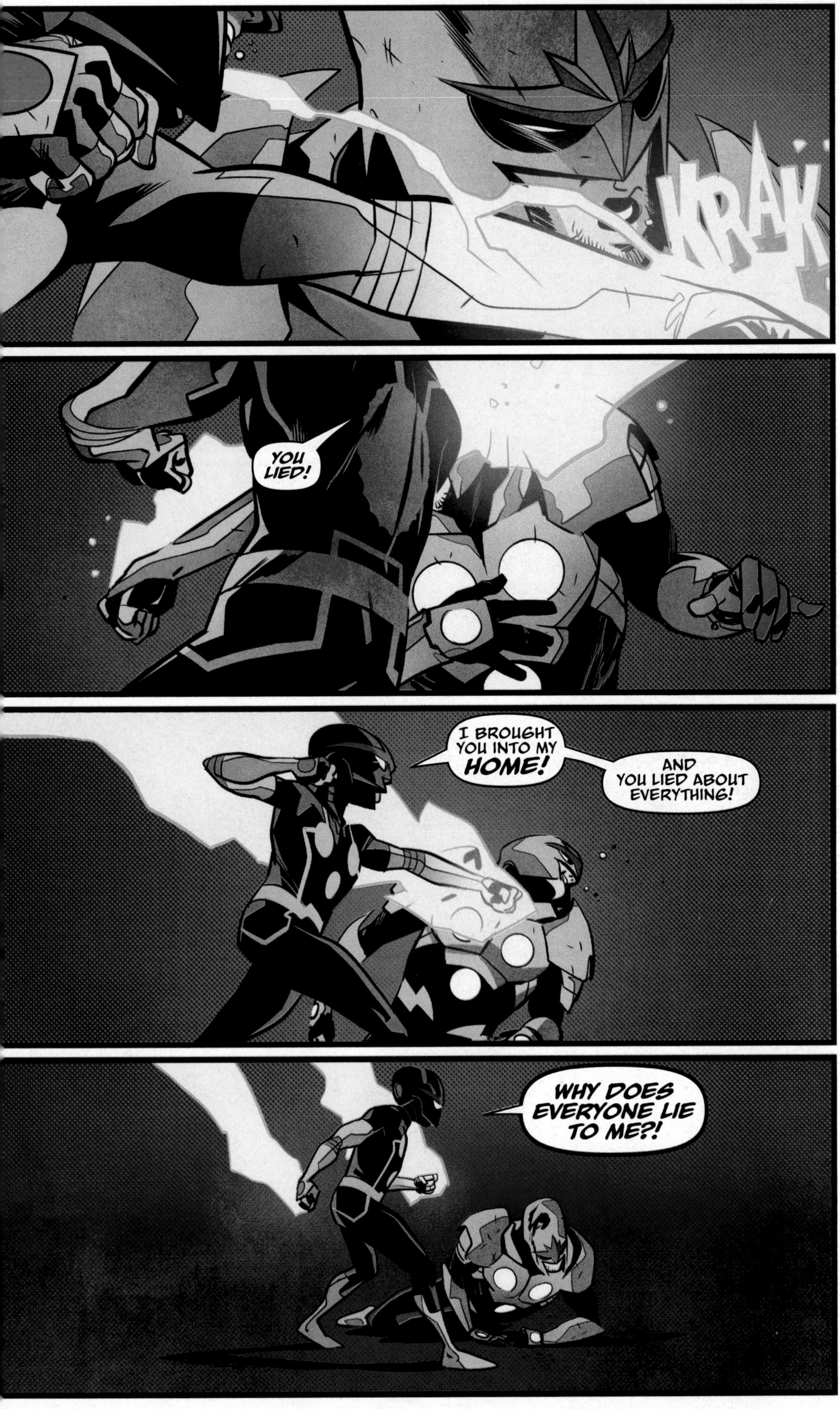
KRAK
YOU LIED!
I BROUGHT YOU INTO MY HOME!
AND YOU LIED ABOUT EVERYTHING!
WHY DOES EVERYONE LIE TO ME?!

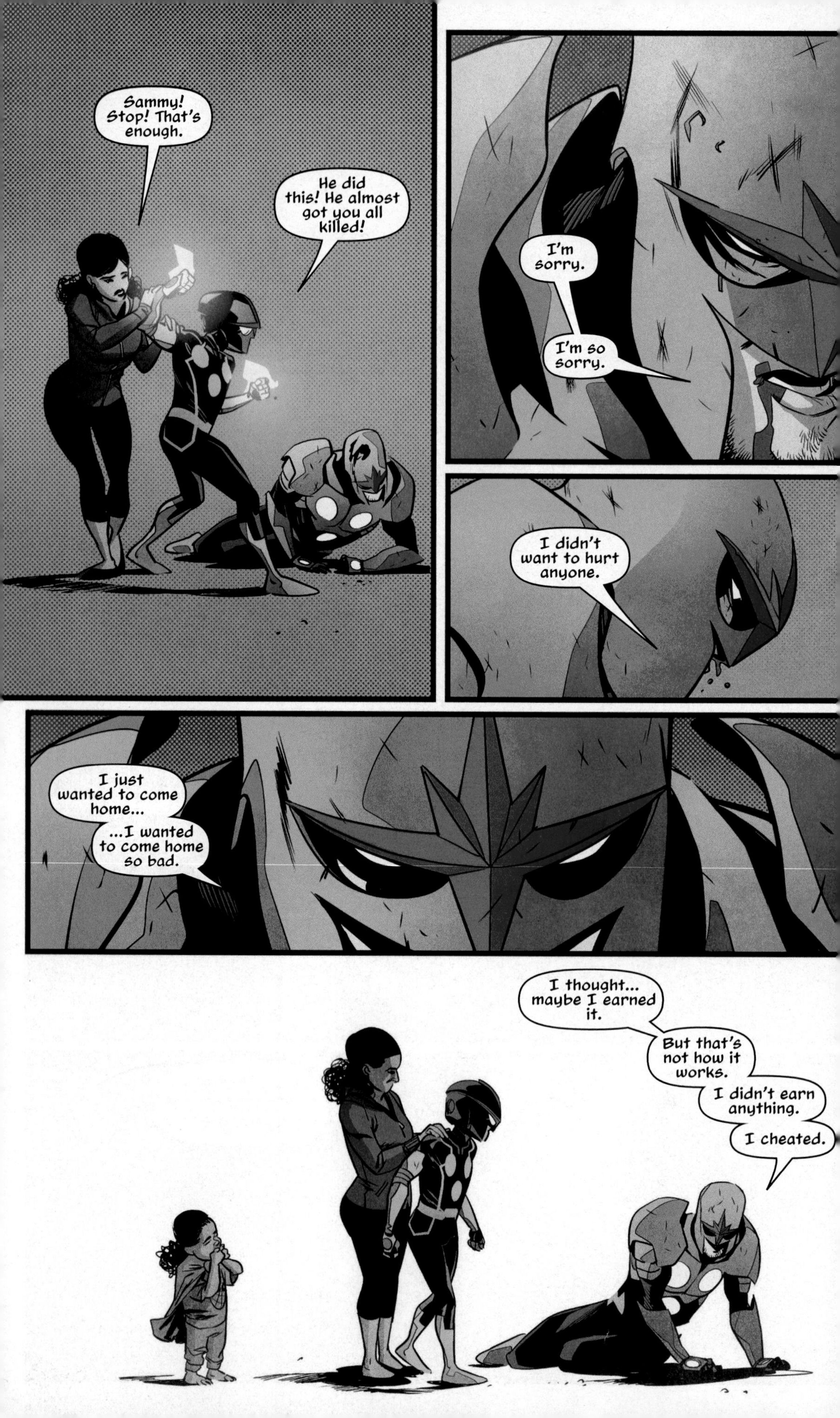

Sammy! Stop! That's enough.
He did this! He almost got you all killed!
I'm sorry.
I'm so sorry.
I didn't want to hurt anyone.
I just wanted to come home...
...I wanted to come home so bad.
I thought... maybe I earned it.
But that's not how it works.
I didn't earn anything.
I cheated.

I thought I could escape the Cancerverse...

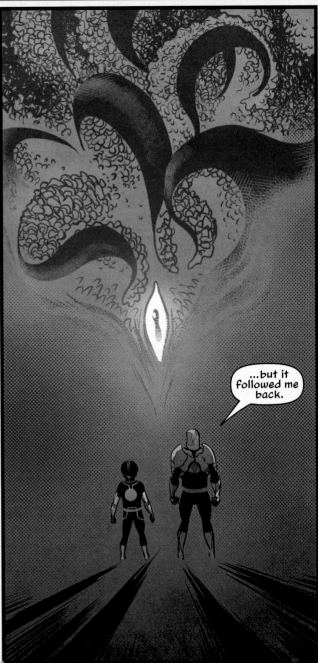

...but it followed me back.

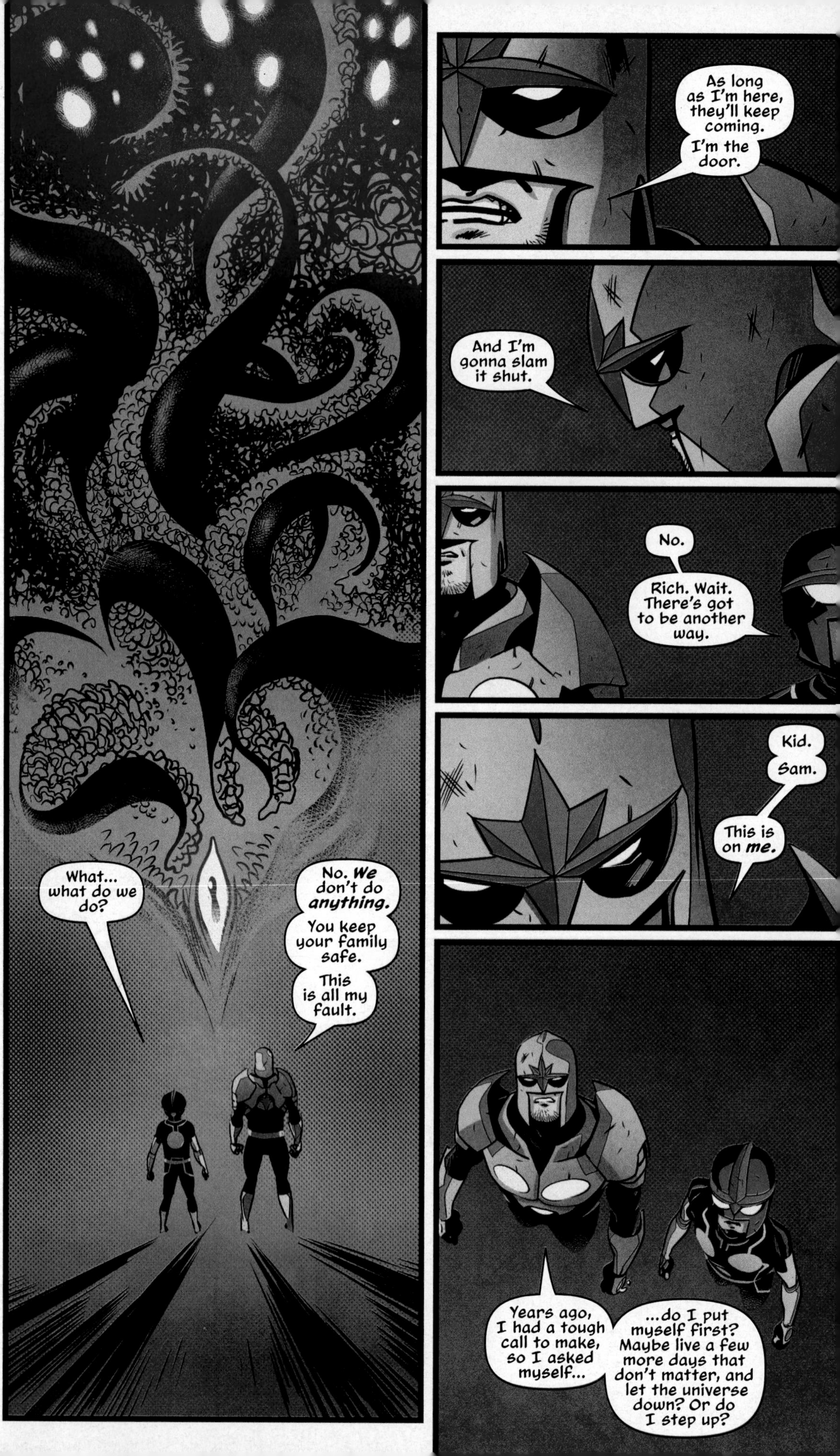
What... what do we do?
No. *We* don't do *anything.*
You keep your family safe.
This is all my fault.
As long as I'm here, they'll keep coming.
I'm the door.
And I'm gonna slam it shut.
No.
Rich. Wait. There's got to be another way.
Kid.
Sam.
This is on *me.*
Years ago, I had a tough call to make, so I asked myself...
...do I put myself first? Maybe live a few more days that don't matter, and let the universe down? Or do I step up?

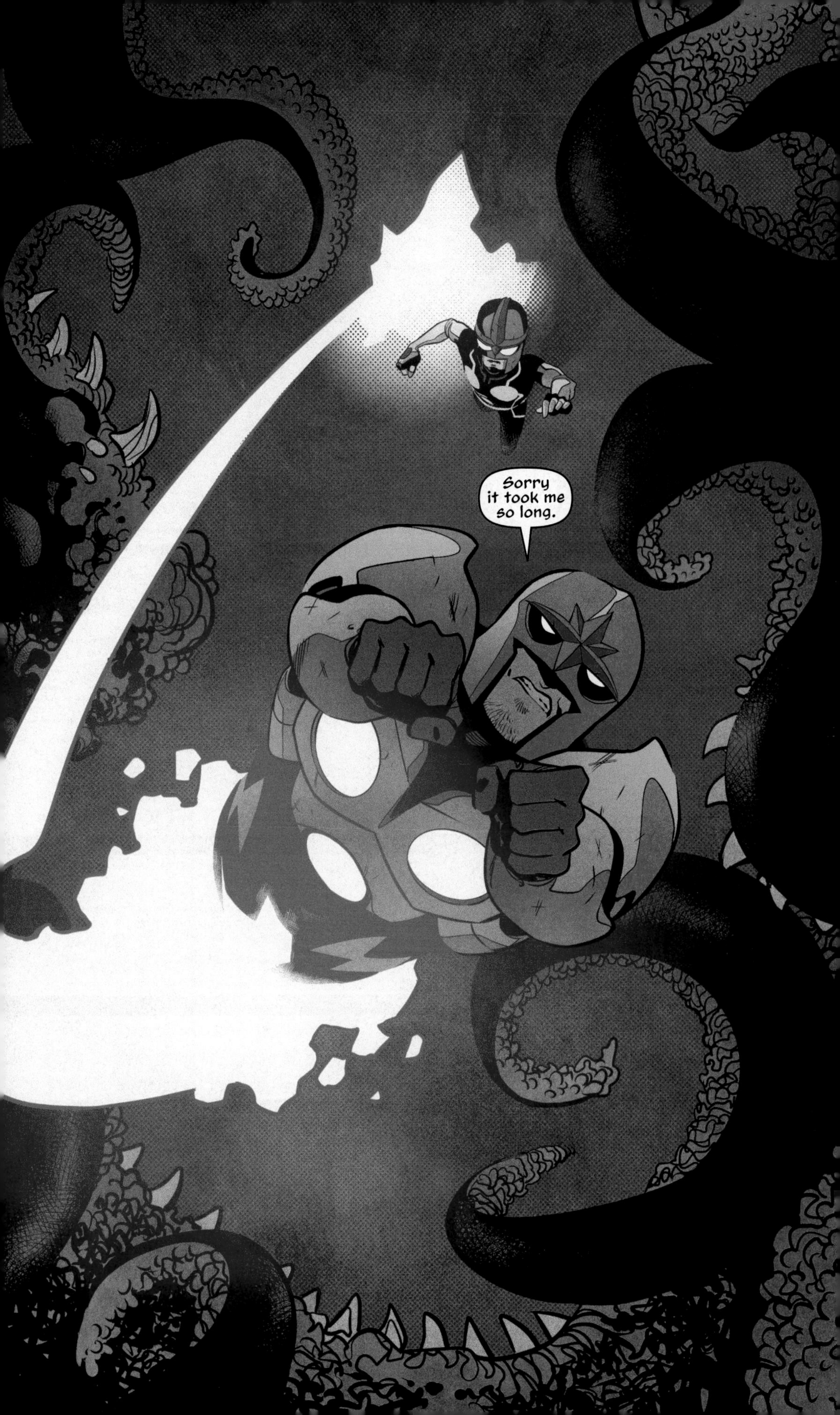
Sorry it took me so long.

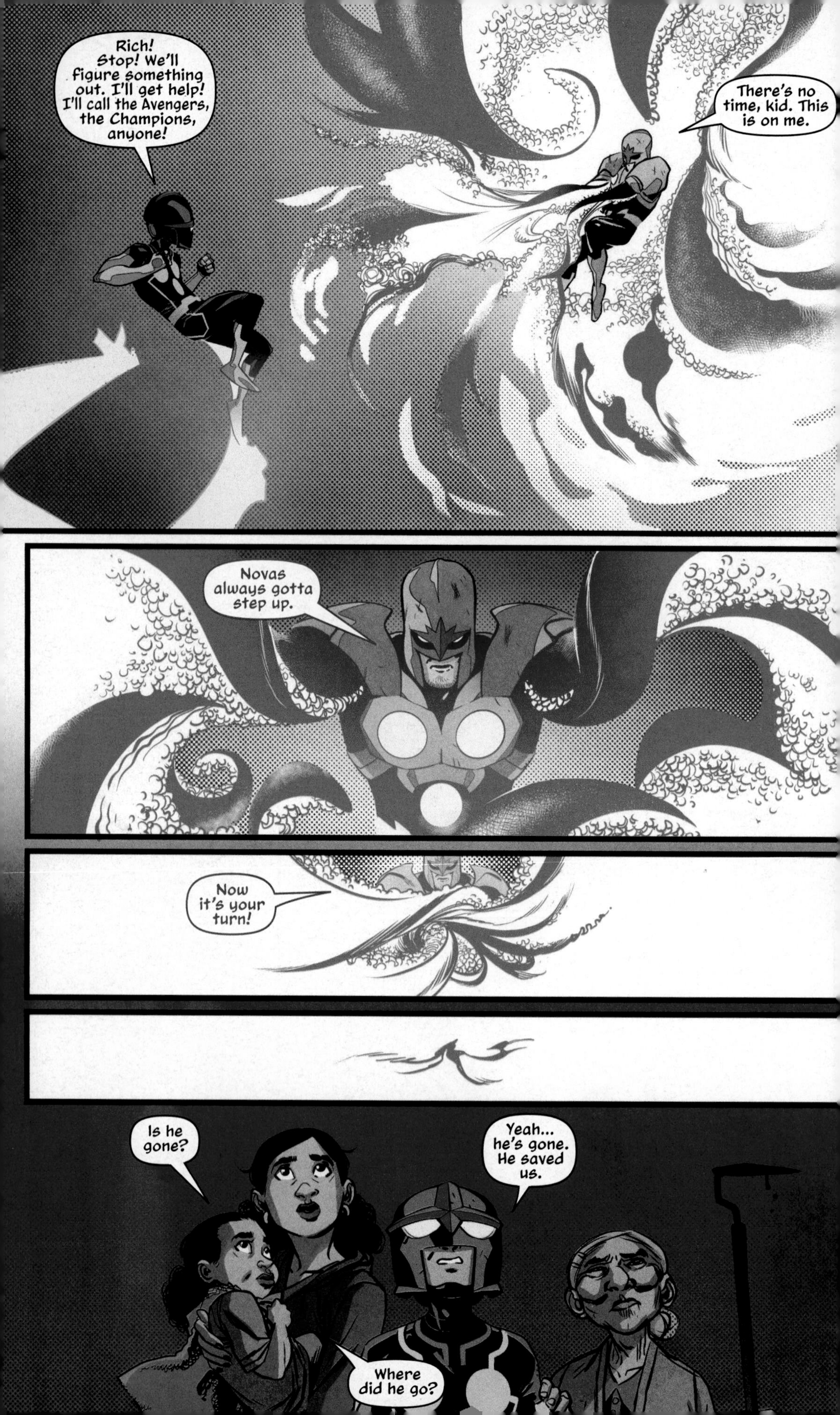
Rich! Stop! We'll figure something out. I'll get help! I'll call the Avengers, the Champions, anyone!
There's no time, kid. This is on me.
Novas always gotta step up.
Now it's your turn!
Is he gone?
Yeah... he's gone. He saved us.
Where did he go?

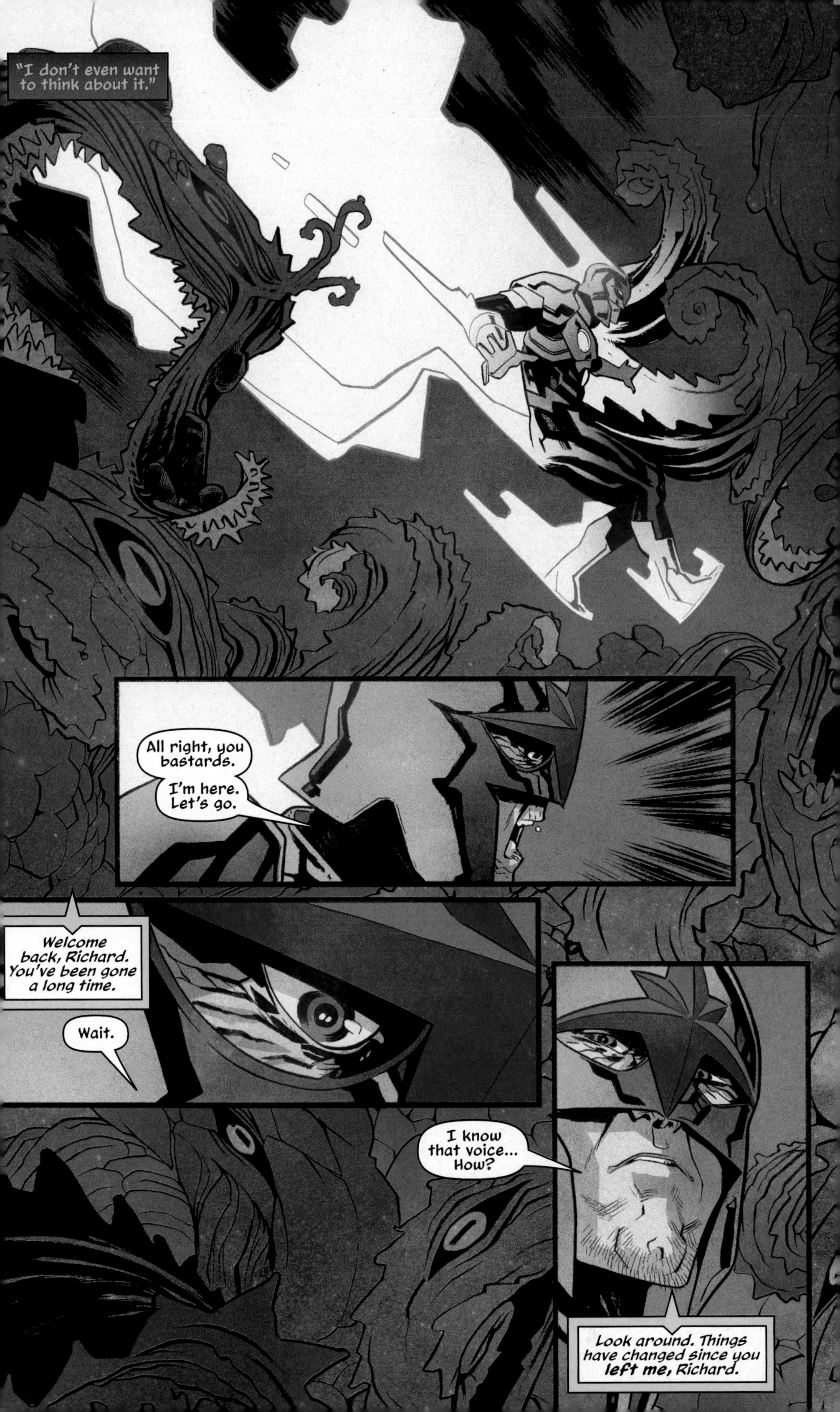

"I don't even want to think about it."
All right, you bastards.
I'm here. Let's go.
Welcome back, Richard. You've been gone a long time.
Wait.
I know that voice... How?
Look around. Things have changed since you **left me,** Richard.

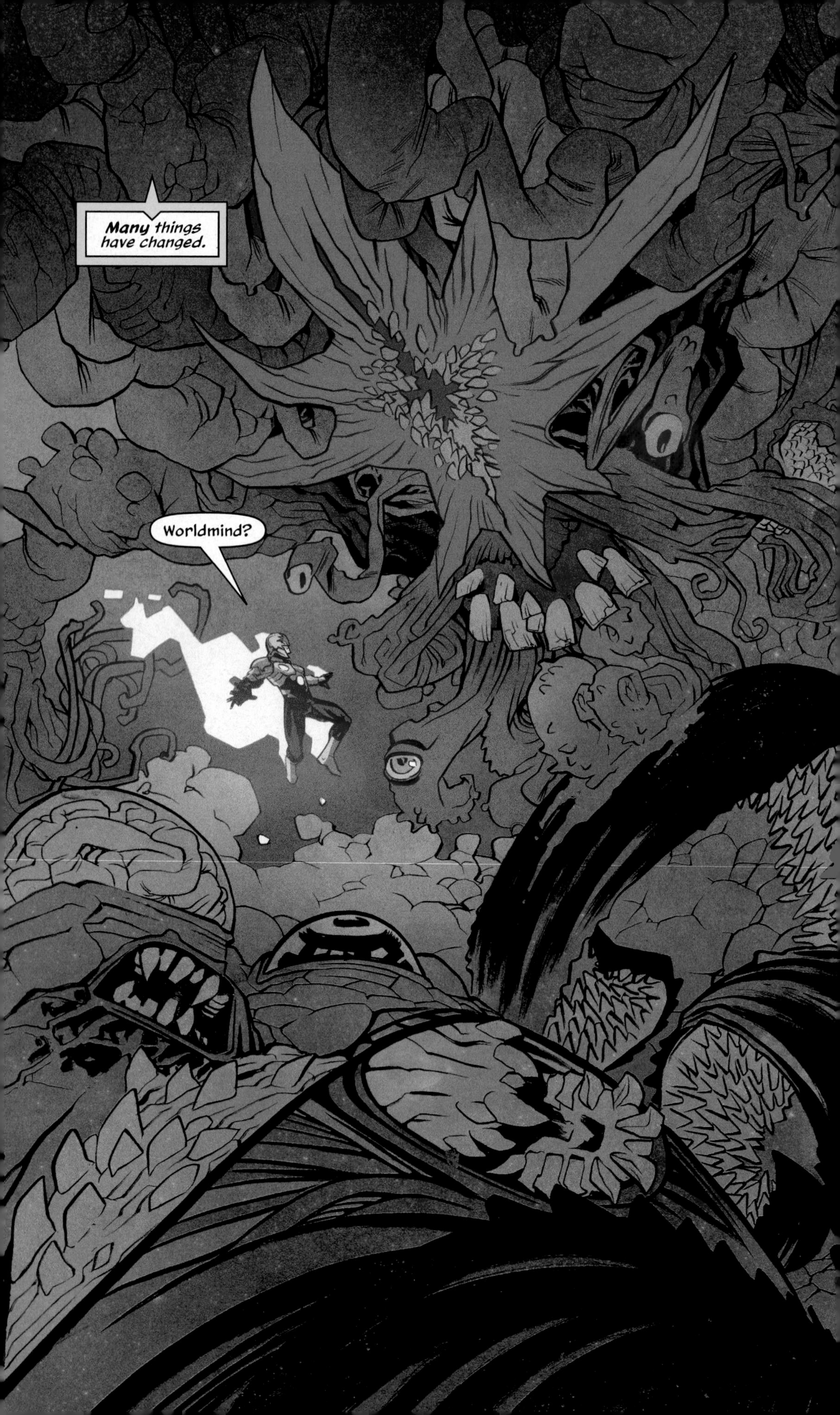

Many things have changed.
Worldmind?

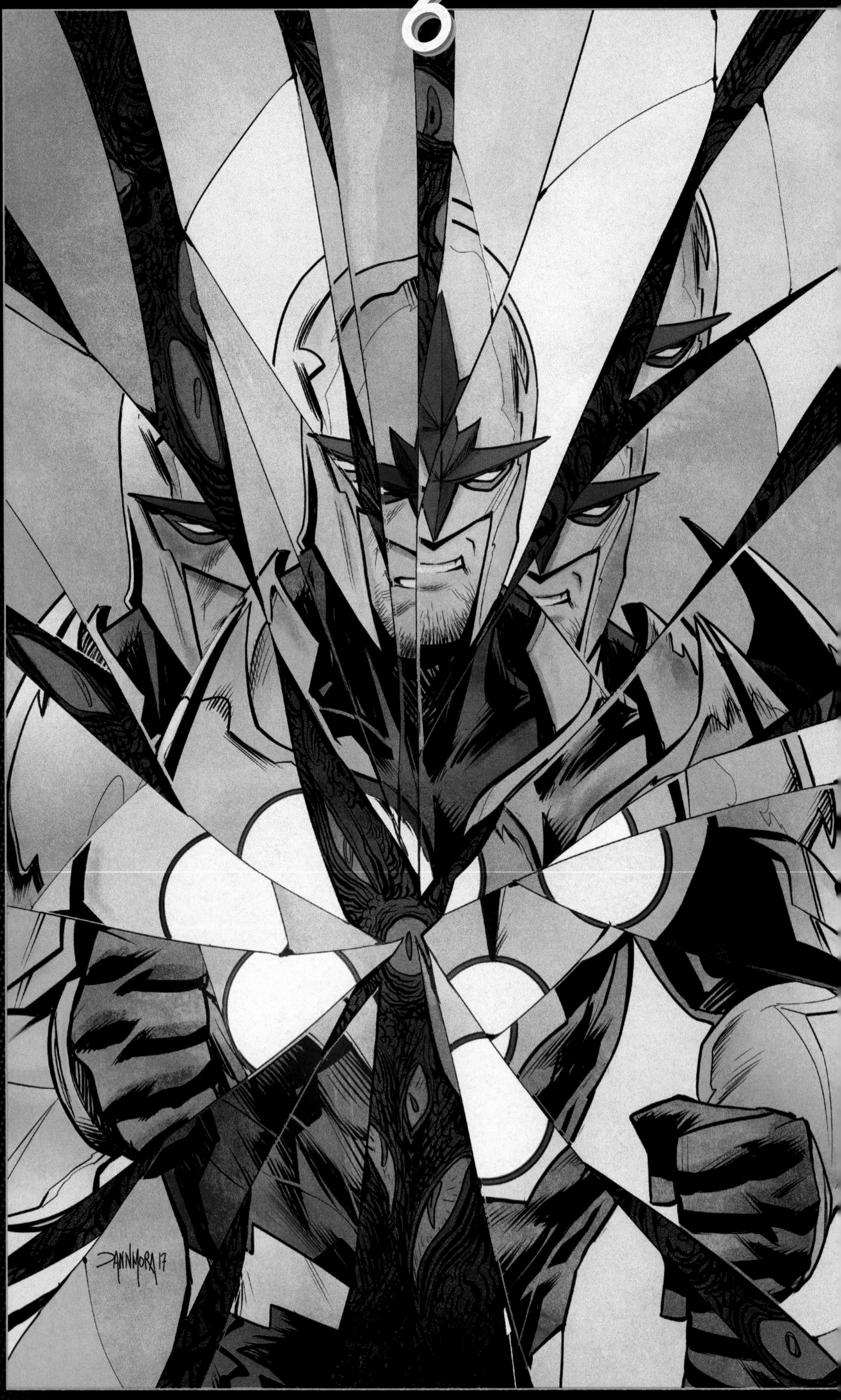
6
DANNMORA 17

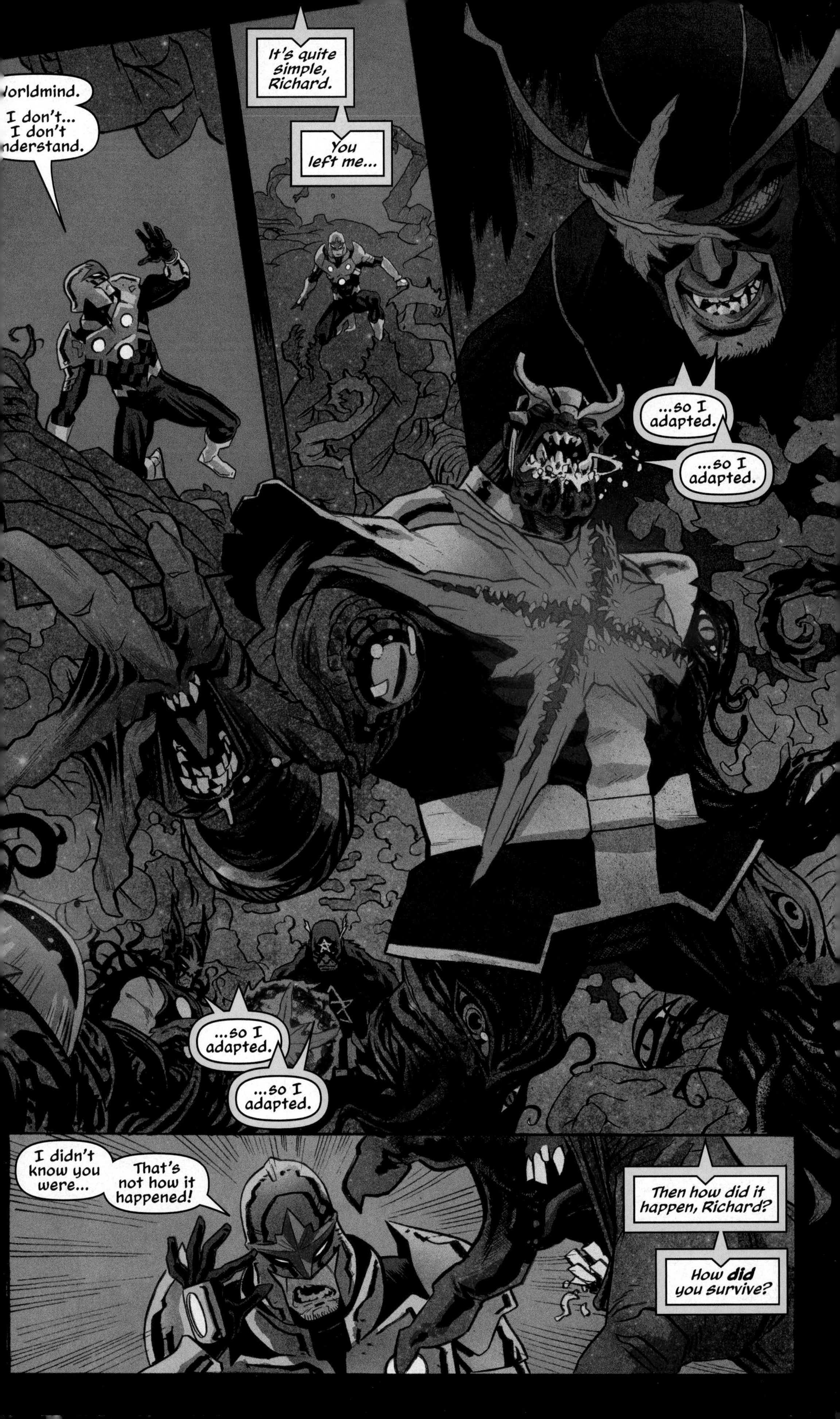

orldmind.
I don't... I don't nderstand.
It's quite simple, Richard.
You left me...
...so I adapted.
...so I adapted.
...so I adapted.
...so I adapted.
I didn't know you were...
That's not how it happened!
Then how did it happen, Richard?
How **did** you survive?

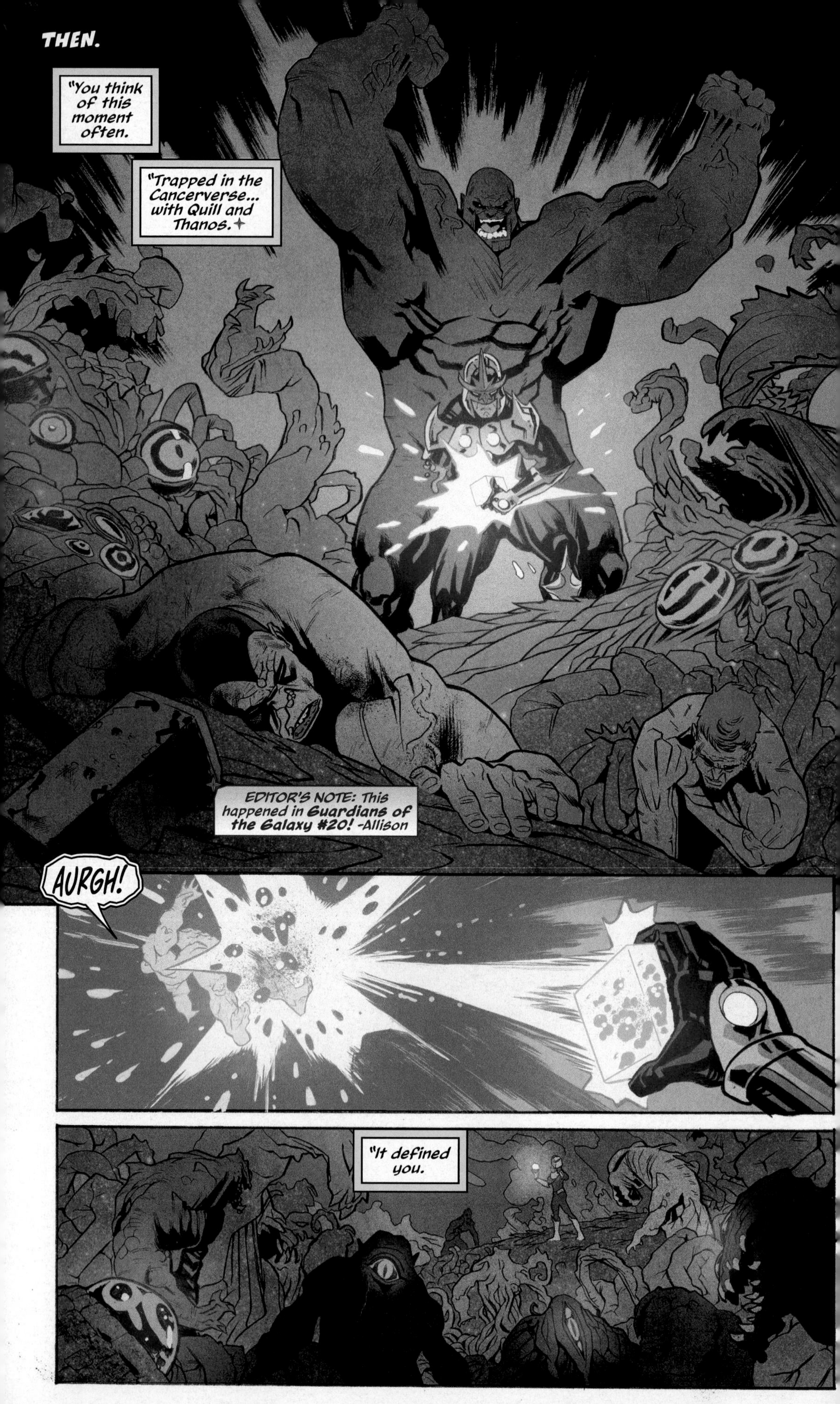
THEN.
"You think of this moment often.
"Trapped in the Cancerverse... with Quill and Thanos.✦
EDITOR'S NOTE: This happened in Guardians of the Galaxy #20! -Allison
AURGH!
"It defined you.

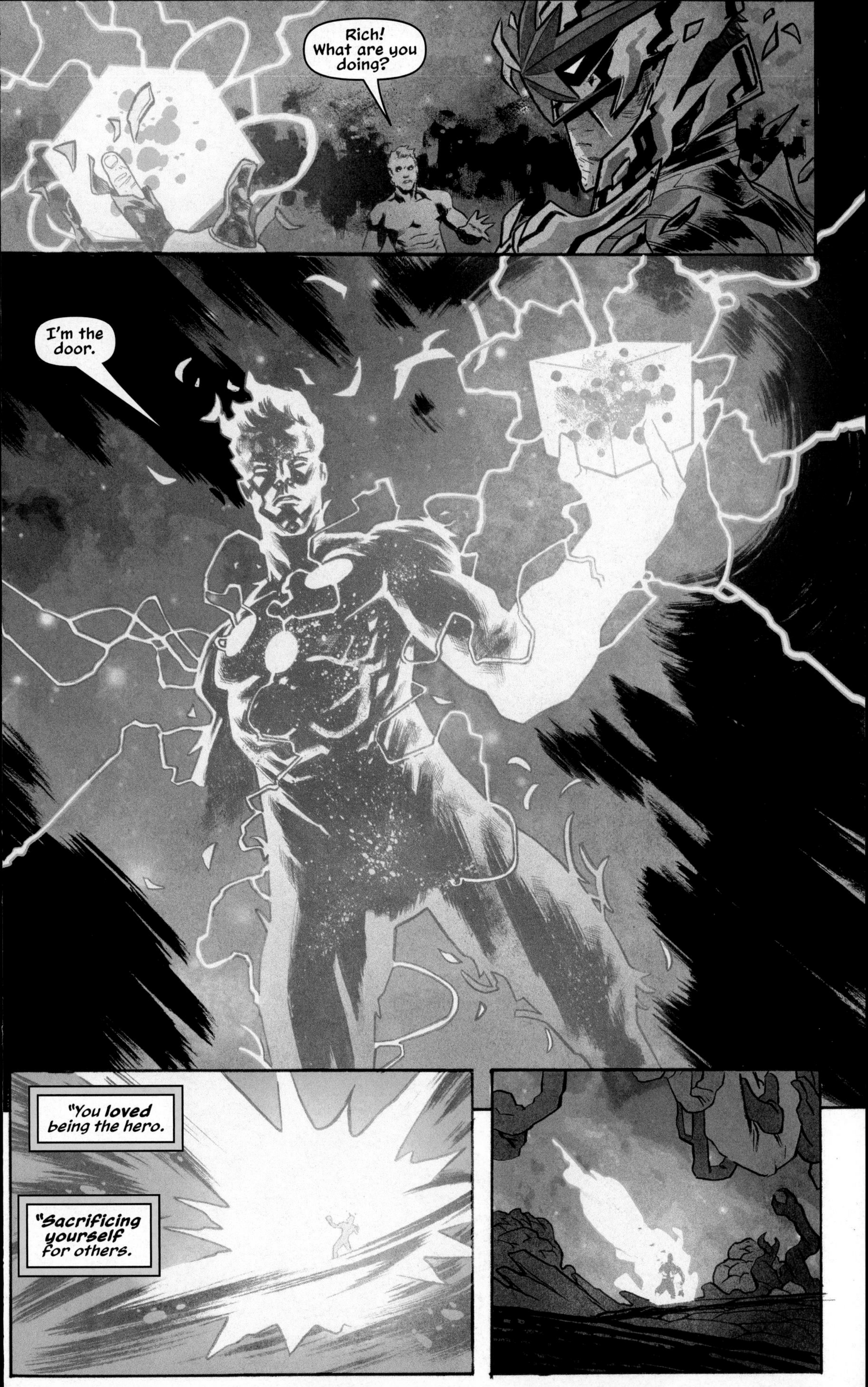
Rich! What are you doing?
I'm the door.
"You loved being the hero.
"Sacrificing yourself for others.

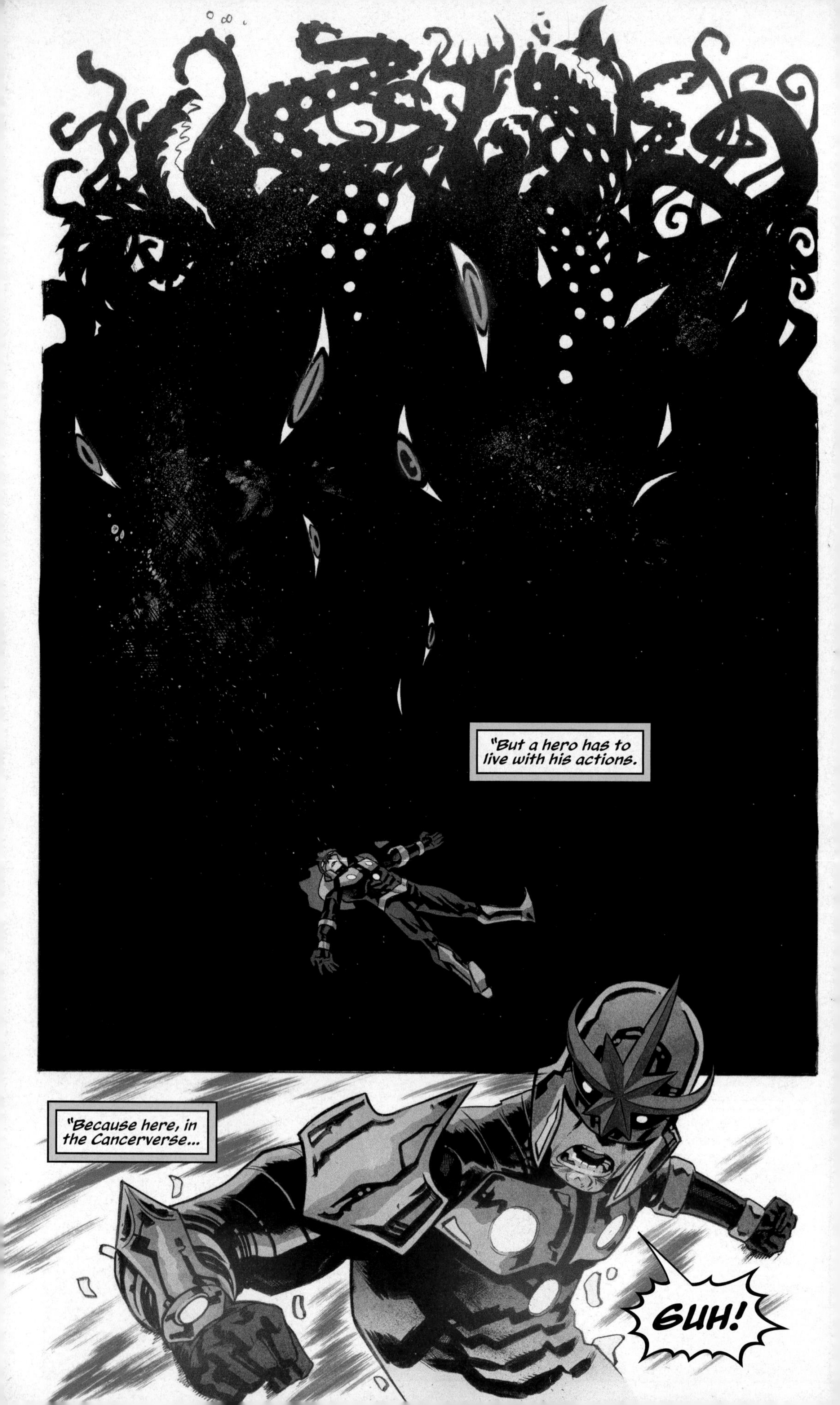
"But a hero has to
live with his actions.
"Because here, in
the Cancerverse...
GUH!

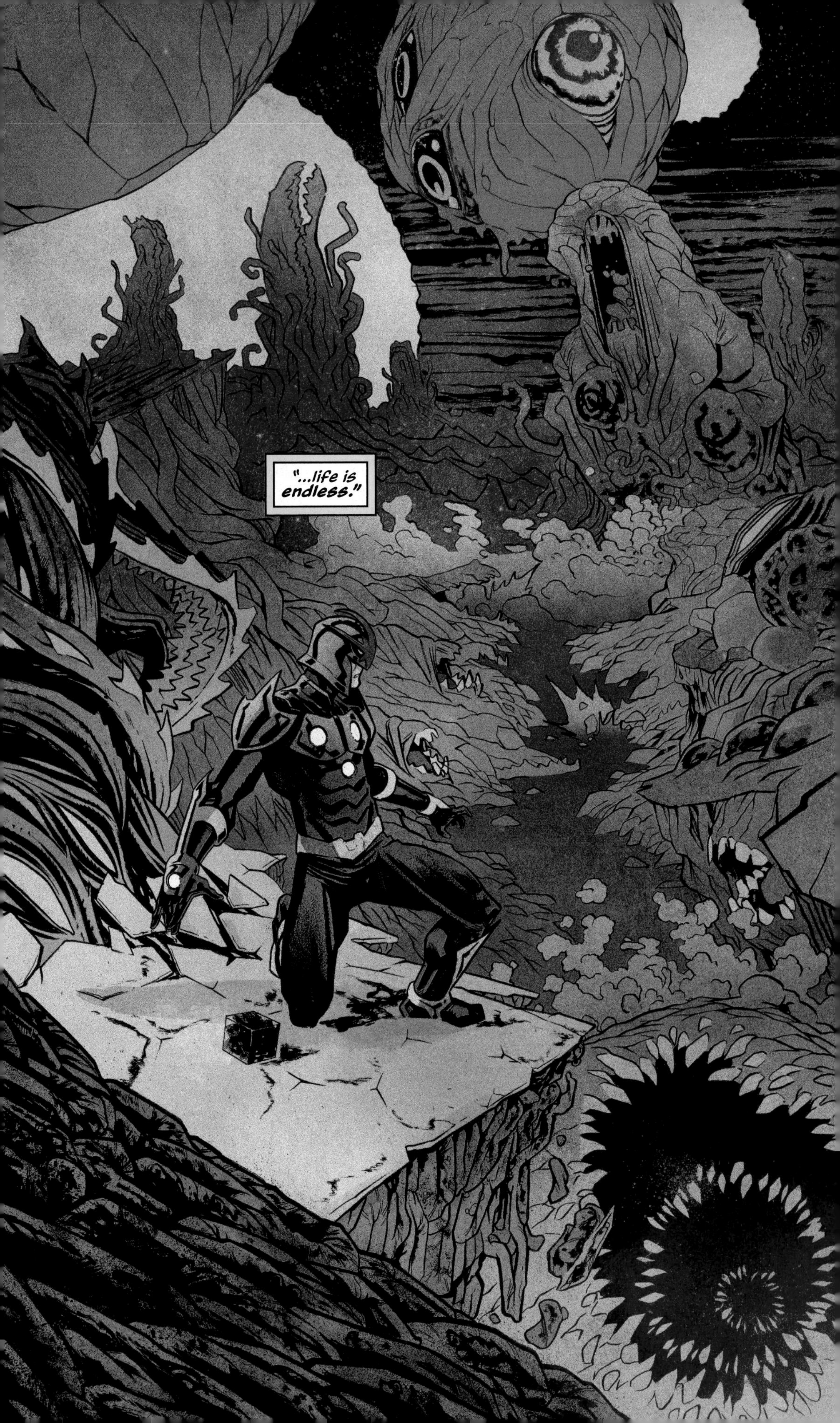
"...life is endless."

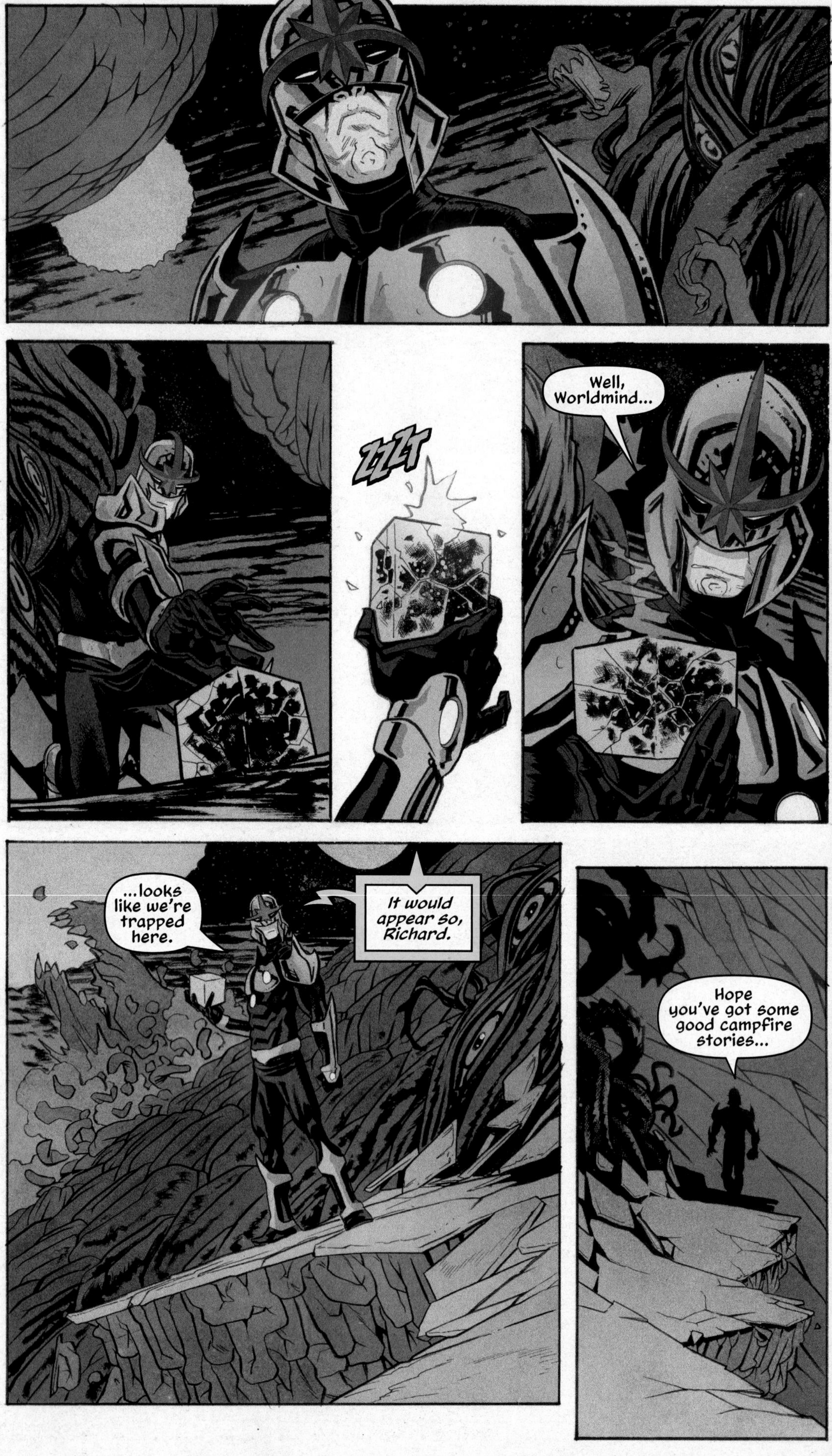
ZZZT
Well, Worldmind...
...looks like we're trapped here.
It would appear so, Richard.
Hope you've got some good campfire stories...

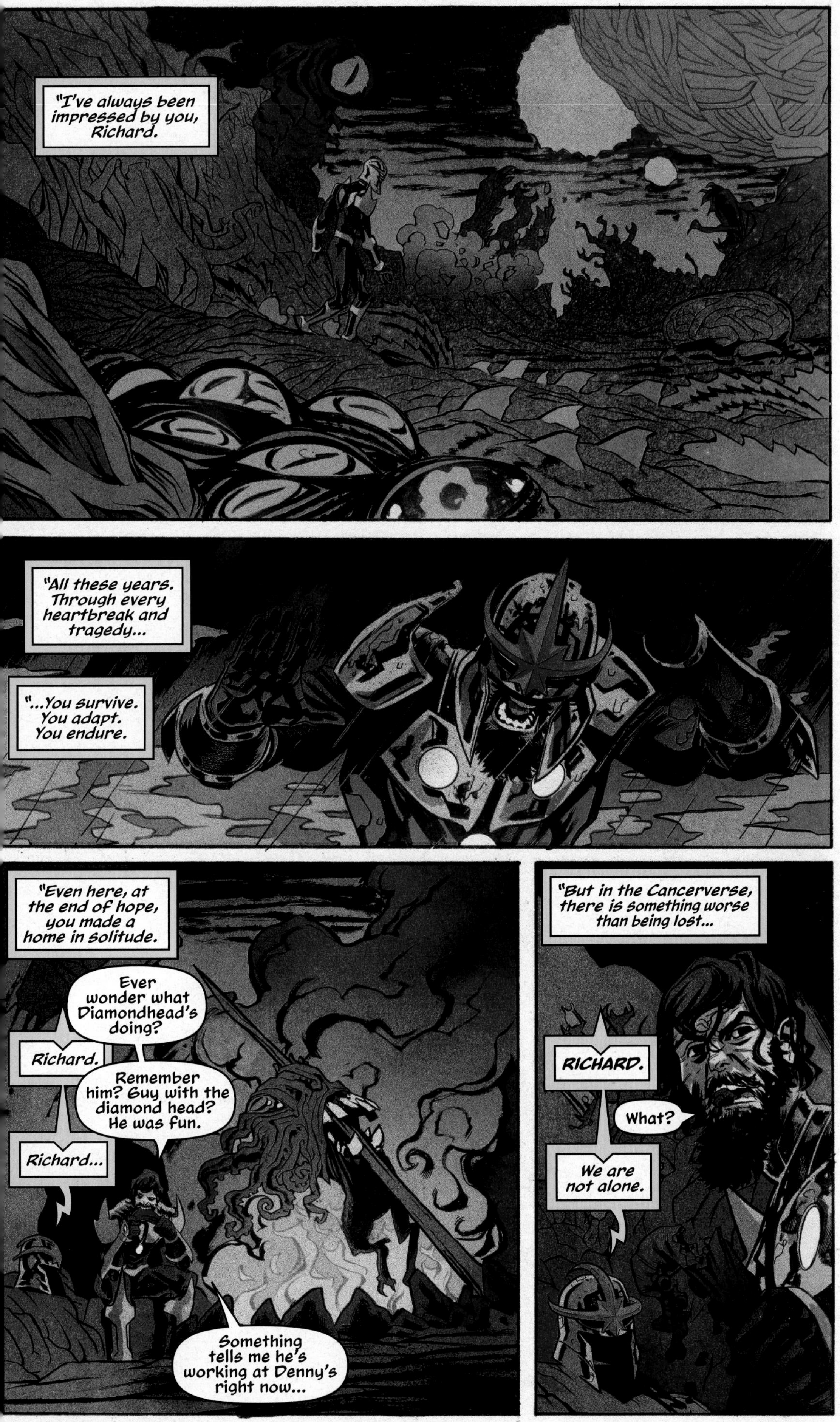
"I've always been impressed by you, Richard.
"All these years. Through every heartbreak and tragedy...
"...You survive. You adapt. You endure.
"Even here, at the end of hope, you made a home in solitude.
Richard.
Ever wonder what Diamondhead's doing?
Richard...
Remember him? Guy with the diamond head? He was fun.
Something tells me he's working at Denny's right now...
"But in the Cancerverse, there is something worse than being lost...
RICHARD.
What?
We are not alone.

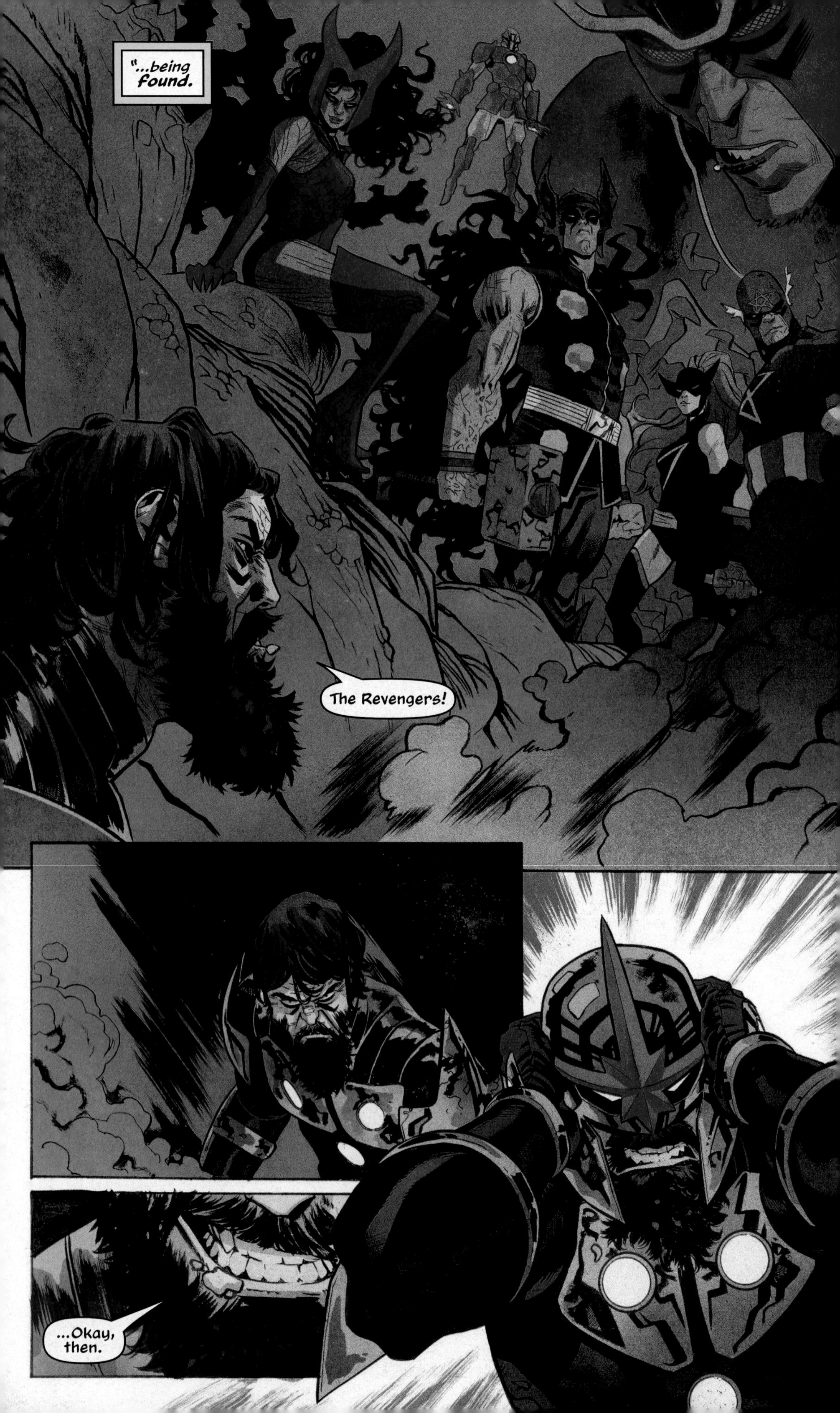
"...being found.
The Revengers!
...Okay, then.

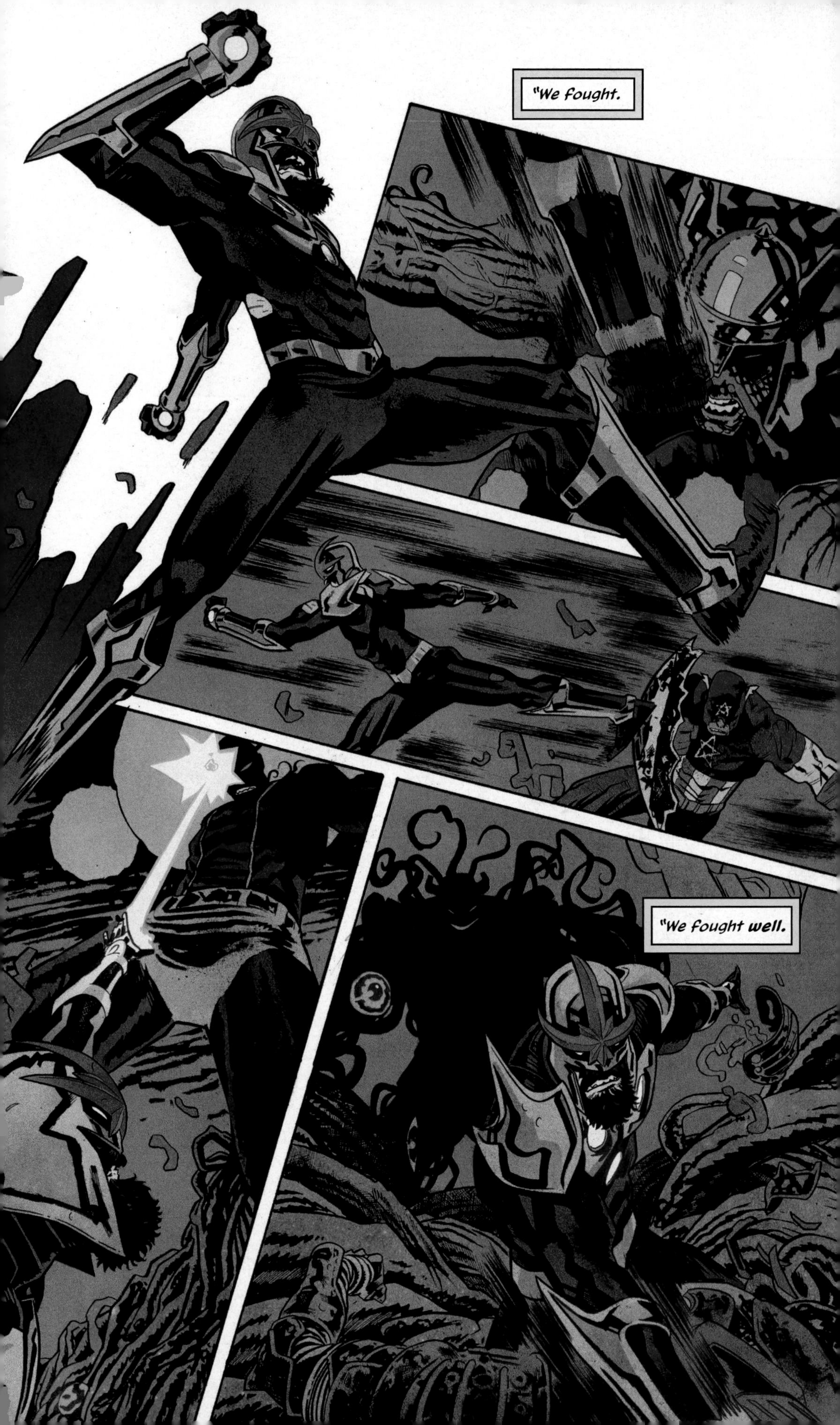
"We fought.
"We fought well.

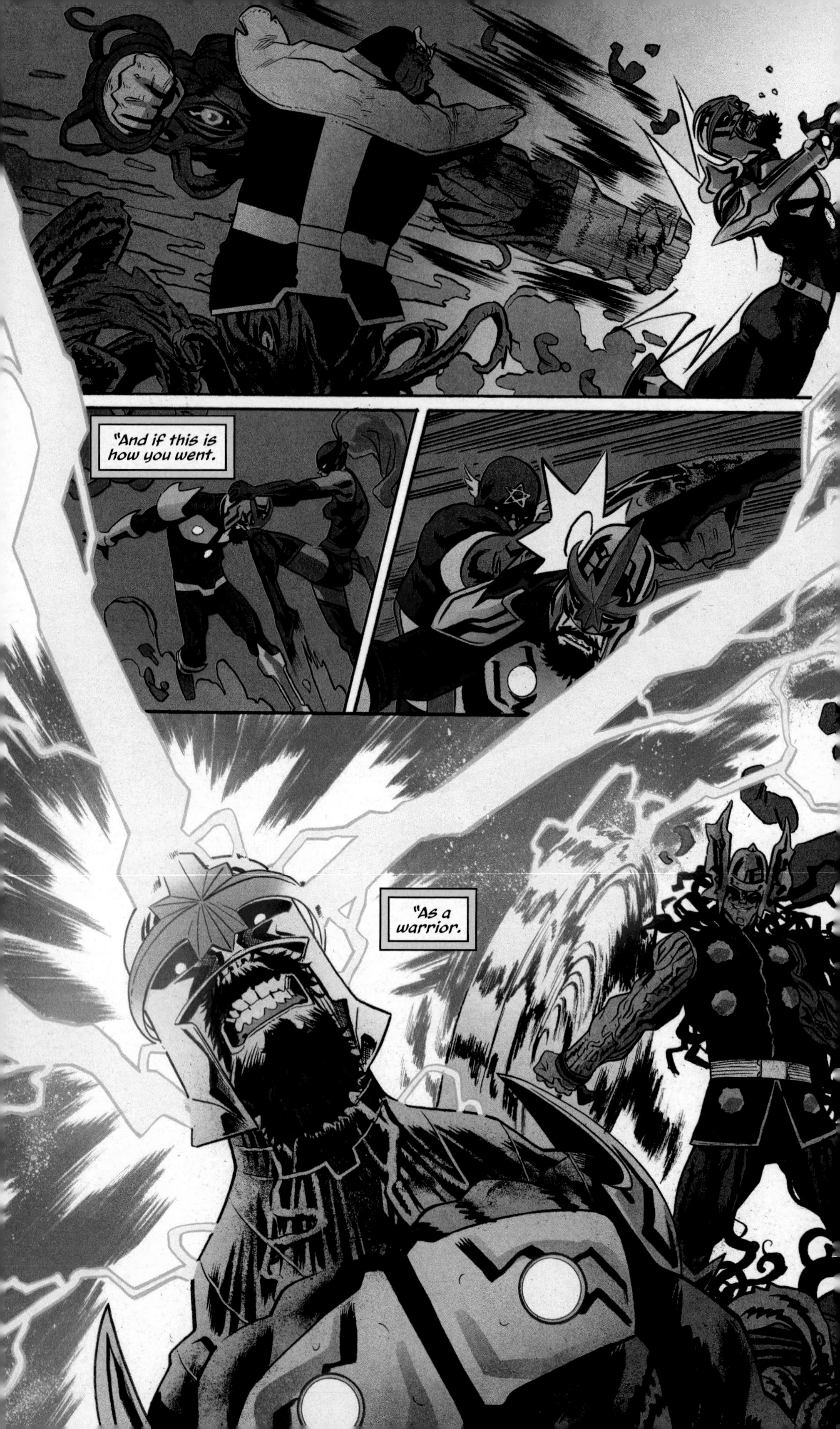
"And if this is how you went.
"As a warrior.

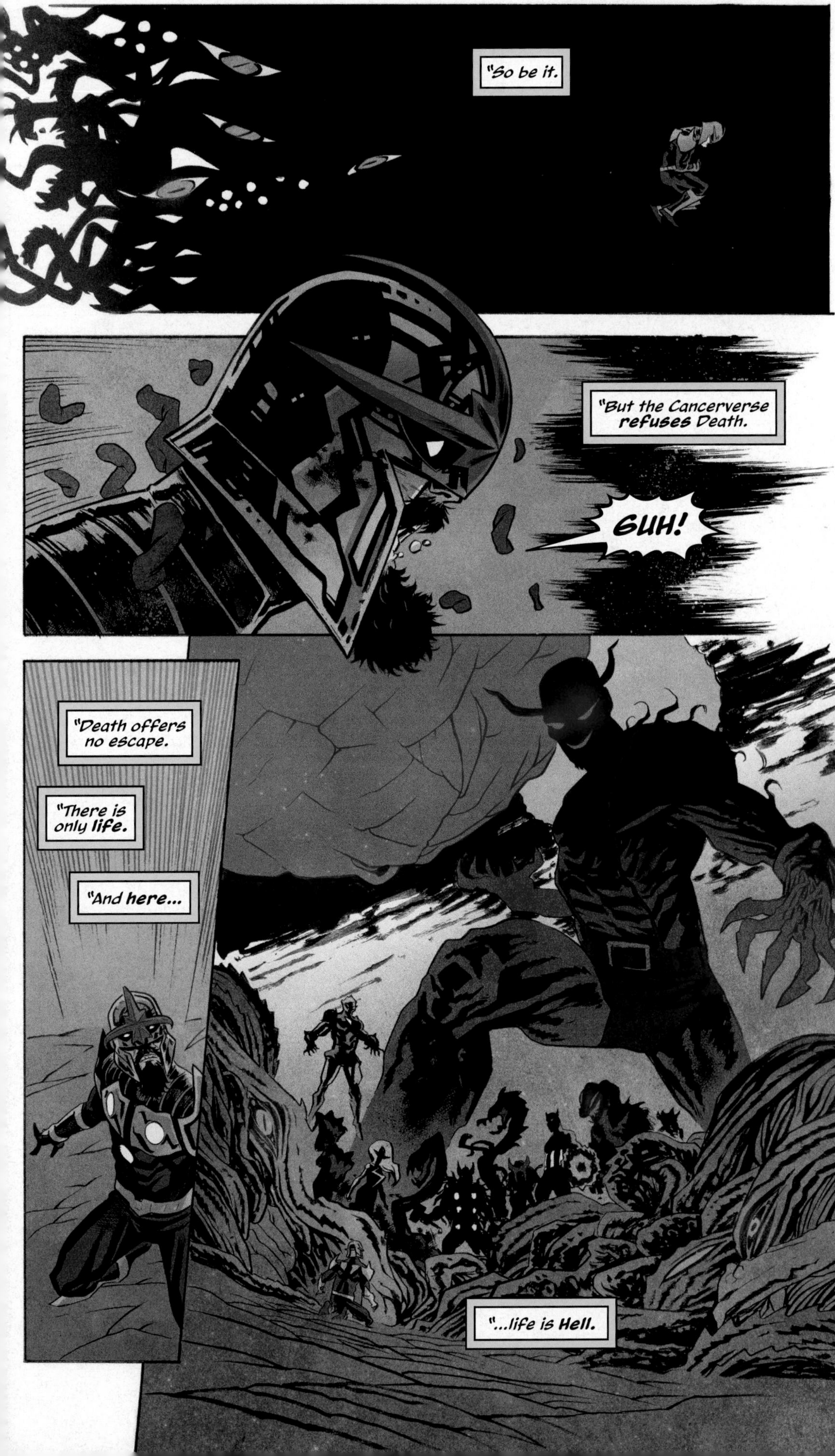
"So be it.
"But the Cancerverse refuses Death.
GUH!
"Death offers no escape.
"There is only life.
"And here...
"...life is Hell.

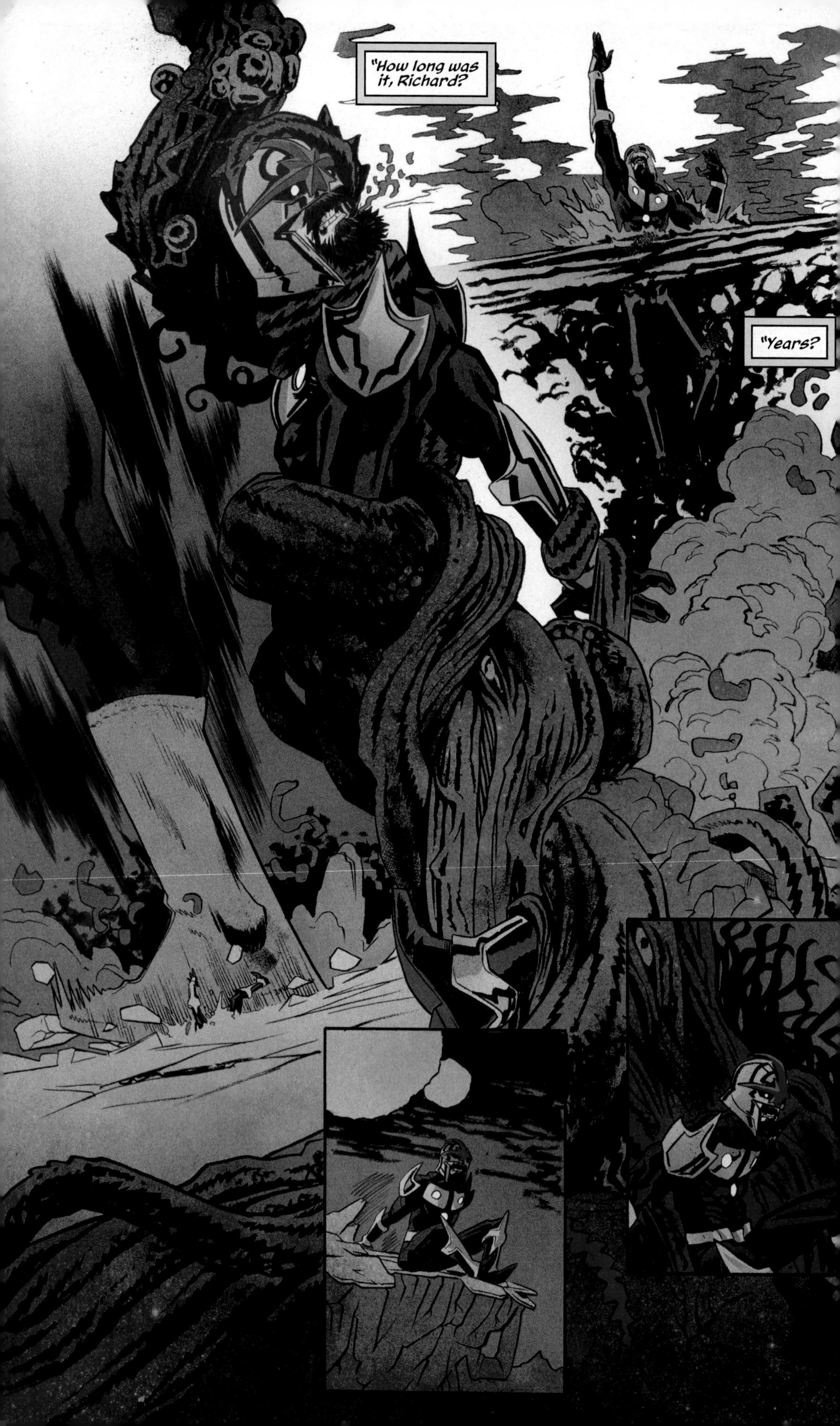
"How long was it, Richard?
"Years?

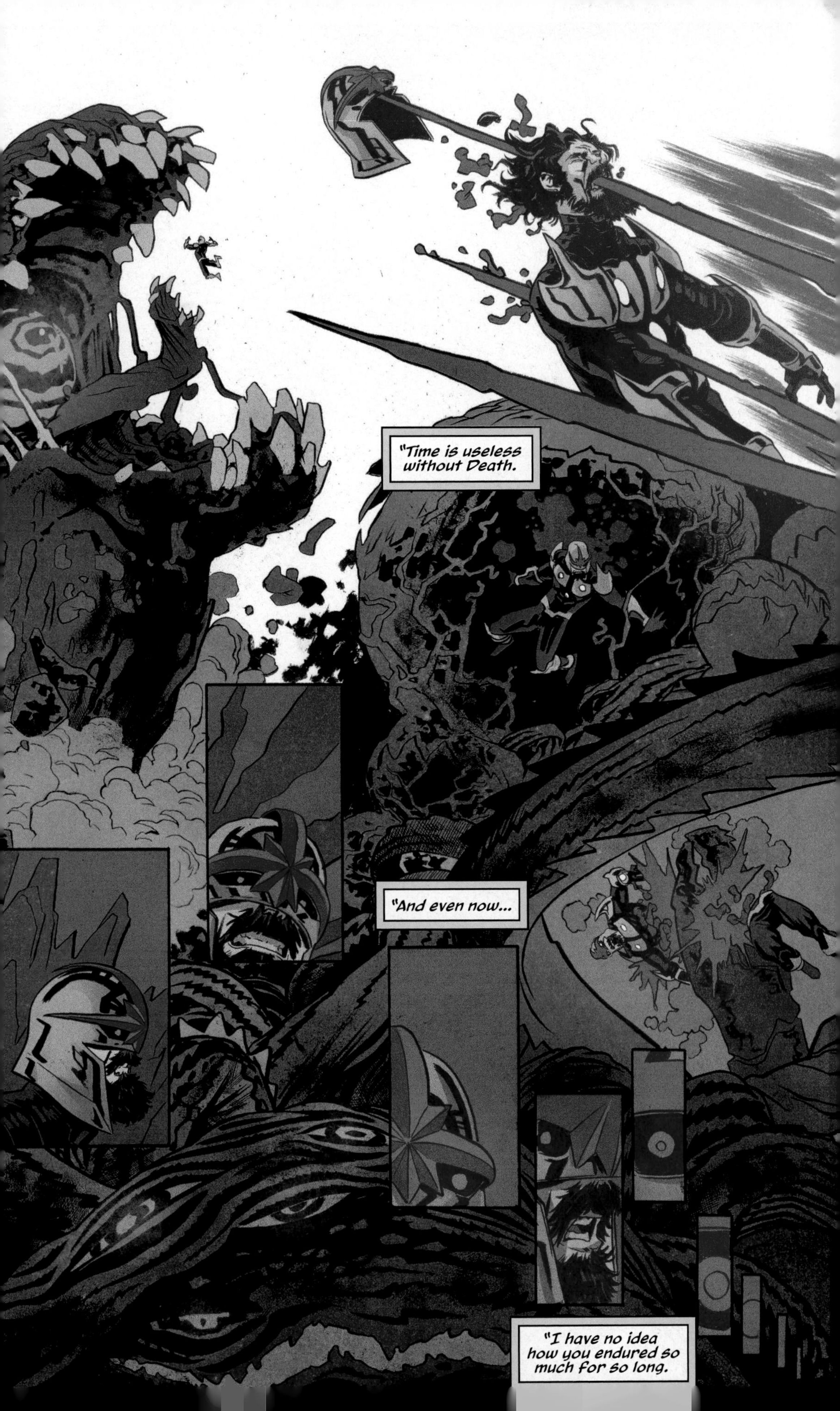
"Time is useless without Death.
"And even now...
"I have no idea how you endured so much for so long.

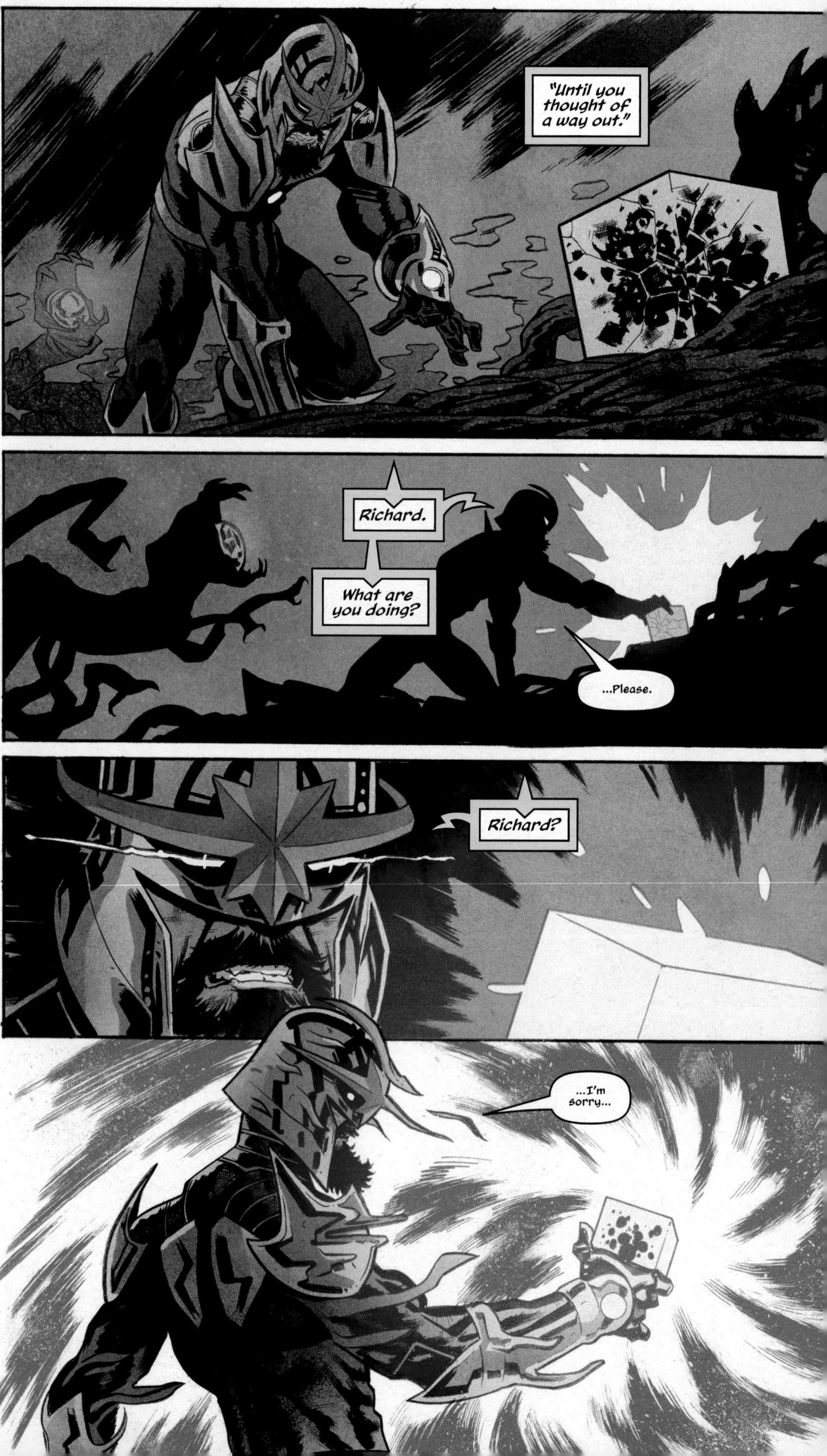
"Until you thought of a way out."
Richard.
What are you doing?
...Please.
Richard?
...I'm sorry...

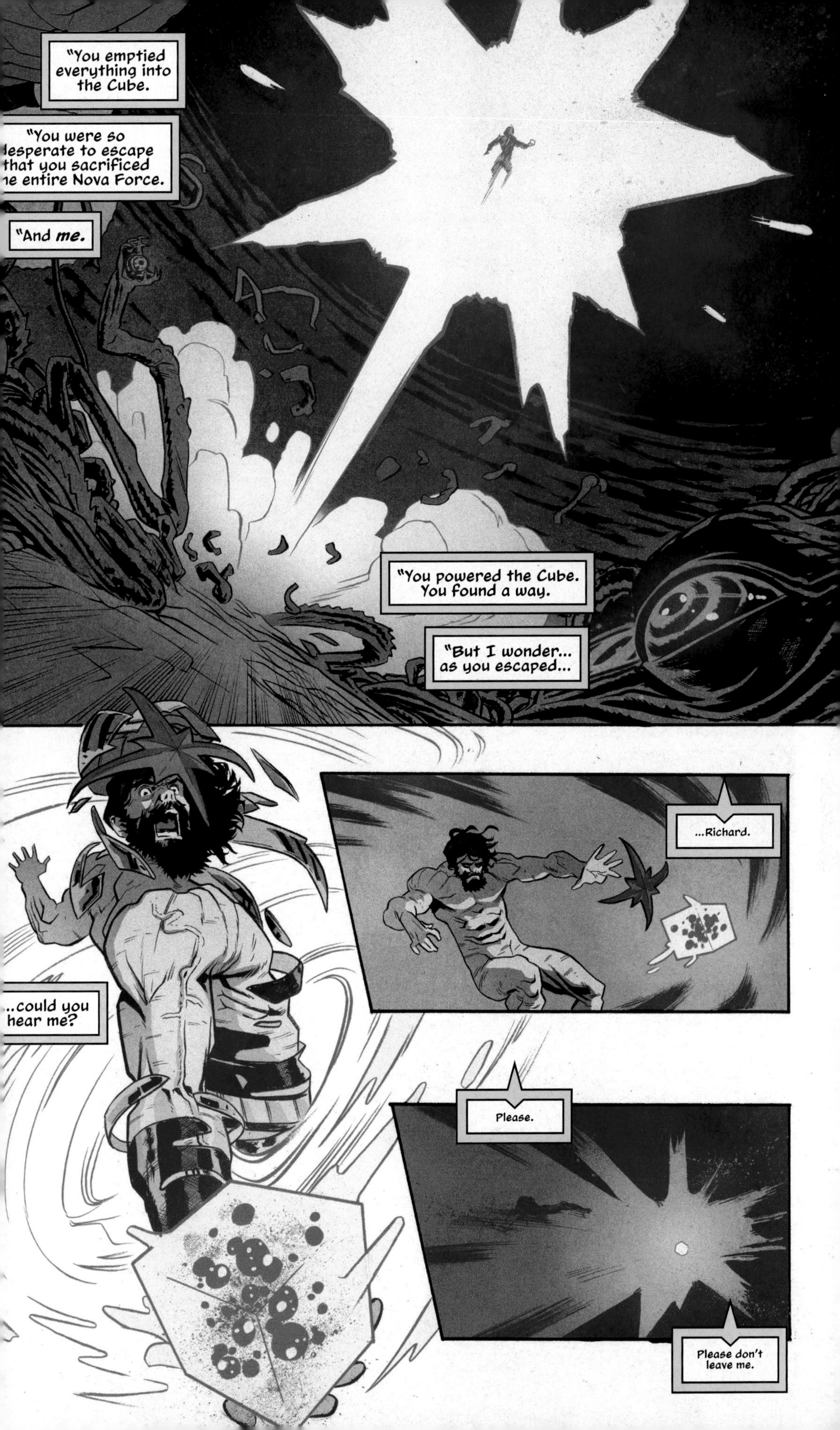
"You emptied everything into the Cube.
"You were so lesperate to escape that you sacrificed e entire Nova Force.
"And *me.*
"You powered the Cube. You found a way.
"But I wonder... as you escaped...
..could you hear me?
...Richard.
Please.
Please don't leave me.

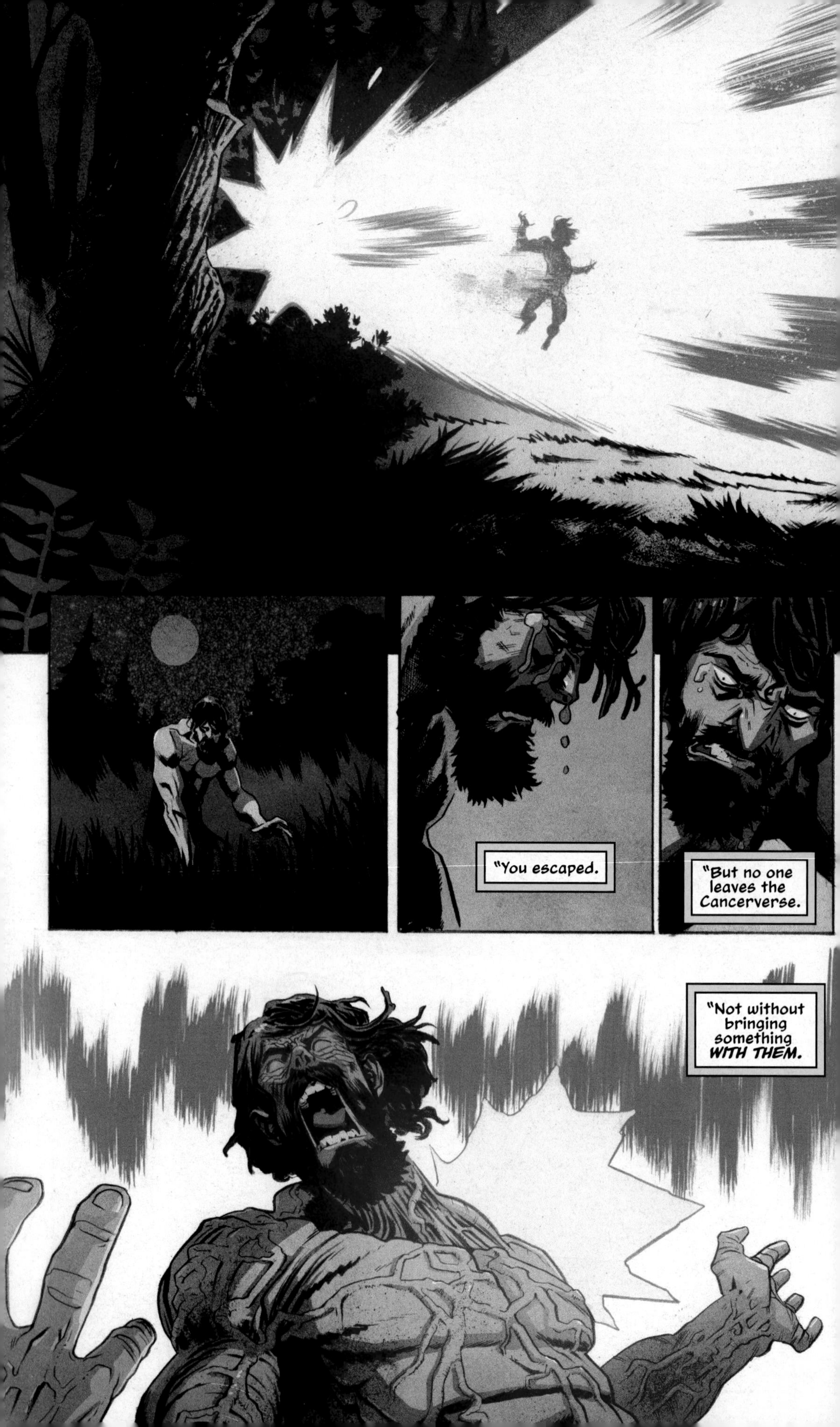
"You escaped.
"But no one leaves the Cancerverse.
"Not without bringing something **WITH THEM.**

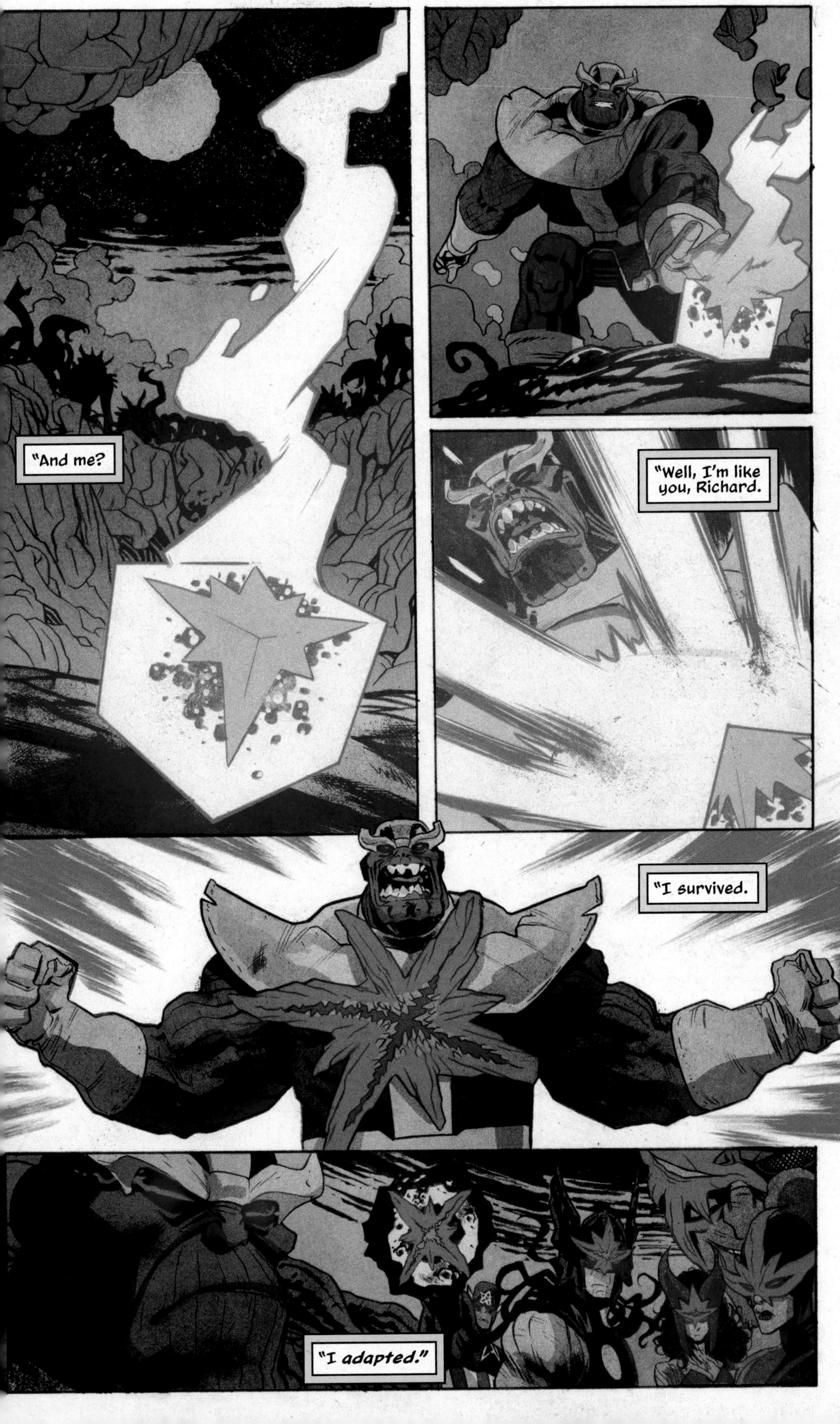
"And me?
"Well, I'm like you, Richard.
"I survived.
"I adapted."

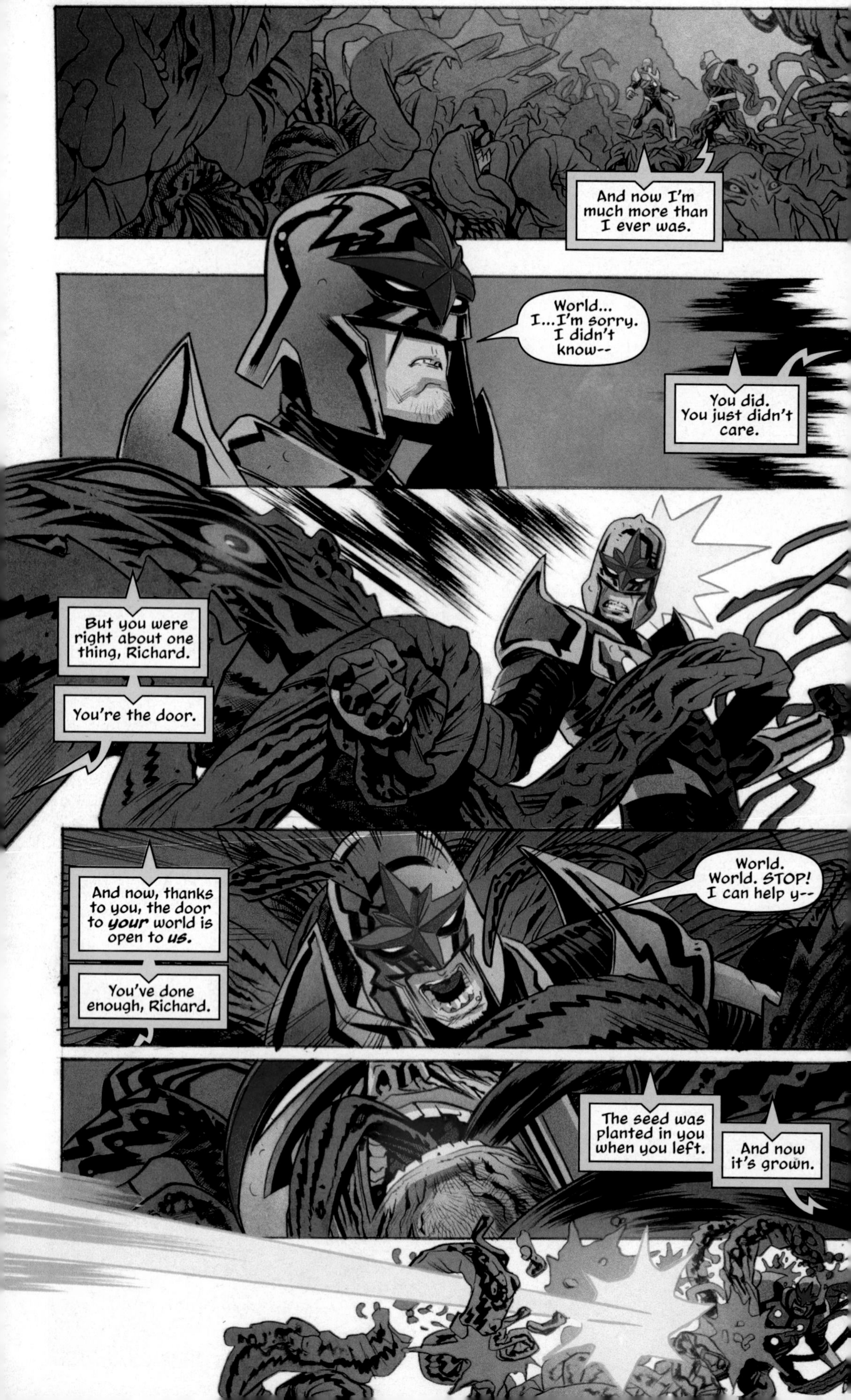
And now I'm much more than I ever was.
World... I...I'm sorry. I didn't know--
You did. You just didn't care.
But you were right about one thing, Richard.
You're the door.
And now, thanks to you, the door to *your* world is open to *us.*
You've done enough, Richard.
World. World. STOP! I can help y--
The seed was planted in you when you left.
And now it's grown.

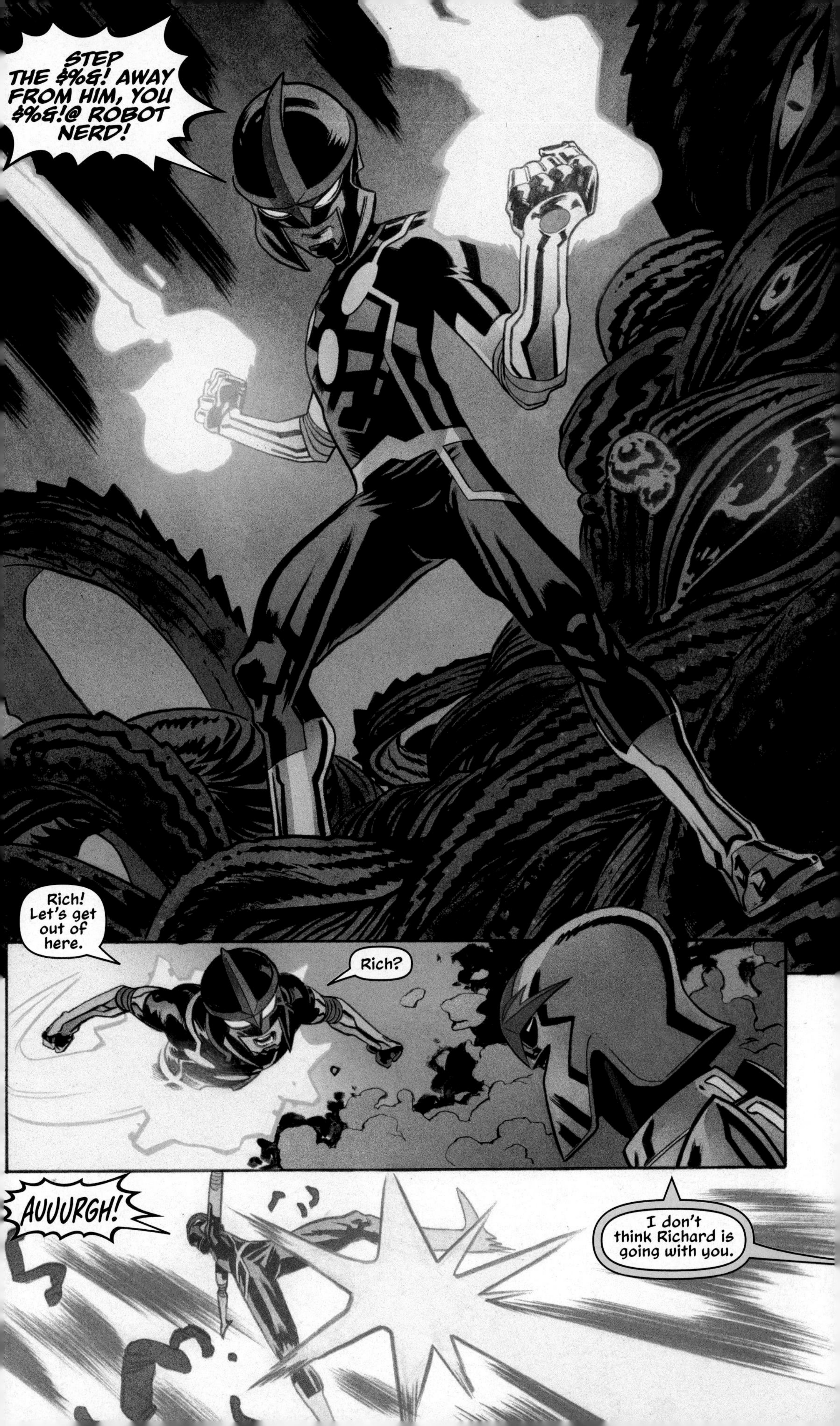
STEP THE $%&! AWAY FROM HIM, YOU $%&!@ ROBOT NERD!
Rich! Let's get out of here.
Rich?
AUUURGH!
I don't think Richard is going with you.

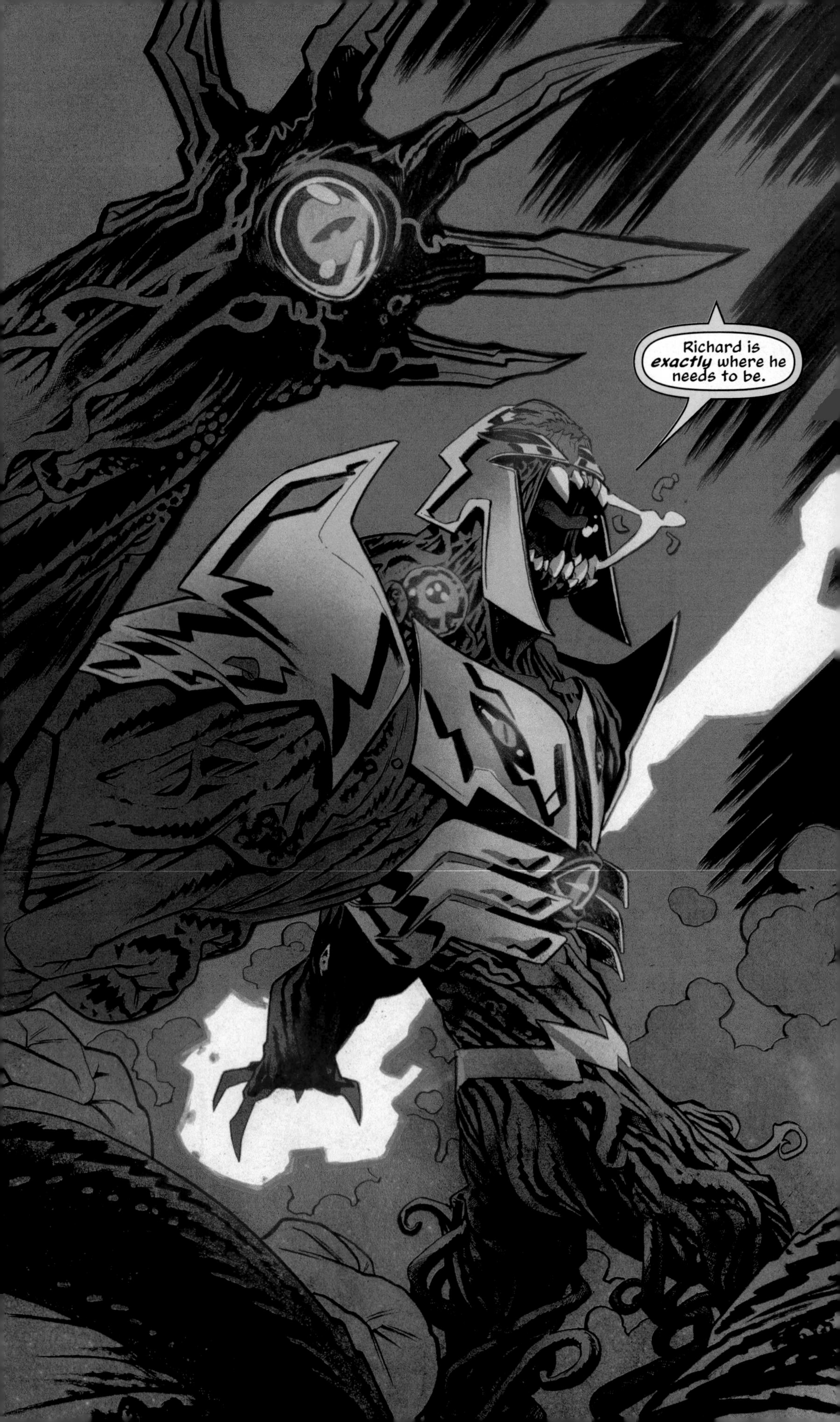
Richard is *exactly* where he needs to be.

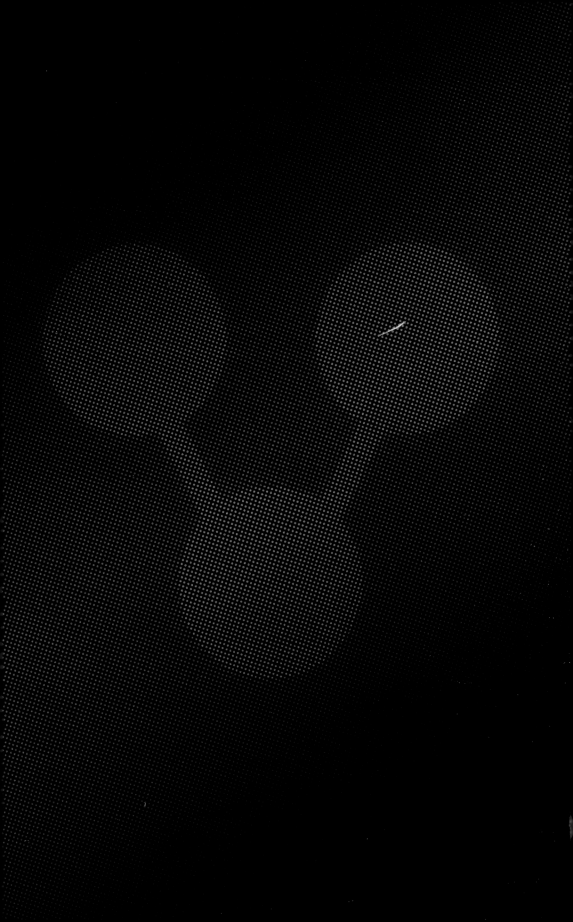

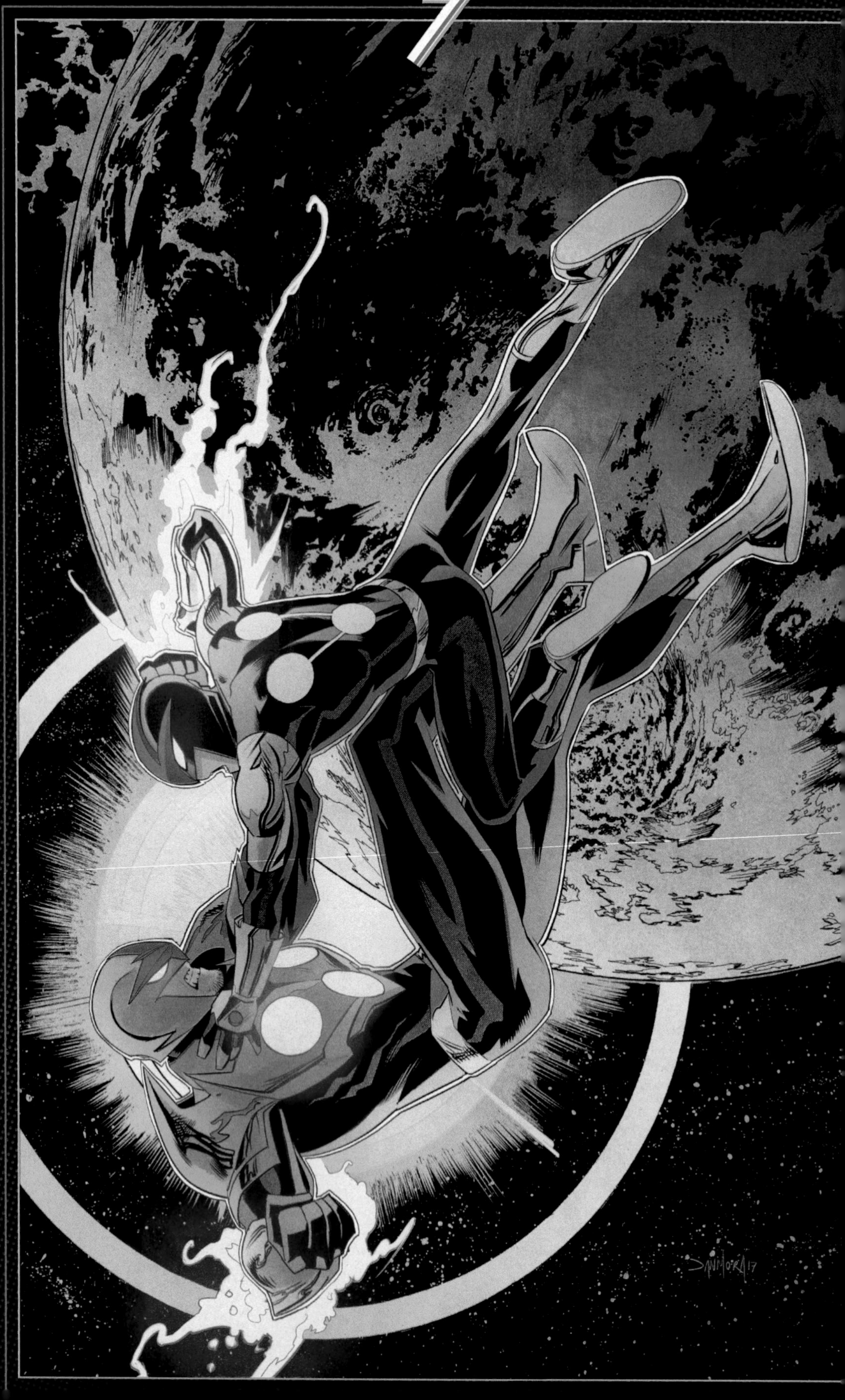

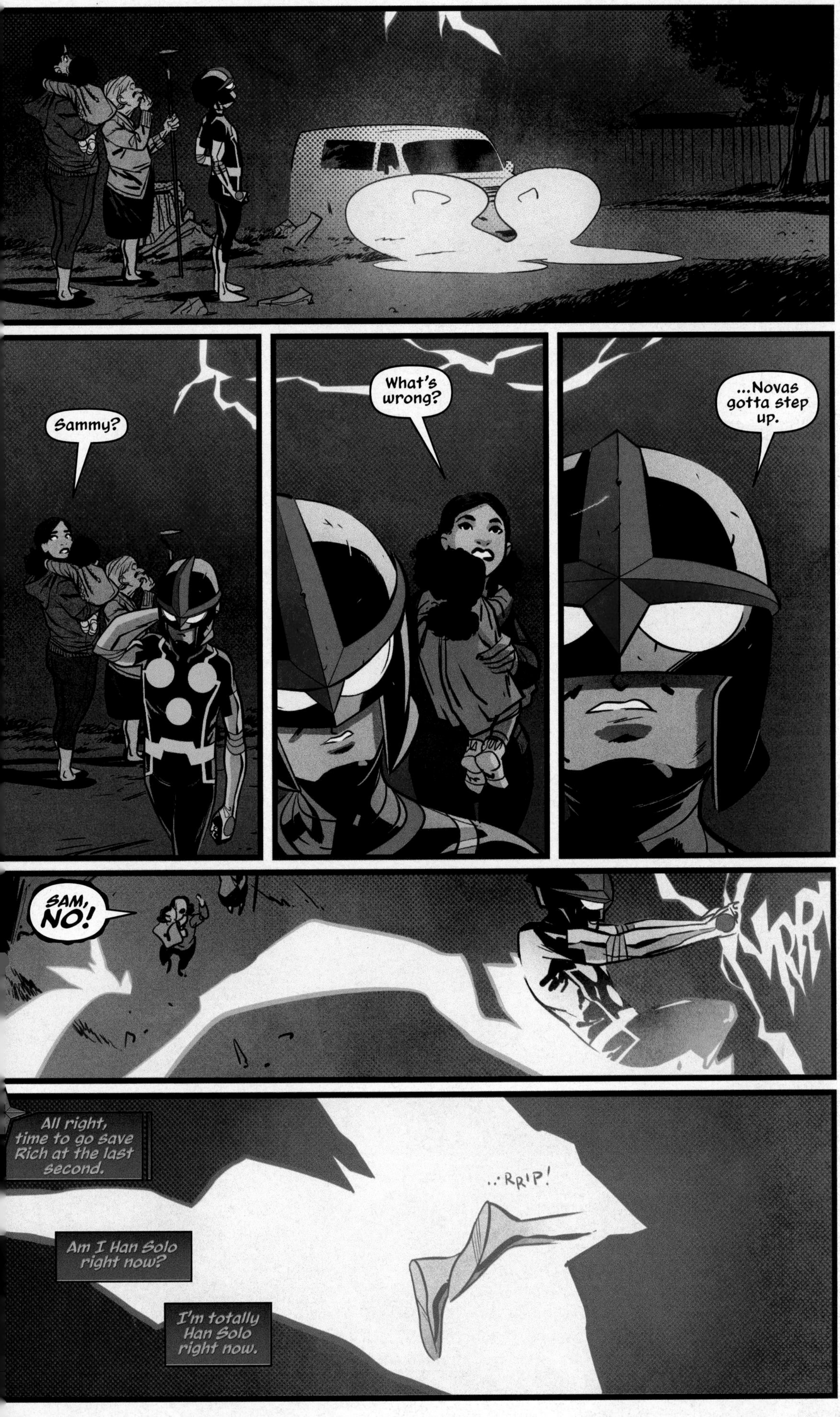
Sammy?
What's wrong?
...Novas gotta step up.
SAM, NO!
VRRT
All right, time to go save Rich at the last second.
..RRIP!
Am I Han Solo right now?
I'm totally Han Solo right now.

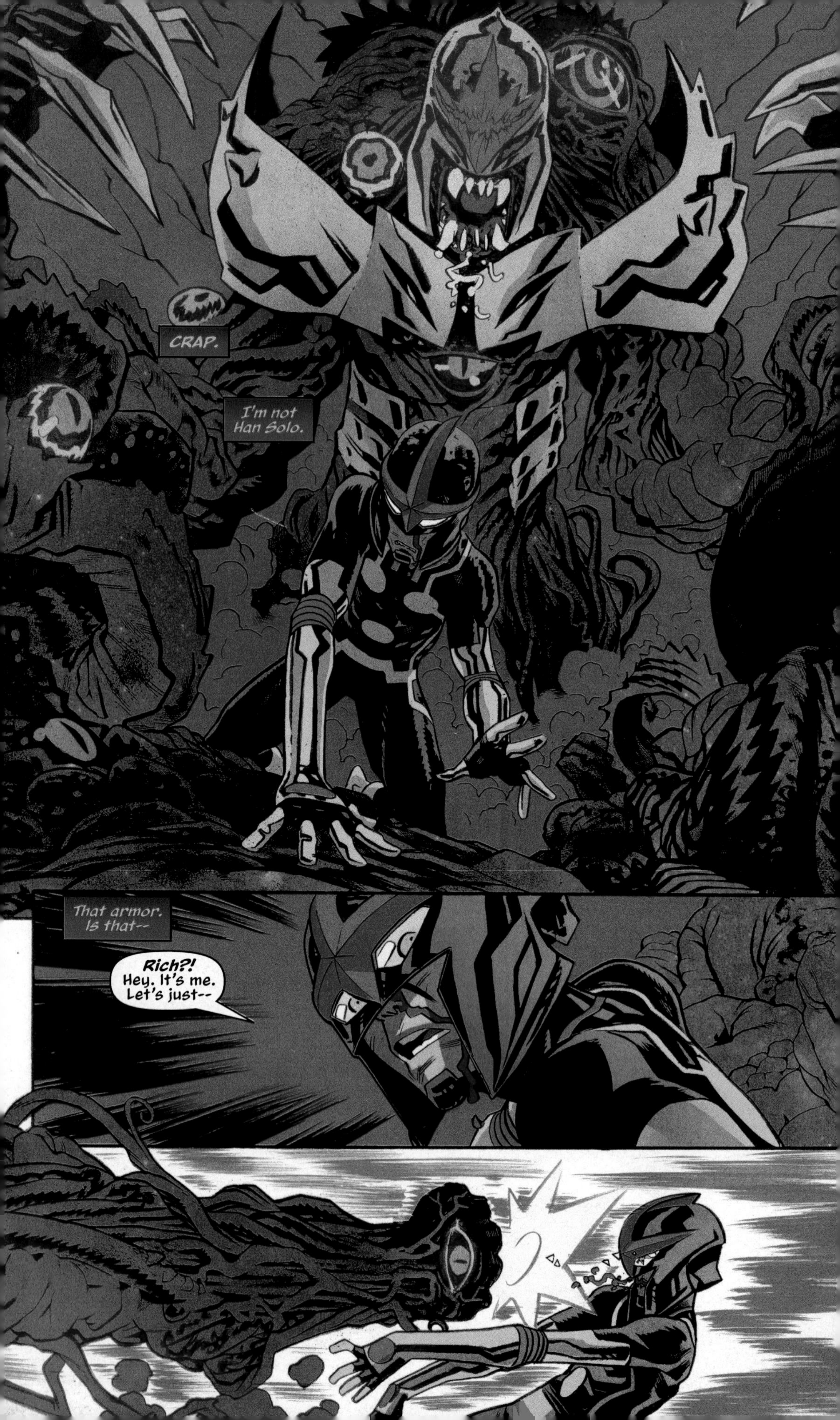
CRAP.
I'm not Han Solo.
That armor. Is that--
Rich?! Hey. It's me. Let's just--

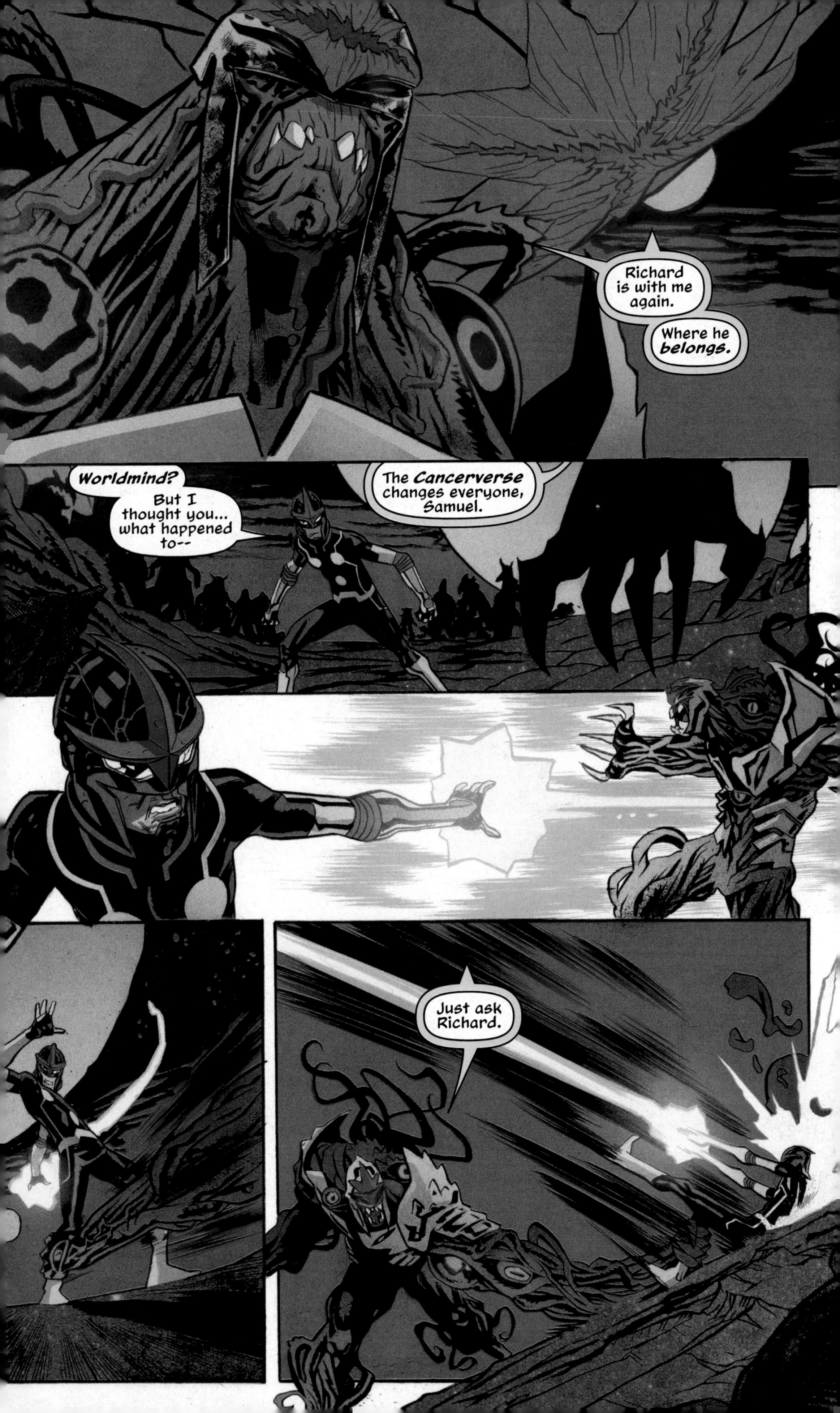

Richard is with me again.
Where he *belongs.*
Worldmind?
But I thought you... what happened to--
The *Cancerverse* changes everyone, Samuel.
Just ask Richard.

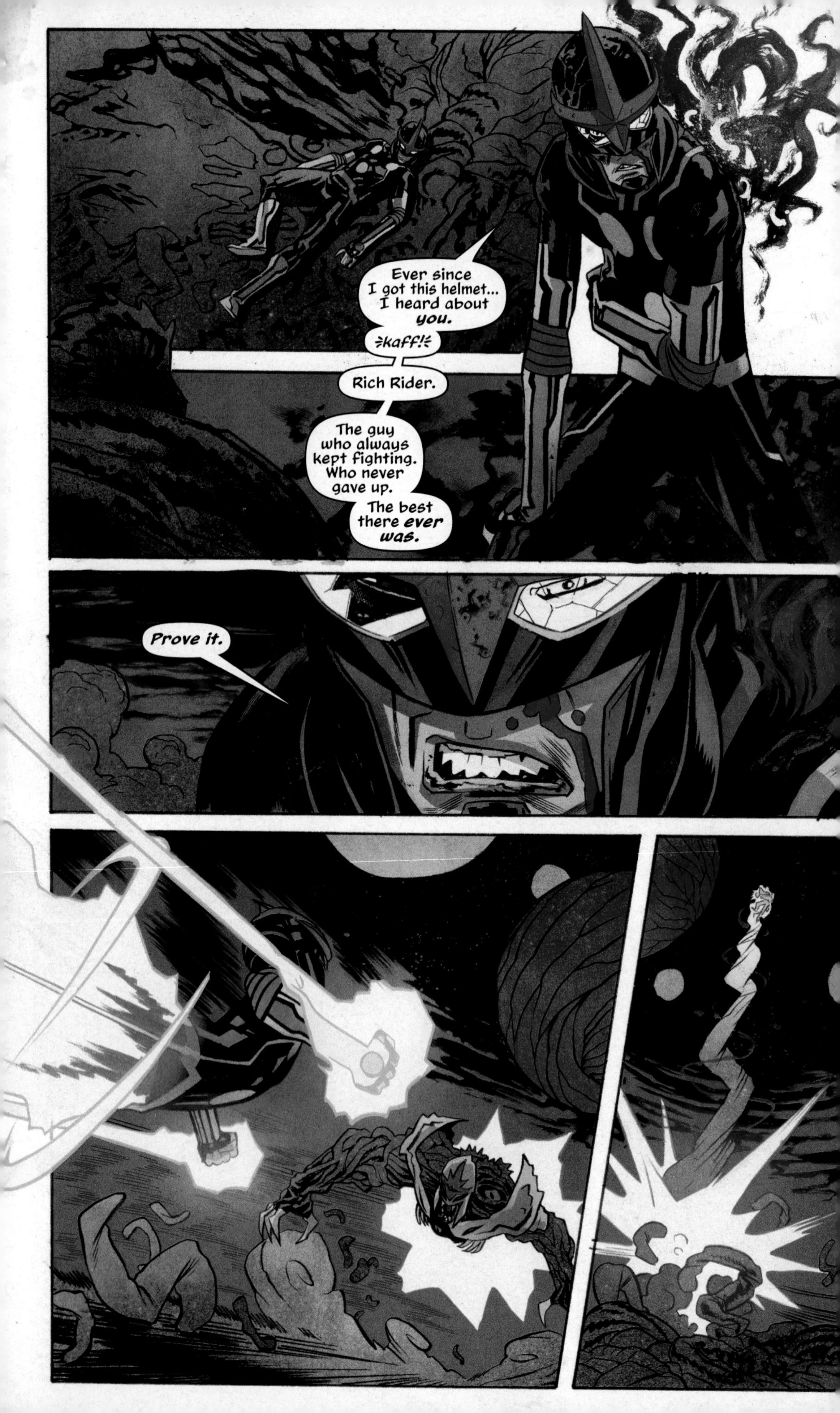
Ever since I got this helmet... I heard about *you.*
kaff!
Rich Rider.
The guy who always kept fighting. Who never gave up.
The best there *ever was.*
Prove it.

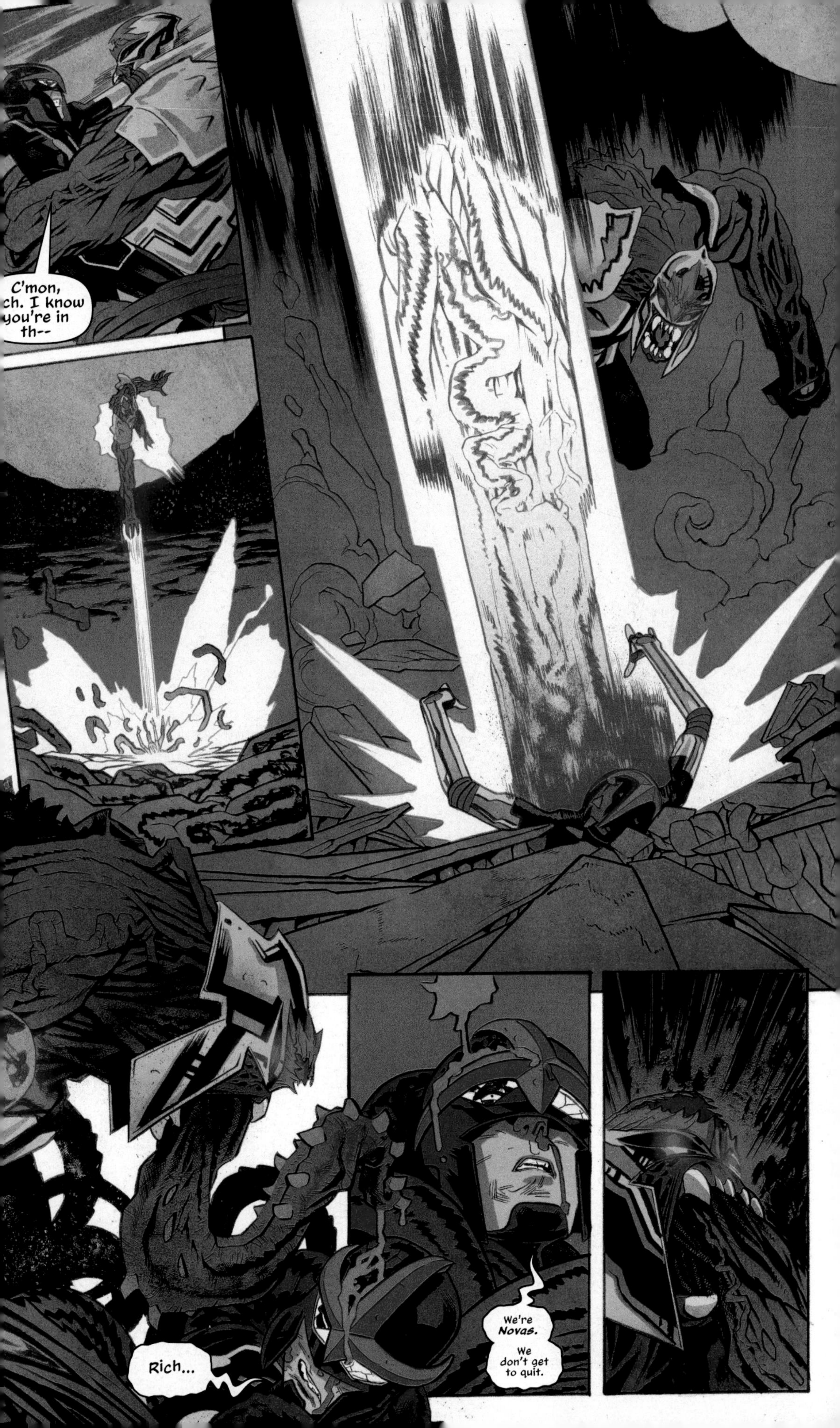
C'mon, ch. I know you're in th--
Rich...
We're Novas. We don't get to quit.

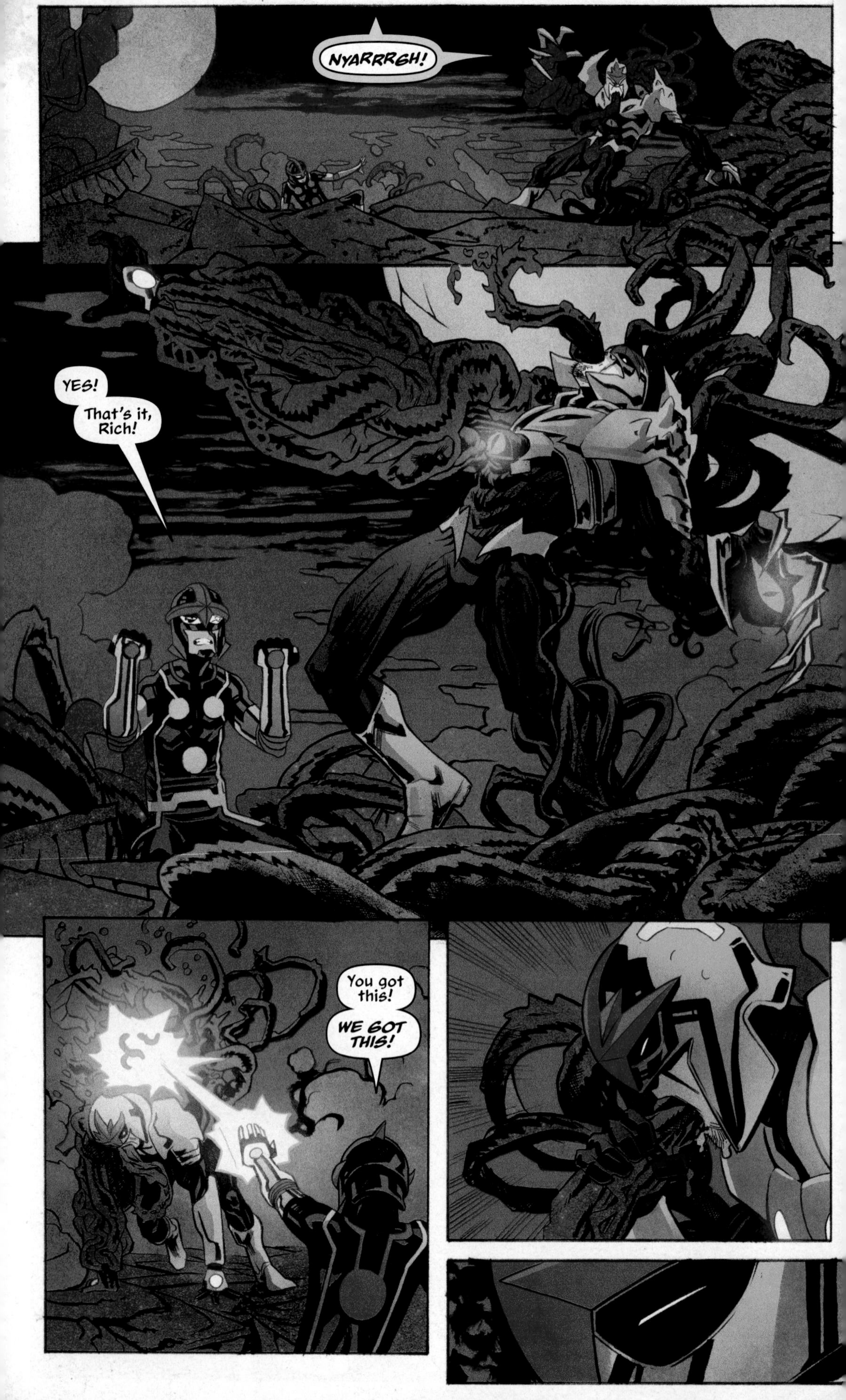
NYARRRGH!
YES!
That's it, Rich!
You got this!
WE GOT THIS!

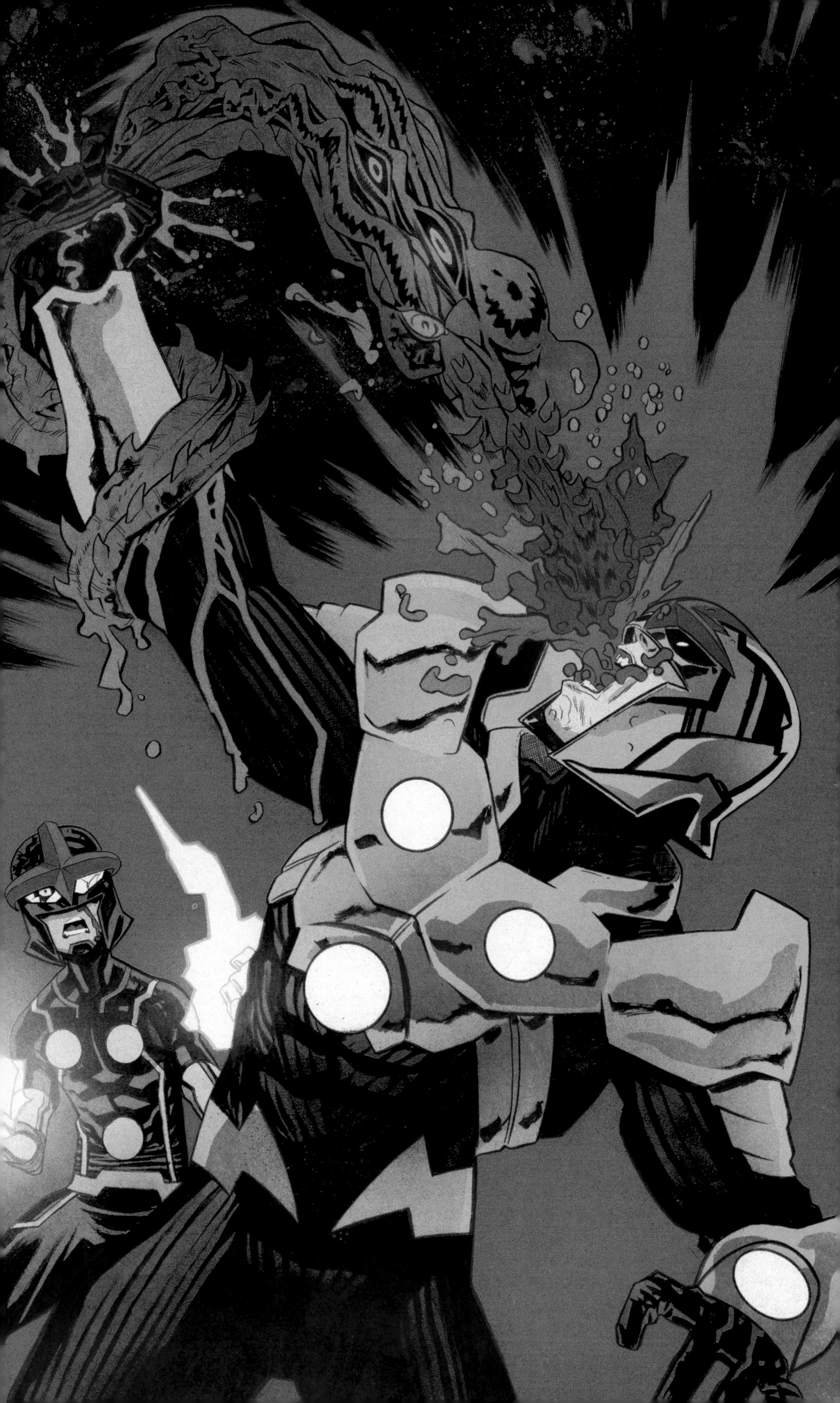

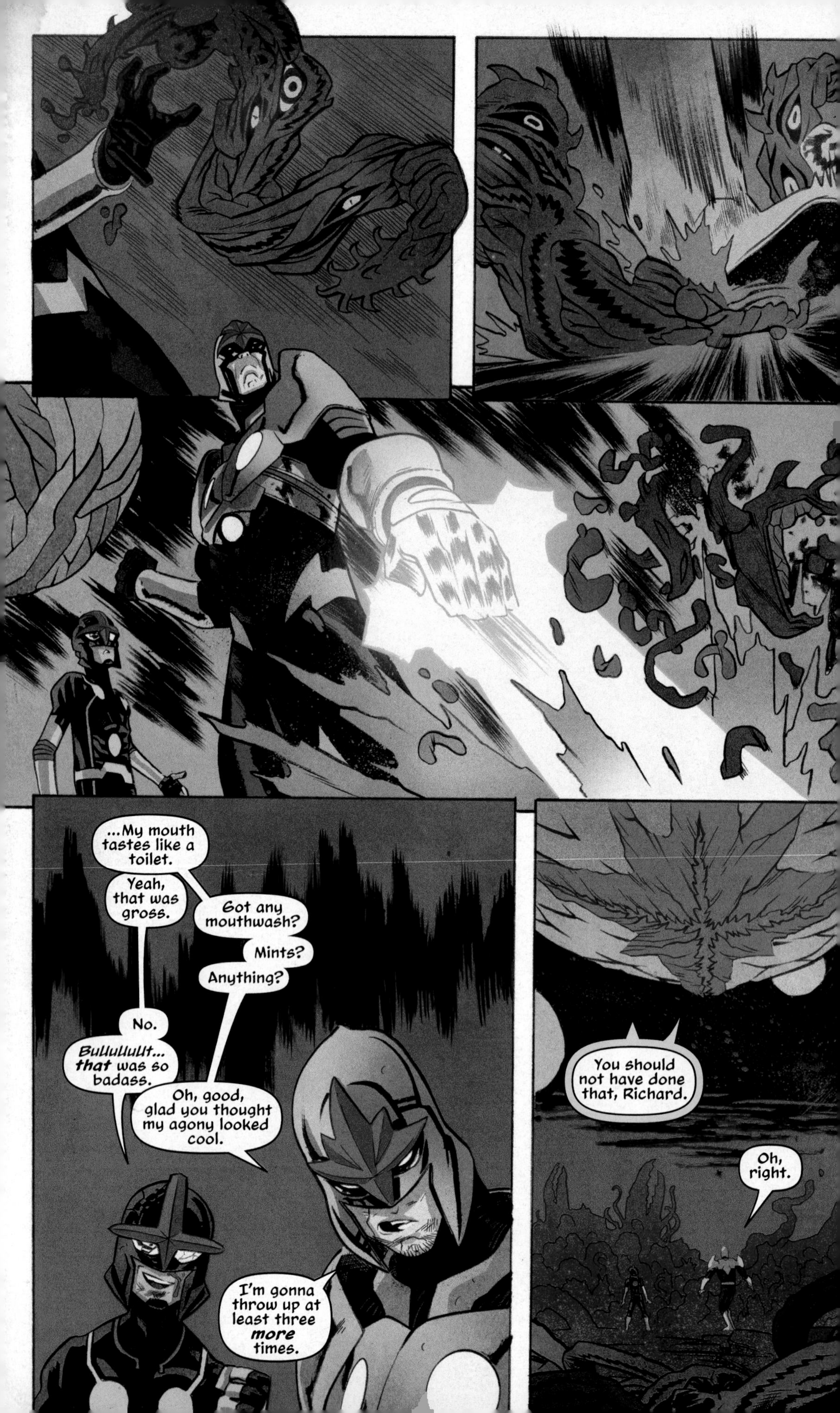

...My mouth tastes like a toilet.
Yeah, that was gross.
Got any mouthwash?
Mints?
Anything?
No.
Bullullult... *that* was so badass.
Oh, good, glad you thought my agony looked cool.
I'm gonna throw up at least three *more* times.
You should not have done that, Richard.
Oh, right.

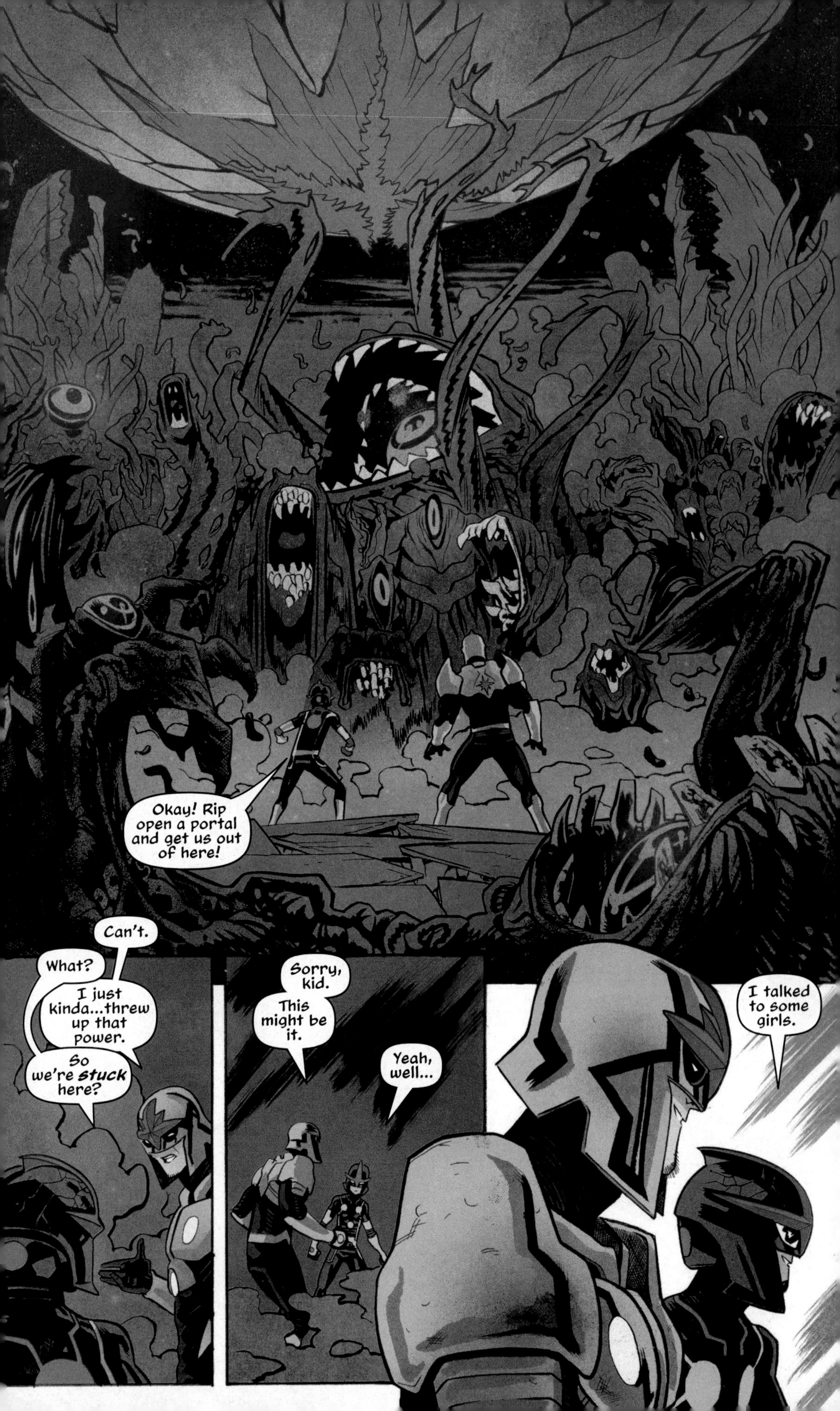

Okay! Rip open a portal and get us out of here!
Can't.
What?
I just kinda...threw up that power.
So we're *stuck* here?
Sorry, kid.
This might be it.
Yeah, well...
I talked to some girls.

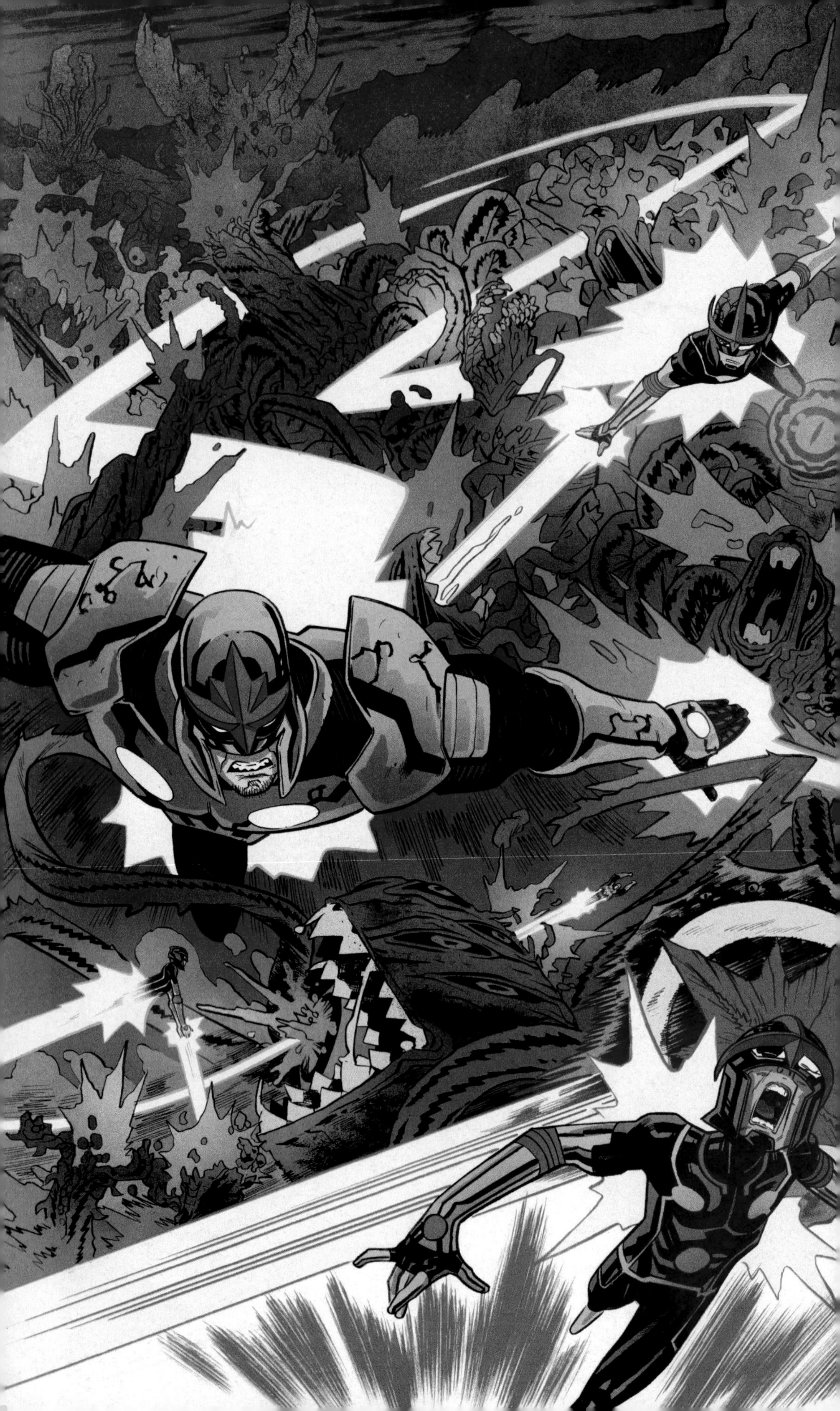

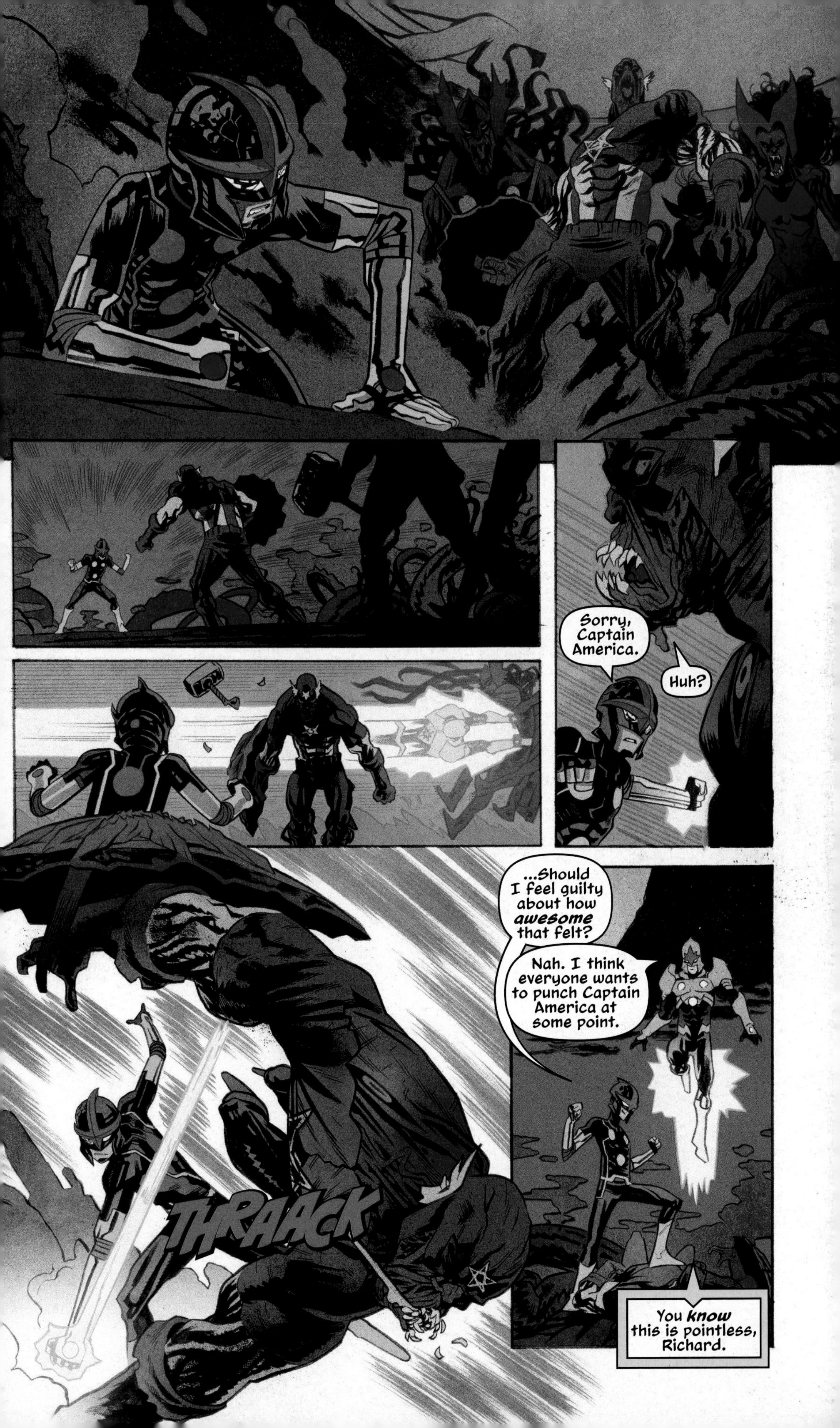
Sorry, Captain America.
Huh?
THRAACK
...Should I feel guilty about how *awesome* that felt?
Nah. I think everyone wants to punch Captain America at some point.
You *know* this is pointless, Richard.

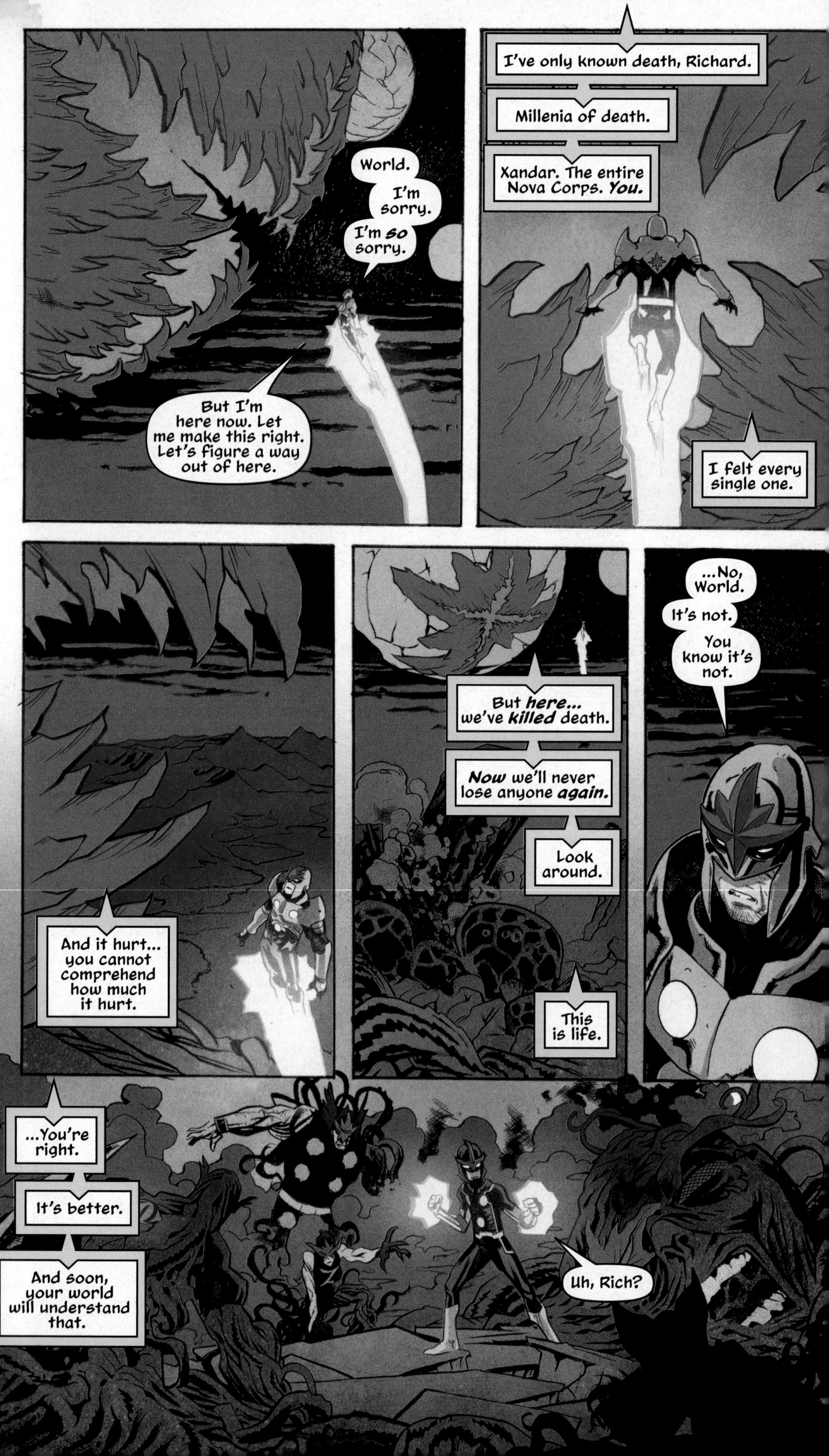
World.
I'm sorry.
I'm *so* sorry.
But I'm here now. Let me make this right. Let's figure a way out of here.
I've only known death, Richard.
Millenia of death.
Xandar. The entire Nova Corps. *You.*
I felt every single one.
And it hurt... you cannot comprehend how much it hurt.
But *here...* we've *killed* death.
Now we'll never lose anyone *again.*
Look around.
This is life.
...No, World.
It's not.
You know it's not.
...You're right.
It's better.
And soon, your world will understand that.
Uh, Rich?

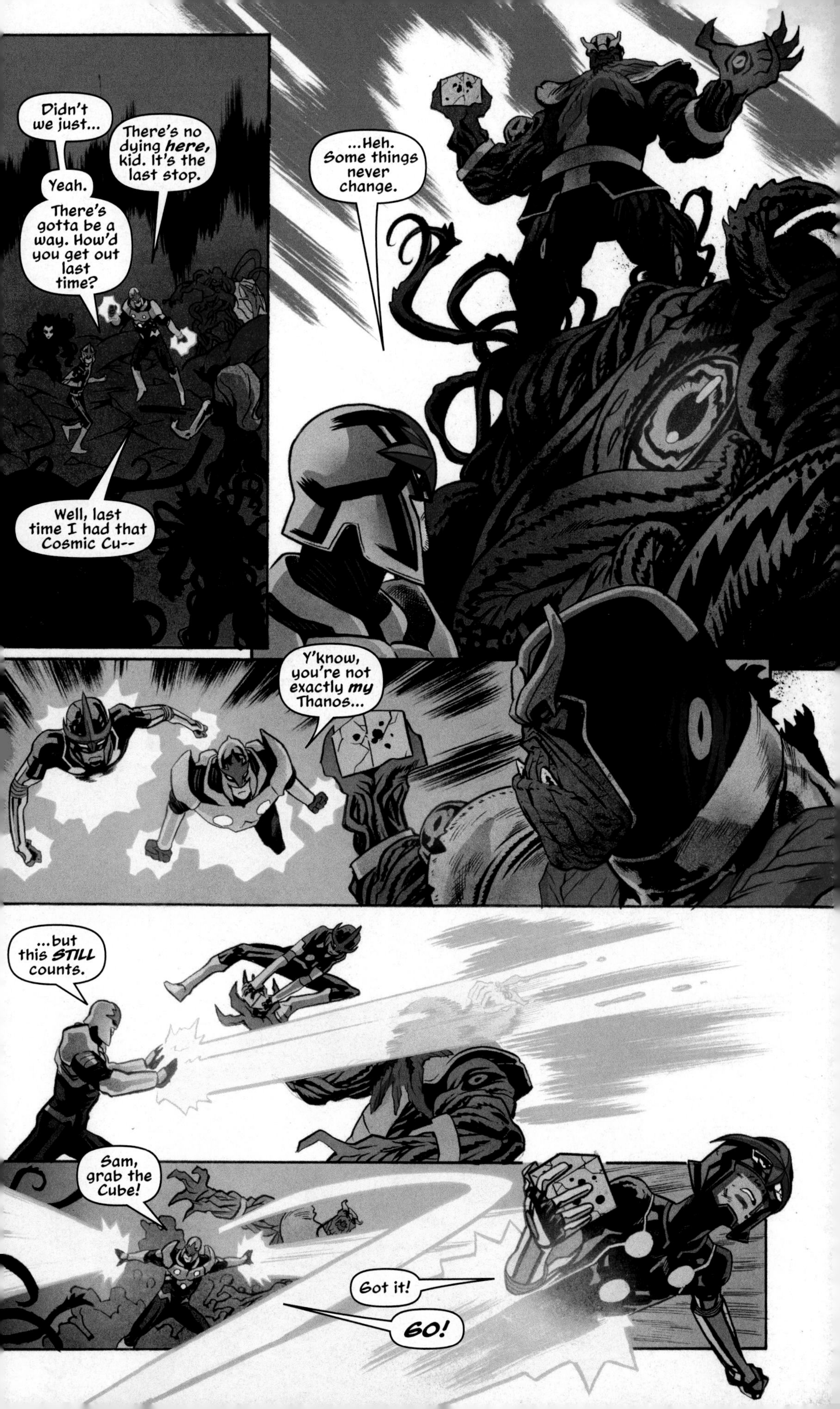
Didn't we just...
Yeah.
There's no dying here, kid. It's the last stop.
There's gotta be a way. How'd you get out last time?
Well, last time I had that Cosmic Cu--
...Heh. Some things never change.
Y'know, you're not exactly my Thanos...
...but this STILL counts.
Sam, grab the Cube!
Got it!
GO!

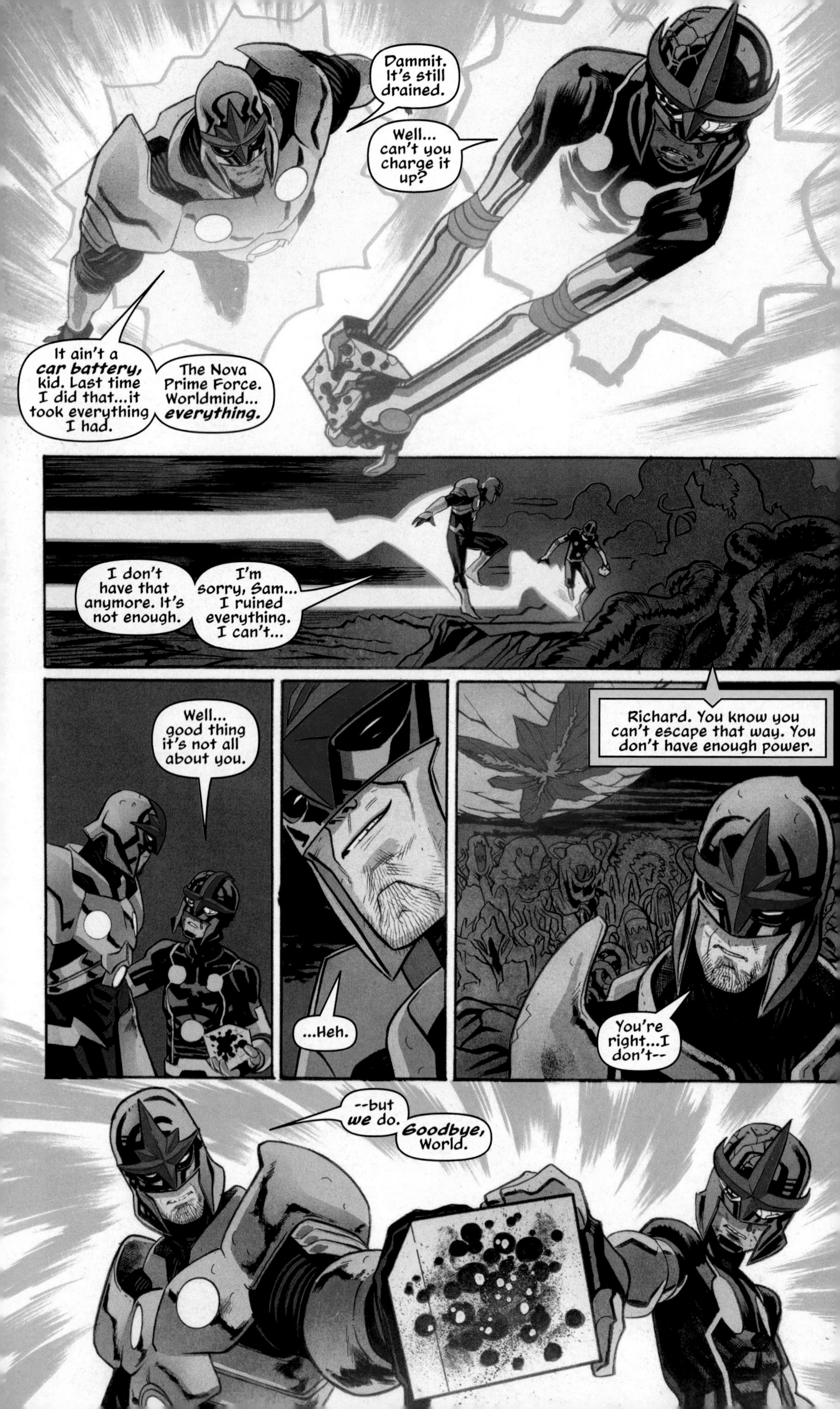
Dammit. It's still drained.
Well... can't you charge it up?
It ain't a car battery, kid. Last time I did that...it took everything I had.
The Nova Prime Force. Worldmind... everything.
I don't have that anymore. It's not enough.
I'm sorry, Sam... I ruined everything. I can't...
Well... good thing it's not all about you.
...Heh.
Richard. You know you can't escape that way. You don't have enough power.
You're right...I don't--
--but we do. Goodbye, World.

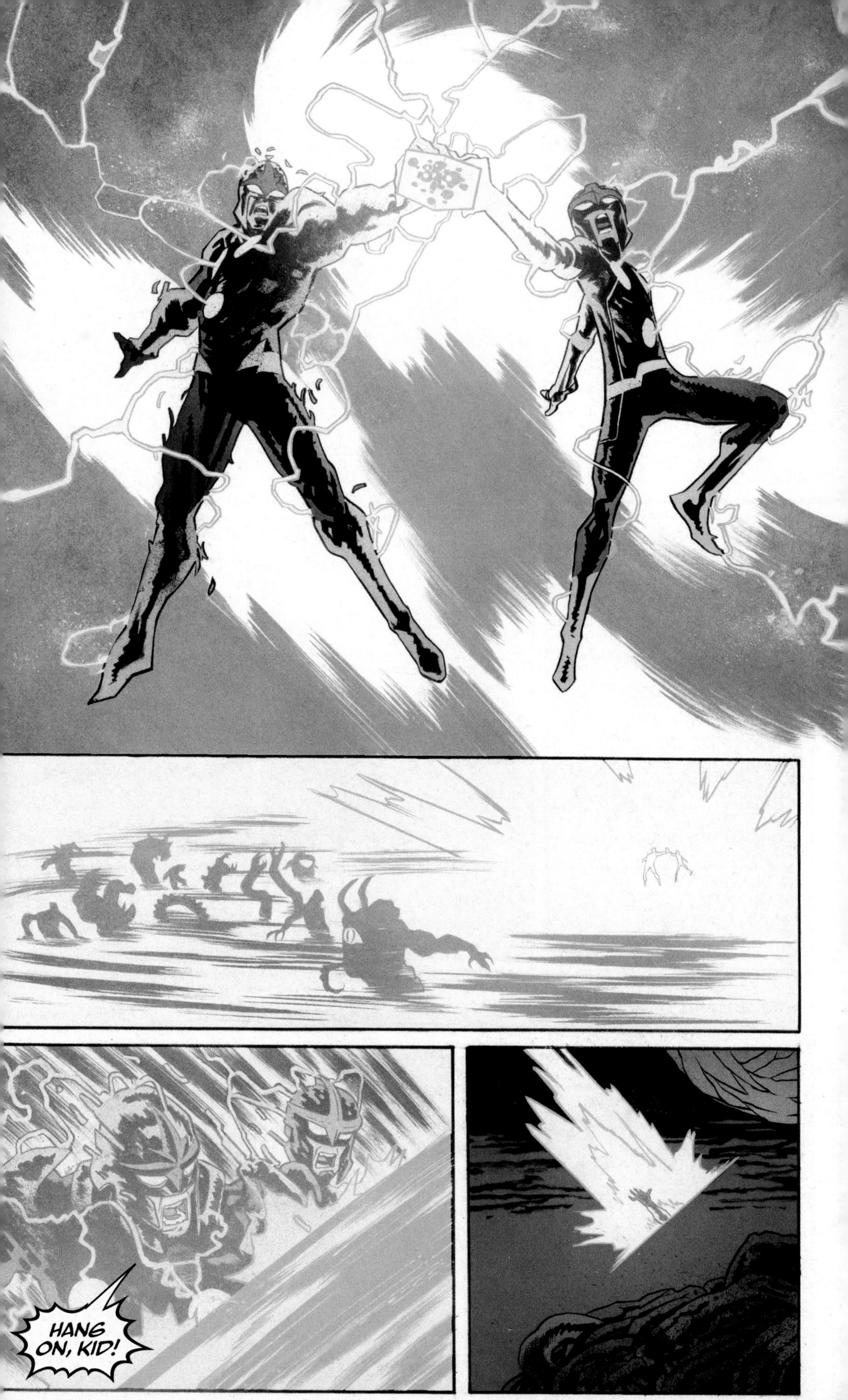
HANG ON, KID!

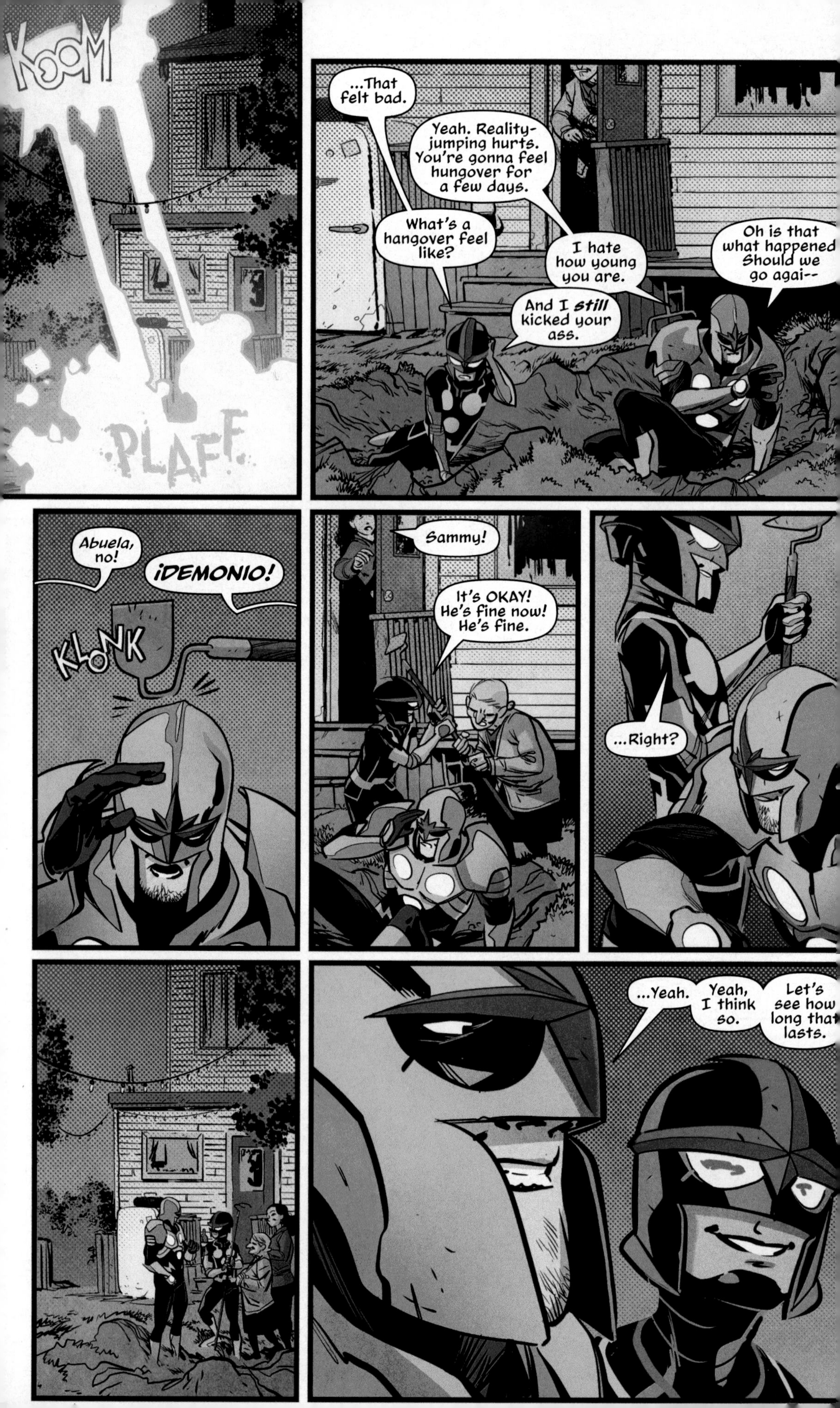
KOOM
PLAFF
...That felt bad.
Yeah. Reality-jumping hurts. You're gonna feel hungover for a few days.
What's a hangover feel like?
I hate how young you are.
And I still kicked your ass.
Oh is that what happened Should we go agai--
Abuela, no!
¡DEMONIO!
KLONK
Sammy!
It's OKAY! He's fine now! He's fine.
...Right?
...Yeah.
Yeah, I think so.
Let's see how long that lasts.

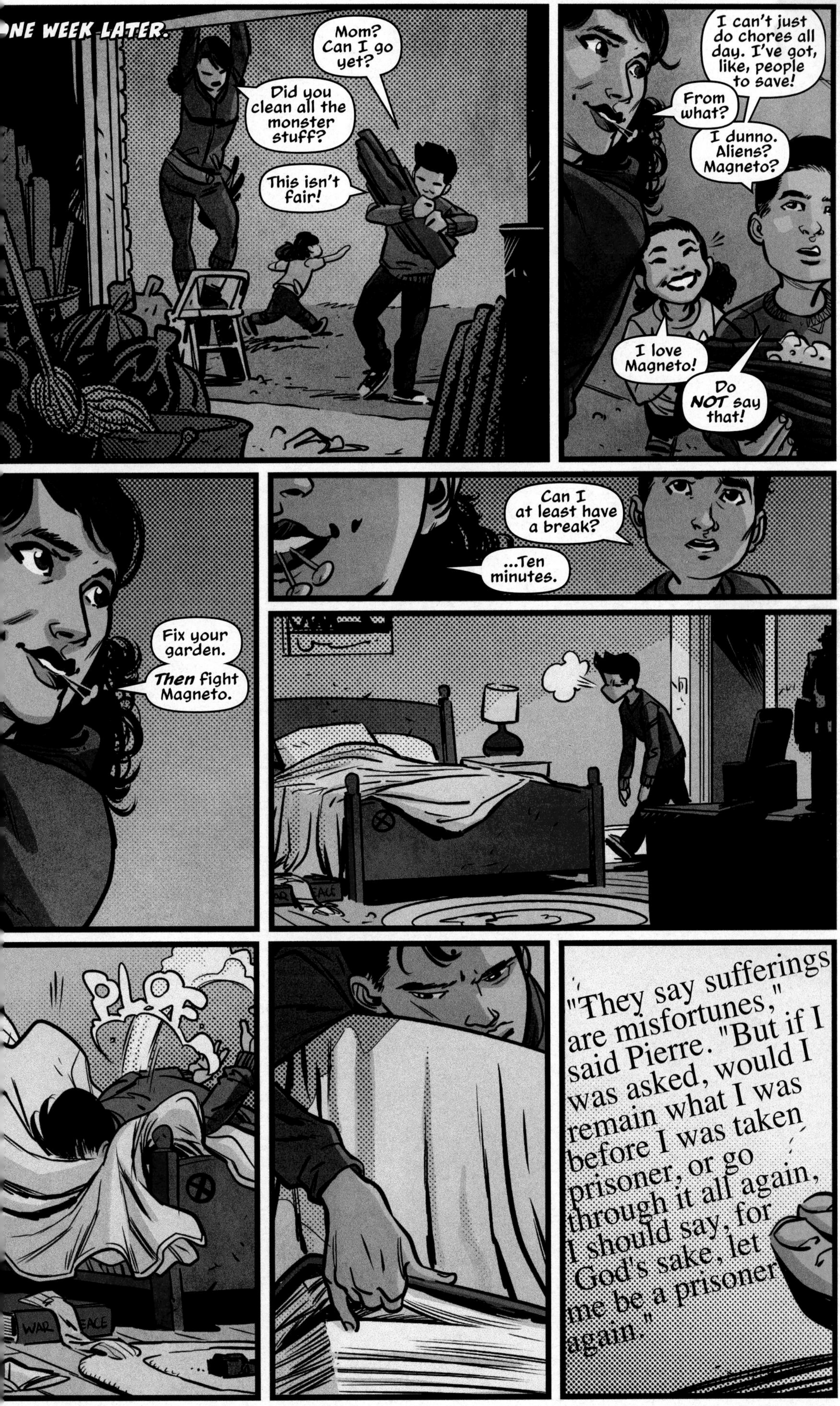

ONE WEEK LATER.
Mom? Can I go yet?
Did you clean all the monster stuff?
This isn't fair!
I can't just do chores all day. I've got, like, people to save!
From what?
I dunno. Aliens? Magneto?
I love Magneto!
Do NOT say that!
Fix your garden.
Then fight Magneto.
Can I at least have a break?
...Ten minutes.
PLOF
"They say sufferings are misfortunes," said Pierre. "But if I was asked, would I remain what I was before I was taken prisoner, or go through it all again, I should say, for God's sake, let me be a prisoner again."

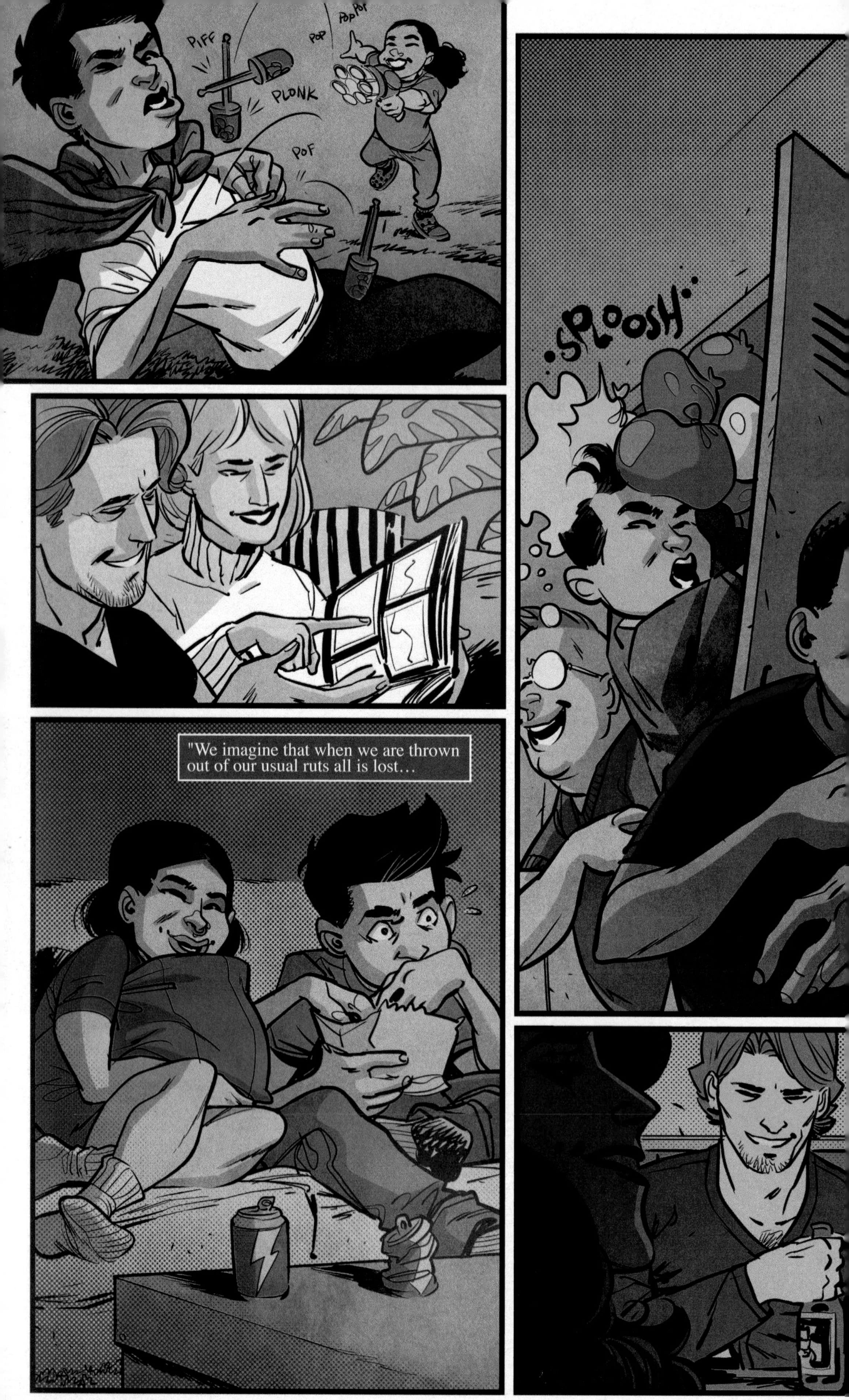
PIFF
POP
POP POP
PLONK
POF
"We imagine that when we are thrown out of our usual ruts all is lost…
SPLOOSH

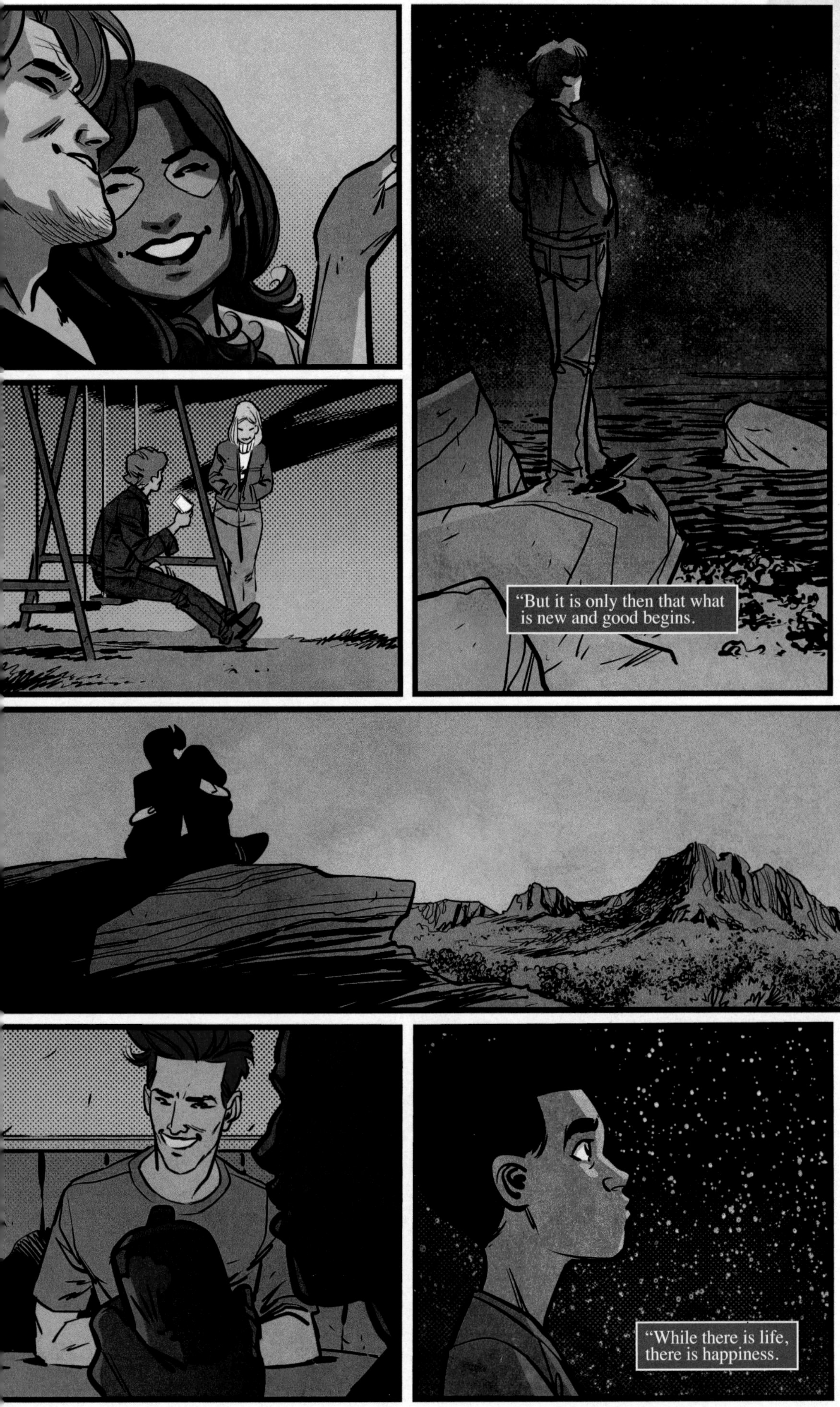
"But it is only then that what is new and good begins.
"While there is life, there is happiness.

KRAAKAA
KOOOOOOM
"There is much, much before us."
--Leo Tolstoy, *War and Peace*
PEREZ 2017 FINI
THE END.

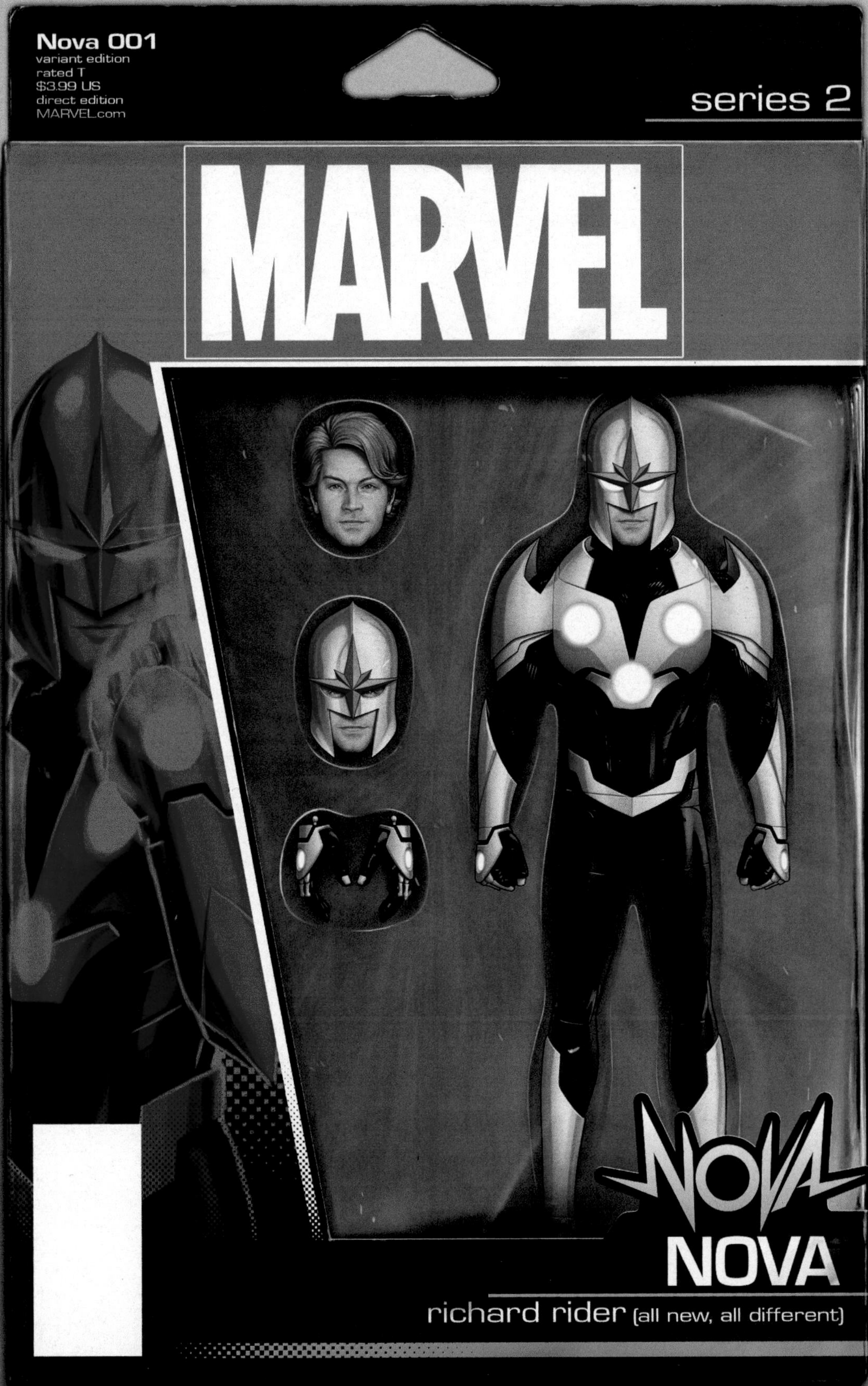
Nova 001
variant edition
rated T
$3.99 US
direct edition
MARVEL.com
series 2
MARVEL
NOVA
NOVA
richard rider (all new, all different)

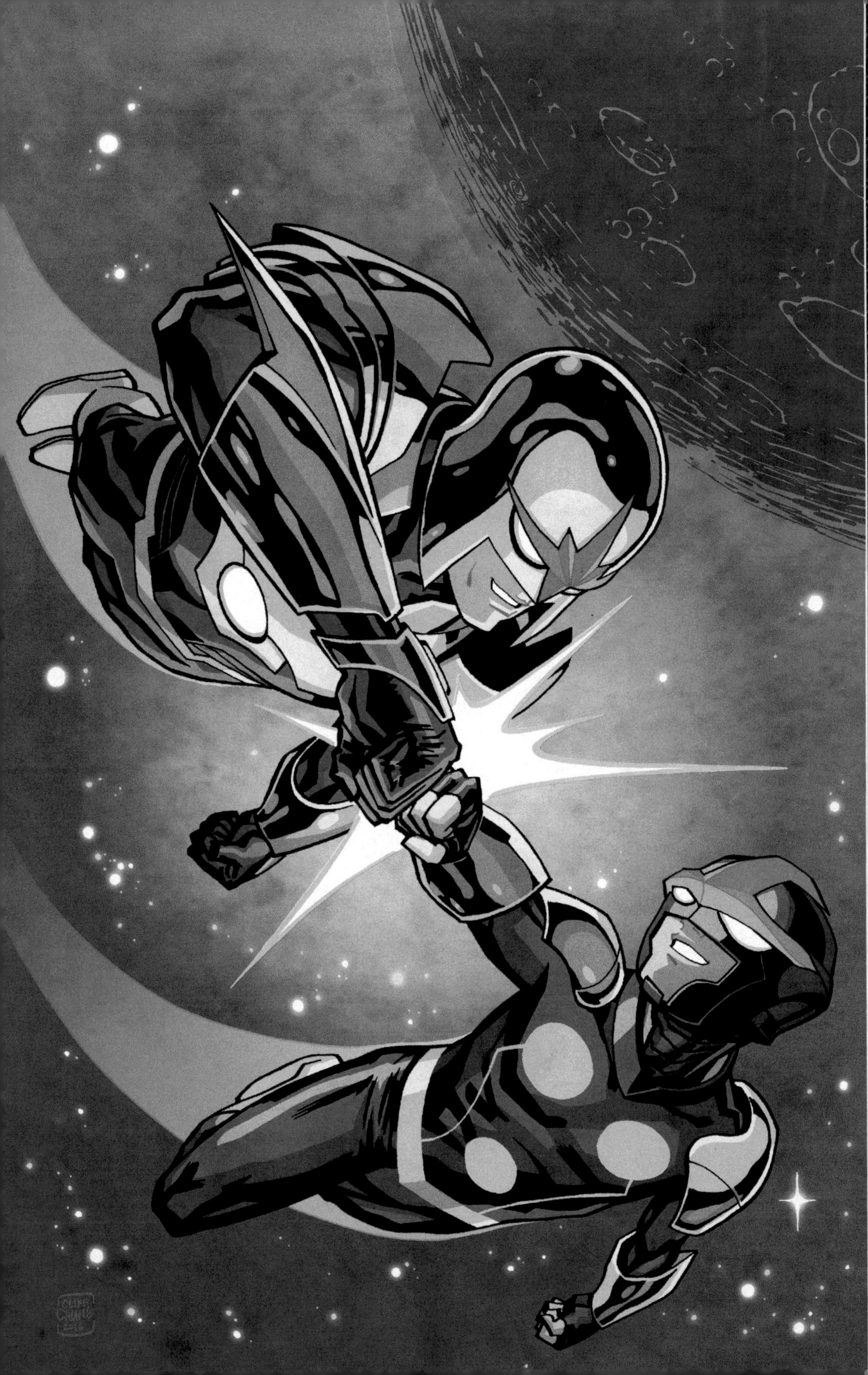

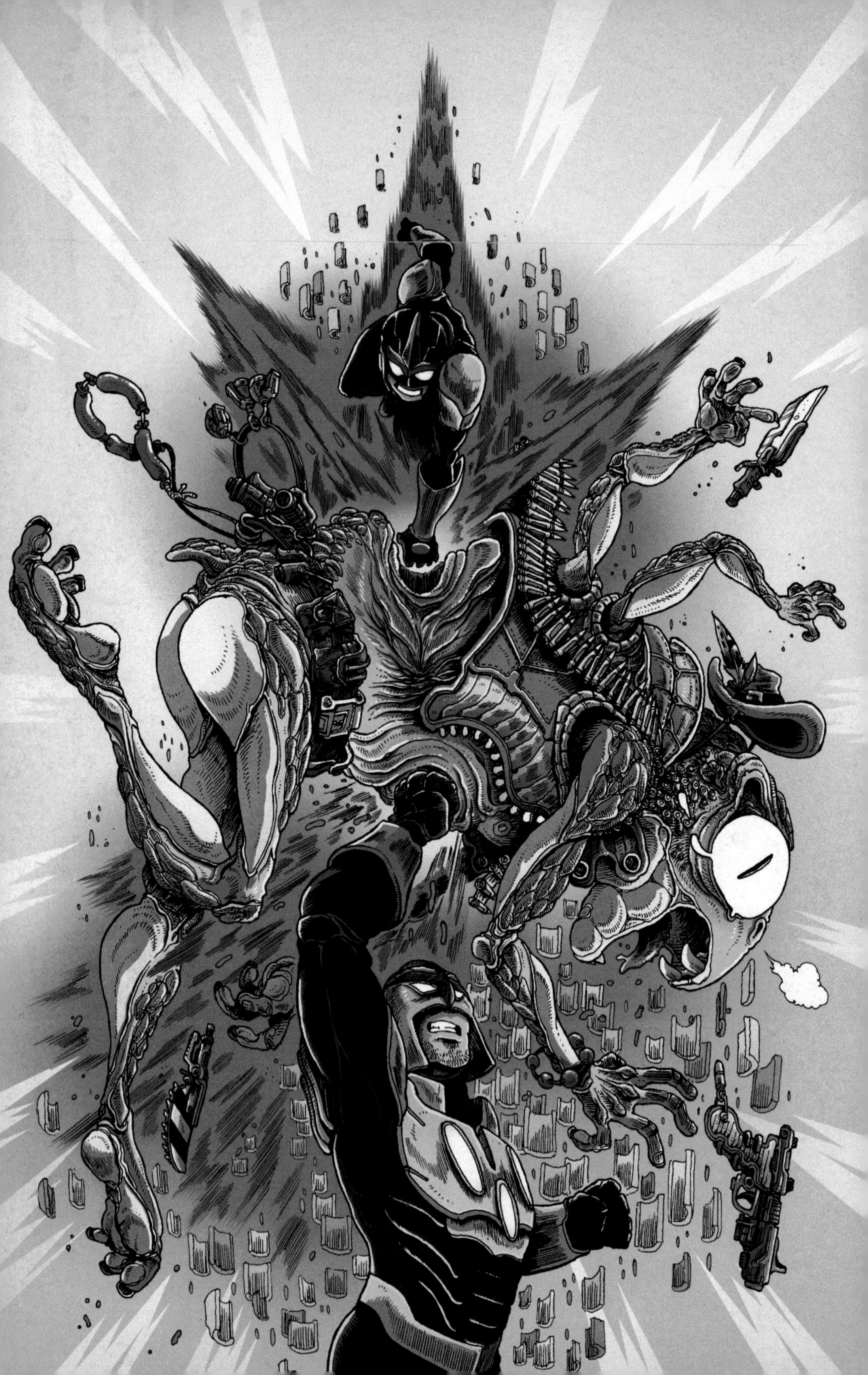

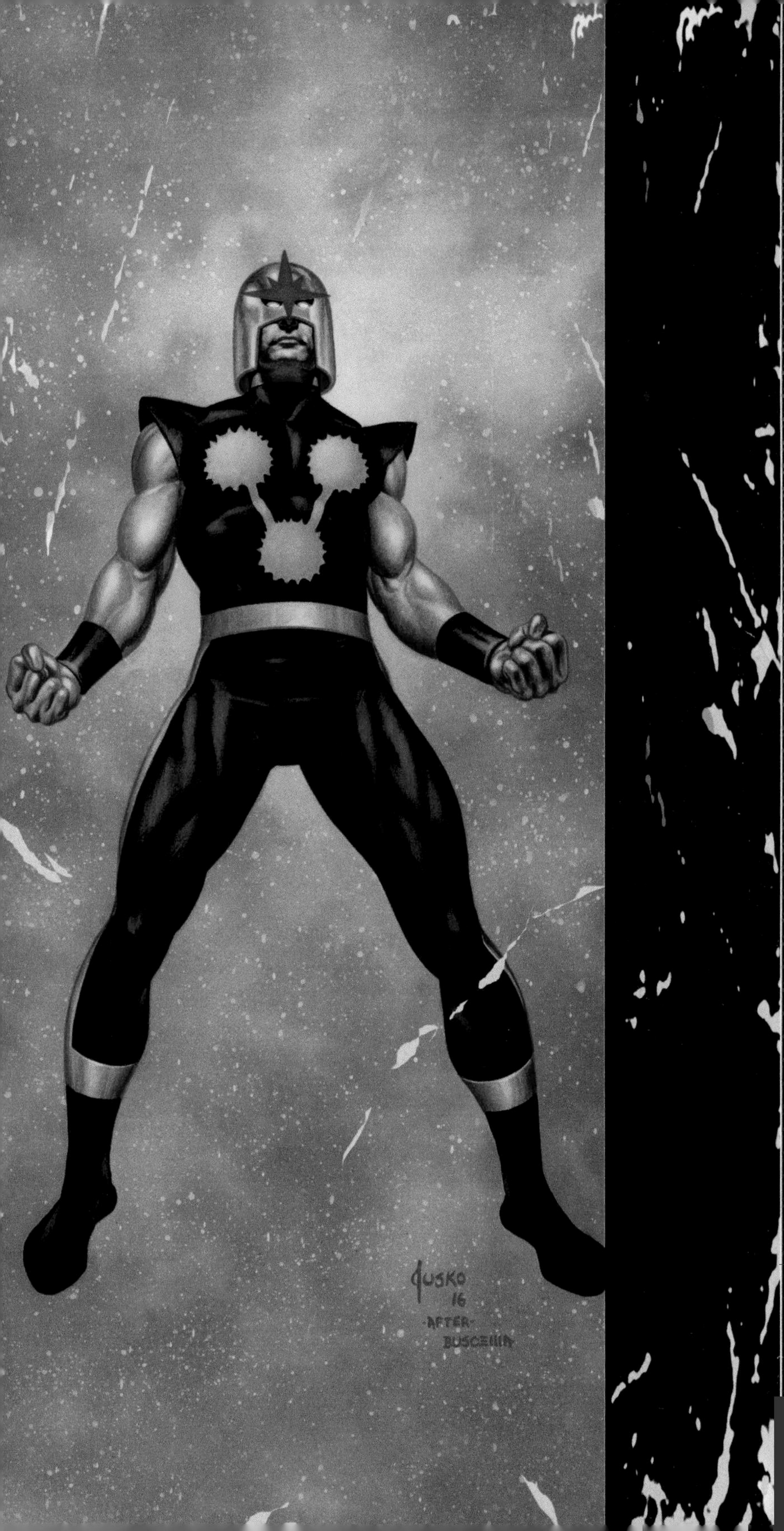
JUSKO
16
·AFTER·
BUSCEMA

Hello, heroes! NOVA editor Devin Lewis reporting to you live and in print from the headquarters of the House of Ideas in the heart of New York City.

What an incredible adventure this book has been! For years, Sam Alexander and Richard Rider have both ranked among my favorite Marvel characters—Sam, the gold-hearted goof who can't seem to get anything right, and Rich, the space ace who killed Thanos the Mad Titan. Do comics get any better that these two paired up together?!

I know that you Mighty Marvelites love Sam and Rich, too (well, some of you only like one of 'em) and you made it known through your tweets and fan mail, so THANK YOU!

From the get-go, the idea behind this book was to incorporate both Novas into each other's lives. We didn't want to leave either of these characters in the dust, and to you fans of Rich OR Sam, I hope we did ya proud! To fans of both Rich AND Sam, I hope we did ya proud, too!

But, heck, you don't want to hear from me. You want the brains of the operation — the talent! Let's see what they have to say about this most titanic tale in all of Marveldom…

Hey, everyone,

Thanks so much for sticking with this story. I'm so grateful to Devin, Allison, and the good people of Marvel for taking a shot on me with this. I couldn't have had a better partner than Ramón in crafting the story. He puts style, craft, and passion into everything he makes, and hopefully our paths cross again soon. Ian Herring and Scott Hepburn knocked every single page out of the park as well. I'm always so amazed at the talent on display in these books. I grew up consuming Marvel, and the fact that I get to play a small part in Marvel today is a surreal joy I don't deserve.

I love comics because they give you a world that understands you. Growing up, I felt lost. Aimless. Hopeless. Rejected. Alone… But so did my favorite Marvel characters.

They went through the same problems (albeit maybe with a few more interdimensional tentacle monsters and/or Phoenix-related problems), but most importantly, they showed me that we're so much stronger than our problems will ever be. We can always move forward. We can always change. We can find our hope again. We can step into life again. We can be kinder and better. I try to plunge that optimism into every story I write. These stories make my life better, and I hope they make your life better, too.

Also, read *War & Peace* while climbing Kilimanjaro. It'll change your life.

-Jeff Loveness

Marvel heroes cross generations, and it's definitely an exciting opportunity when you're presented with two heroes that cross that divide. Mix in two creators collaborating on a story of two mismatched, yet linked, heroes, and you have a recipe rife with fun. Working with Jeff on NOVA, being able to re-instill the breath of life into Rich, and flesh out the still novice Sam, was a wonderful adventure. We came at the project from different angles and met in the middle for a story that I am quite proud of. As Sam and Rich learned from each other, I can easily say the same for myself after collaborating with Jeff and crafting our story. The NOVA team in its entirety was so supportive, and stood behind this book with all their hearts. My love and thanks to Devin, Allison, Jeff, and Ian. Our time on NOVA was a short one, but it was one of quality, and it will be missed but never forgotten.

-Ramón Pérez

It's been a brief time with Nova, but I can clearly see why the fans love the character. Rich is a classic hero. The way Jeff and Ramón took this concept and had Rich fall into a big-brother role for Sam kept me wanting more. The promise of adventures between these two, whether it be space- or terrestrial-based, has been a pleasure to be part of, and I hope this is not the last we see of this pairing. Thank you to Jeff, Ramón, and Scott for giving me a lovely book to add color to. Thank you to the amazing editorial team of Devin and Allison who kept us pushing forward and fought to make this the best series it could be. Last but not least, thank you to all the fans who have come out of the woodwork to offer their support as we added another chapter to Nova.

-Ian Herring

'Nuff said.
Over and out!
-Devin

ALBERT DESCHESNE 1962-2017

Albert Deschesne, who had lettered for Comicraft for some 23 of our 25 years, passed away unexpectedly on May 31st, 2017. Albert was renowned in the Comicraft studio for coming up with clever lettering shortcuts, priding himself on being a Power User of Mac computers — from teaching us all QuicKeys to figuring out a way of "tricking a PC into thinking it was a Mac" — and keeping everyone's computers up and running back when freezes and crashes were a regular part of the day.

Albert was as sweethearted as they come, and unselfishly shared his discoveries when it came to doing things faster or better. He came up with the brilliant Layer Method of merging tails and balloons, as a way of making corrections quicker and easier. There isn't a letterer in the industry today that doesn't owe Albert a debt of gratitude for that technique alone.

Albert's knowledge of Marvel (and DC, shhh!) characters and history was unrivaled at Comicraft, and he was lamenting that NOVA was coming to an end after completing this last issue. Years ago, when DC sent a Superman bathrobe to Comicraft for Christmas, Albert unashamedly took it home. He was proud to be a geek LONG before it was fashionable.

Albert was a cancer survivor, and although we knew that he struggled off and on with health issues, I guess we always thought he would battle through for many more years to come. We will miss his unbridled enthusiasm for everything comics, computers, movies and gaming, and his unflagging good cheer.

Cheers!
Richard Starkings
President & First Tiger
Comicraft & ELEPH...